Richard G. Moulton, G. Moulton Richard

Shakespeare As A Dramatic Artist

Richard G. Moulton, G. Moulton Richard

Shakespeare As A Dramatic Artist

ISBN/EAN: 9783348011808

Printed in Europe, USA, Canada, Australia, Japan

Cover: Foto ©ninafisch / pixelio.de

More available books at **www.hansebooks.com**

SHAKESPEARE

AS A DRAMATIC ARTIST

MOULTON

a

SHAKESPEARE

A DRAMATIC ARTIST

A POPULAR ILLUSTRATION OF
THE PRINCIPLES OF SCIENTIFIC CRITICISM

BY

RICHARD G. MOULTON, M.A.

LATE SCHOLAR OF CHRIST'S COLLEGE
CAMBRIDGE UNIVERSITY (EXTENSION) LECTURER IN LITERATURE

Oxford

AT THE CLARENDON PRESS

1885

PREFACE.

I HAVE had three objects before me in writing this book. The first concerns the general reader. No one needs assistance in order to perceive Shakespeare's greatness; but an impression is not uncommonly to be found, especially amongst English readers, that Shakespeare's greatness lies mainly in his deep knowledge of human nature, while, as to the technicalities of Dramatic Art, he is at once careless of them and too great to need them. I have endeavoured to combat this impression by a series of Studies of Shakespeare as a Dramatic Artist. They are chiefly occupied with a few master-strokes of art, sufficient to illustrate the revolution Shakespeare created in the Drama of the world—a revolution not at once perceived simply because it had carried the Drama at a bound so far beyond Dramatic Criticism that the appreciation of Shakespeare's plays was left to the uninstructed public, while the trained criticism that ought to have recognised the new departure was engaged in clamouring for other views of dramatic treatment, which it failed to perceive that Shakespeare had rendered obsolete.

While the earlier chapters are taken up with these Studies,

a 3

the rest of the work is an attempt, in very brief form, to present Dramatic Criticism as a regular Inductive Science. If
I speak of this as a new branch of Science I am not ignoring
the great works on Shakespeare-Criticism which already
exist, the later of which have treated their subject in an
inductive spirit. What these still leave wanting is a *recognition*
of method in application to the study of the Drama : my
purpose is to claim for Criticism a position amongst the
Inductive Sciences, and to sketch in outline a plan for the
Dramatic side of such a Critical Science.

A third purpose has been to make the work of use as an
educational manual. Shakespeare now enters into every
scheme of liberal education ; but the annotated editions of
his works give the student little assistance except in the explanation of language and allusions ; and the idea, I believe,
prevails that anything like the discussion of literary characteristics or dramatic effect is out of place in an educational
work—is, indeed, too 'indefinite' to be 'examined on.' Ten
years' experience in connection with the Cambridge University Extension, during which my work has been to teach
literature apart from philology, has confirmed my impression
that the subject-matter of literature, its exposition and
analysis from the sides of science, history, and art, is as good
an educational discipline as it is intrinsically valuable in
quickening literary appreciation.

There are two special features of the book to which I may
here draw attention. Where practicable, I have appended in
the margin references to the passages of Shakespeare on which
my discussion is based. (These references are to the Globe
Edition.) I have thus hoped to reduce to a minimum the

element of personal opinion, and to give to my treatment at least that degree of definiteness which arises when a position stands side by side with the evidence supporting it. I have also endeavoured to meet a practical difficulty in the use of Shakespeare-Criticism as an educational subject. It is usual in educational schemes to name single plays of Shakespeare for study. Experience has convinced me that methodical study of the subject-matter is not possible within the compass of a single play On the other hand, few persons in the educational stage of life can have the detailed knowledge of Shakespeare's plays as a whole which is required for a full treatment of the subject. The present work is so arranged that it assumes knowledge of only five plays—*The Merchant of Venice, Richard III, Macbeth, Julius Cæsar,* and *King Lear.* Not only in the Studies, but also in the final review, the matter introduced is confined to what can be illustrated out of these five plays. These are amongst the most familiar of the Shakespearean Dramas, or they can be easily read before commencing the book ; and if the arrangement is a limitation involving a certain amount of repetition, yet I believe the gain will be greater than the loss. For the young student, at all events, it affords an opportunity of getting what will be the best of all introductions to the whole subject—a thorough knowledge of five plays.

In passing the book through the press I have received material assistance from my brother, Dr. Moulton, Master of the Leys School, and from my College friend, Mr. Joseph Jacobs. With the latter, indeed, I have discussed the work in all its stages, and have been under continual obligation to his stores of knowledge and critical grasp in all departments of literary study. I cannot even attempt to name the many friends—chiefly fellow-workers in the University Extension Movement—through whose active interest in my Shakespeare teaching I have been encouraged to seek for it publication.

RICHARD G. MOULTON.

April, 1885.

CONTENTS.

———◆———

INTRODUCTION.

PLEA FOR AN INDUCTIVE SCIENCE OF LITERARY
CRITICISM.

————

PART FIRST.

SHAKESPEARE CONSIDERED AS A DRAMATIC ARTIST,
IN TEN STUDIES.

VI.

VII.

VIII.

IX.

X.

PART SECOND.

SURVEY OF DRAMATIC CRITICISM AS AN INDUCTIVE SCIENCE.

XI.

XII

XIII.

XIV.

INTRODUCTION.

PLEA FOR AN INDUCTIVE SCIENCE
OF LITERARY CRITICISM.

INTRODUCTION.

IN the treatment of literature the proposition which seems *Proposi-* to stand most in need of assertion at the present *tion* moment is, *that there is an inductive science of literary criticism.* As botany deals inductively with the phenomena of vegetable life and traces the laws underlying them, as economy reviews and systematises on inductive principles the facts of commerce, so there is a criticism not less inductive in character which has for its subject-matter literature.

The presumption is clearly that literary criticism should *Presump-* follow other branches of thought in becoming inductive. *tion in favour of* Ultimately, science means no more than organised thought; *inductive* and amongst the methods of organisation induction is the *literary* most practical. To begin with the observation of facts; to *criticism.* advance from this through the arrangement of observed facts; to use *à priori* ideas, instinctive notions of the fitness of things, insight into far probabilities, only as side-lights for suggesting convenient arrangements, the value of which is tested only by the actual convenience in arranging they afford; to be content with the sure results so obtained as 'theory' in the interval of waiting for still surer results based on a yet wider accumulation of facts: this is a regimen for healthy science so widely established in different tracts of thought as almost to rise to that universal acceptance which we call common sense. Indeed the whole progress of science consists in winning fresh fields of thought to the inductive methods.

B

Yet the great mass of literary criticism at the present moment is of a nature widely removed from induction. The prevailing notions of criticism are dominated by the idea of *assaying*, as if its function were to test the soundness and estimate the comparative value of literary work. Lord Macaulay, than whom no one has a better right to be heard on this subject, compares his office of reviewer to that of a king-at-arms, versed in the laws of literary precedence, marshalling authors to the exact seats to which they are entitled. And, as a matter of fact, the bulk of literary criticism, whether in popular conversation or in discussions by professed critics, occupies itself with the merits of authors and works; founding its estimates and arguments on canons of taste, which are either assumed as having met with general acceptance, or deduced from speculations as to fundamental conceptions of literary beauty.

It becomes necessary then to recognise two different kinds of literary criticism, as distinct as any two things that can be called by the same name. The difference between the two may be summed up as the difference between the work of a *judge* and of an *investigator*. The one is the enquiry into what ought to be, the other the enquiry into what is. Judicial criticism compares a new production with those already existing in order to determine whether it is inferior to them or surpasses them; criticism of investigation makes the same comparison for the purpose of identifying the new product with some type in the past, or differentiating it and registering a new type. Judicial criticism has a mission to watch against variations from received canons; criticism of investigation watches for new forms to increase its stock of species. The criticism of taste analyses literary works for grounds of preference or evidence on which to found judgments; inductive criticism analyses them to get a closer acquaintance with their phenomena.

Let the question be of Ben Jonson. Judicial criticism

starts by holding Ben Jonson responsible for the decay of the English Drama.

Inductive criticism takes objection to the word ' decay ' as suggesting condemnation, but recognises Ben Jonson as the beginner of a new tendency in our dramatic history.

But, judicial criticism insists, the object of the Drama is to pourtray human nature, whereas Ben Jonson has painted not men but caricatures.

Induction sees that this formula cannot be a sufficient definition of the Drama, for the simple reason that it does not take in Ben Jonson; its own mode of putting the matter is that Ben Jonson has founded a school of treatment of which the law is caricature.

But Ben Jonson's caricatures are palpably impossible.

Induction soon satisfies itself that their point lies in their impossibility; they constitute a new mode of pourtraying qualities of character, not by resemblance, but by analysing and intensifying contrasts to make them clearer.

Judicial criticism can see how the poet was led astray; the bent of his disposition induced him to sacrifice dramatic propriety to his satiric purpose.

Induction has another way of putting the matter : that the poet has utilised dramatic form for satiric purpose; thus by the ' cross-fertilisation ' of two existing literary species he has added to literature a third including features of both.

At all events, judicial criticism will maintain, it must be admitted that the Shakespearean mode of pourtraying is infinitely the higher : a sign-painter, as Macaulay points out, can imitate a deformity of feature, while it takes a great artist to bring out delicate shades of expression.

Inductive treatment knows nothing about higher or lower, which lie outside the domain of science. Its point is that science is indebted to Ben Jonson for a new species ; if the new species be an easier form of art it does not on that account lose its claim to be analysed.

The critic of merit can always fall back upon taste : who would not prefer Shakespeare to Ben Jonson ?

But even from this point of view scientific treatment can plead its own advantages. The inductive critic reaps to the full the interest of Ben Jonson, to which the other has been forcibly closing his eyes ; while, so far from liking Shakespeare the less, he appreciates all the more keenly Shakespeare's method of treatment from his familiarity with that which is its antithesis.

The two criticisms confused.

It must be conceded at once that both these kinds of criticism have justified their existence. Judicial criticism has long been established as a favourite pursuit of highly cultivated minds ; while the criticism of induction can shelter itself under the authority of science in general, seeing that it has for its object to bring the treatment of literature into the circle of the inductive sciences. It is unfortunate, however,

conception of critical method limited to judicial method.

that the spheres of the two have not been kept distinct. In the actual practice of criticism the judicial method has obtained an illegitimate supremacy which has thrown the other into the shade ; it has even invaded the domain of the criticism that claims to be scientific, until the word *criticism* itself has suffered, and the methodical treatment of literature has by tacit assumption become limited in idea to the judicial method.

Partly a survival of Renaissance influence.

Explanation for this limited conception of criticism is not far to seek. Modern criticism took its rise before the importance of induction was recognised : it lags behind other branches of thought in adapting itself to inductive treatment chiefly through two influences. The first of these is connected with the revival of literature after the darkness of the middle ages. The birth of thought and taste in modern Europe was the Renaissance of classical thought and taste ; by Roman and Greek philosophy and poetry the native powers of our ancestors were trained till they became strong enough to originate for themselves. It was natural for their earliest criticism to take the form of applying the

classical standards to their own imitations: now we have *and its testing by classical models.*
advanced so far that no one would propose to test ex-
clusively by classical models, but nevertheless the idea of
testing still lingers as the root idea in the treatment of literature. Other branches of thought have completely shaken off
this attitude of submission to the past: literary criticism
differs from the rest only in being later to move. This is
powerfully suggested by the fact that so recent a writer
as Addison couples science in general with criticism in
his estimate of probable progress; laying down the startling
proposition that 'it is impossible for us who live in the later
ages of the world to make observations in criticism, in
morality, *or in any art or science,* which have not been
touched upon by others'!

And even for this lateness a second influence goes far to *Partly that methods of journalism have invaded systematic criticism.*
account. The grand literary phenomenon of modern times is
journalism, the huge apparatus of floating literature of which
one leading object is to review literature itself. The vast increase of production consequent upon the progress of printing
has made production itself a phenomenon worthy of study, and
elevated the sifting of production into a prominent literary
occupation; by the aid of book-tasters alone can the
ordinary reader keep pace with production. It is natural
enough that the influence of journalism should pass beyond
its natural sphere, and that the review should tend to usurp
the position of the literature for which reviewing exists. Now
in journalism testing and valuation of literary work have a
real and important place. It has thus come about that in
the great preponderance of ephemeral over permanent
literature the machinery adapted to the former has become
applied to the latter: methods proper to journalism have
settled the popular conception of systematic treatment; and
the bias already given to criticism by the Renaissance has
been strengthened to resist the tendency of all kinds of
thought towards inductive methods.

History will thus account for the way in which the criticism of taste and valuation tends to be identified with criticism in general: but attempts are not wanting to give the identification a scientific basis. Literary appreciation, it is said, is a thing of culture. A critic in the reviewer's sense is one who has the literary faculty both originally acute and developed by practice: he thus arrives quickly and with certainty at results which others would reach laboriously and after temporary misjudgments. Taste, however arbitrary in appearance, is in reality condensed experience; judicial criticism is a wise economy of appreciation, the purpose of which is to anticipate natural selection and universal experience. He is a good critic who, by his keen and practised judgment, can tell you at once the view of authors and works which you would yourself come to hold with sufficient study and experience.

Now in the first place there is a flaw in this reasoning: it omits to take into account that the judicial attitude of mind is itself a barrier to appreciation, as being opposed to that delicacy of receptiveness which is a first condition of sensibility to impressions of literature and art. It is a matter of commonest experience that appreciation may be interfered with by prejudice, by a passing unfavourable mood, or even by uncomfortable external surroundings. But it is by no means sufficient that the reader of literature should divest himself of these passive hindrances to appreciation: poets are pioneers in beauty, and considerable activity of effort is required to keep pace with them. Repetition may be necessary to catch effects—passages to be read over and over again, more than one author of the same school to be studied, effect to be compared with kindred effect each helping the other. Or an explanation from one who has already caught the idea may turn the mind into a receptive attitude. Training again is universally recognised as a necessity for appreciation, and to train is to make receptive.

Beyond all these conditions of perception, and including *On the* them, is yet another. It is a foundation principle in art- *other hand sympathy* culture, as well as in human intercourse, that *sympathy is the* *the great* *grand interpreter:* secrets of beauty will unfold themselves to *interpreter.* the sunshine of sympathy, while they will wrap themselves all the closer against the tempest of sceptical questionings. Now a judicial attitude of mind is highly unreceptive, for it necessarily implies a restraint of sympathy: every one, remarks Hogarth, is a judge of painting except the connoisseur. The judicial mind has an appearance of receptiveness, because it seeks to shut out prejudice: but what if the idea of judging be itself a prejudice? On this view the very consciousness of fairness, involving as it does limitation of sympathy, will be itself unfair. In practical life, where we have to act, the formation of judgments is a necessity. In art we can escape the obligation, and here the judicial spirit becomes a wanton addition to difficulties of appreciation already sufficiently great; the mere notion of condemning may be enough to check our receptivity to qualities which, as we have seen, it may need our utmost effort to catch. So that the judicial attitude of mind comes to defeat its own purpose, and disturbs unconsciously the impression it seeks to judge; until, as Emerson puts it, 'if you criticise a fine genius the odds are that you are out of your reckoning, and instead of the poet are censuring your caricature of him.'

But the appeal made is to experience: to experience let *The theory* it go. It will be found that, speaking broadly, *the whole* *refuted by* *experience:* *history of criticism has been a triumph of authors over critics:* *the history* so long as criticism has meant the gauging of literature, so *of criticism* long its progress has consisted in the reversal of critical *of authors* judgments by further experience. I hesitate to enlarge upon *over critics.* this part of my subject lest I be inflicting upon the reader the tedium of a thrice-told tale. But I believe that the ordinary reader, however familiar with notable blunders of criticism, has little idea of that which is the essence of my argument—the degree of regularity, amounting to absolute law, with which criticism, where it has set itself in opposition to freedom of authorship, has been found in time to have pronounced upon the wrong side, and has, after infinite waste of obstructive energy, been compelled at last to accept innovations it had pronounced impossible under penalty of itself becoming obsolete.

Case of the Shakespearean Drama · retiring waves of critical opposition

Shakespeare-criticism affords the most striking illustration. Its history is made up of wave after wave of critical opposition, each retiring further before the steady advance of Shakespeare's fame. They may almost be traced in the varying apologetic tones of the successive *Variorum* editors, until Reed, in the edition of 1803, is content to leave the poet's renown as established on a basis which will 'bid defiance to the caprices of fashion and the canker of time.'

1. Unmeasured attack.

The first wave was one of unmeasured virulent attack. Rymer, accepted in his own day as the champion of 'regular' criticism, and pronounced by Pope one of the best critics England ever had, says that in Tragedy Shakespeare appears quite out of his element:

> His brains are turned; he raves and rambles without any coherence, any spark of reason, or any rule to control him or set bounds to his phrensy.

The shouting and battles of his scenes are necessary to keep the audience awake, 'otherwise no sermon would be so strong an opiate.' Again:

> In the neighing of an horse, or in the growling of a mastiff, there is a meaning, there is as lively an expression, and, may I say, more humanity, than many times in the tragical flights of Shakespeare.

The famous Suggestion Scene in *Othello* has, in Rymer's view, no point but 'the mops, the mows, the grimace, the grins, the gesticulation.' On Desdemona's

> O good Iago,
> What shall I do to win my lord again?

he remarks that no woman bred out of a pig-stye would talk so meanly. Speaking of Portia he says, 'she is scarce one remove from a natural, she is own cousin-german, of one piece, the very same impertinent flesh and blood with Desdemona.' And Rymer's general verdict of *Othello*—which he considers the best of Shakespeare's tragedies—is thus summed up:

> There is in this play some burlesque, some humour and ramble of comical wit, some show and some mimicry to divert the spectators: but the tragical part is plainly none other than a bloody farce, without salt or savour.

In the eighteenth century Lord Lansdowne, writing on 'Unnatural Flights in Poetry,' could refuse to go into the question of Shakespeare's soliloquies, as being assured that 'not one in all his works could be excused by reason or nature.' The same tone was still later kept up by Voltaire, who calls Shakespeare a writer of monstrous farces called tragedies; says that nature had blended in him all that is most great and elevating with all the basest qualities that belong to barbarousness without genius; and finally proceeds to call his poetry the fruit of the imagination of an intoxicated savage.—Meanwhile a second wave of opinion had arisen, *2. The Shakespearean Drama held inadmissible, yet attractive.* not conceiving a doubt as to the total inadmissibility of the Shakespearean Drama, yet feeling its attraction. This is perhaps most exactly illustrated in the forgotten critic Edwards, who ruled that 'poor Shakespeare'—the expression is his own—must be excluded from the number of good tragedians, yet 'as Homer from the Republic of Plato, with marks of distinction and veneration.' But before this the more celebrated dramatists of the Restoration had shown the double feeling in the way they reconstructed Shakespeare's plays, and turned them into 'correct' dramas. Thus Otway made the mediæval Capulets and Montagus presentable by giving them a classical dress as followers of Marius and Sulla; and even Dryden joined in a polite version of *The*

Tempest, with an original touch for symmetry's sake in the addition to the heroine Miranda, a maid who had never seen a man, of a suitable hero, a man who had never seen a

3. The Shake-spearean Drama ad-mitted with excuses.

maid.—Against loud abuse and patronising reconstruction the silent power of Shakespeare's works made itself more and more felt, and we reach a third stage when the Shakespearean Drama is accepted as it stands, but with excuses. Excuse is made for the poet's age, in which the English nation was supposed to be struggling to emerge from barbarism. Heywood's apology for uniting light and serious matter is allowed, that 'they who write to all must strive to please all.' Pope points out that Shakespeare was dependent for his subsistence on pleasing the taste of tradesmen and mechanics; and that his 'wrong choice of subjects' and 'wrong conduct of incidents,' his 'false thoughts and forced expressions' are the result of his being forced to please the lowest of the people and keep the worst of company. Similarly Theobald considers that he schemed his plots and characters from romances simply for want of classical information.—With the last name we pass to yet

4. The Shake-spearean Drama not felt to need defence as a whole, but praised and blamed in its parts.

another school, with whom Shakespeare's work as a whole is not felt to need defence, and the old spirit survives only in their distribution of praise and blame amongst its different parts. Theobald opens his preface with the comparison of the Shakespearean Drama to a splendid pile of buildings, with 'some parts finished up to hit the taste of a connoisseur, others more negligently put together to strike the fancy of a common beholder.' Pope—who reflects the most various schools of criticism, often on successive pages—illustrates this stage in his remark that Shakespeare has excellences that have elevated him above all others, and almost as many defects; 'as he has certainly written better so he has perhaps written worse than any other.' Dr. Johnson sets out by describing Shakespeare as 'having begun to assume the dignity of an ancient'—the highest commendation in his eyes. But he goes on to point out the inferiority of Shakespeare's Tragedy to his Comedy, the former the outcome of skill rather than instinct, with little felicity and always leaving something wanting; how he seems without moral purpose, letting his precepts and axioms drop casually from him, dismissing his personages without further care, and leaving the examples to operate by chance; how his plots are so loosely formed that they might easily be improved, his set speeches cold and weak, his incidents imperfectly told in many words which might be more plainly described in few. Then in the progress of his commentary, he irritates the reader, as Hallam points out, by the magisterial manner in which he dismisses each play like a schoolboy's exercise.—At last comes a revolution in *5. Finally* criticism and a new order of things arises: with Lessing *criticism comes* to 'lead the way in Germany and Coleridge in England, a *round en-* school of critics appear who are in complete harmony with *tirely to Shake-* their author, who question him only to learn the secrets *speare.* of his art. The new spirit has not even yet leavened the whole of the literary world; but such names as Goethe, Tieck, Schlegel, Victor Hugo, Ulrici, Gervinus suggest how many great reputations have been made, and reputations already great have been carried into a new sphere of greatness, by the interpretation and unfolding of Shakespeare's greatness: not one critic has in recent years risen to eminence by attacking Shakespeare.

And the Shakespearean Drama is only the most illustrious *Other ex-* example of authors triumphing over the criticism that at- *amples.* tempted to judge them. It is difficult for a modern reader *Milton.* to believe that even Rymer could refer to the *Paradise Lost* as 'what some are pleased to call a poem'; or that Dr. Johnson could assert of the minor poems of Milton that they exhibit 'peculiarity as distinguished from excellence,' ' if they differ from others they differ for the worse.' He says of *Comus* that it is ' inelegantly splendid and tediously instructive'; and of *Lycidas*, that its diction is harsh, its rhymes uncertain, its numbers unpleasing, that 'in this poem there is no nature for there is no truth, there is no art for there is nothing new,' that it is 'easy, vulgar, and therefore disgusting,'—after which he goes through the different parts of the poem to show what Milton should have done in each. Hallam has pointed out how utterly impotent Dr. Johnson has been to fix the public taste in the case of these poems; yet even Hallam could think the verse of the poet who wrote *Paradise Lost* sufficiently described by the verdict, 'some-

Shake-speare's Sonnets.

times wanting in grace and almost always in ease.' In the light of modern taste it is astonishing indeed to find Steevens, with his devotion of a lifetime to Shakespeare, yet omitting the Sonnets from the edition of 1793, 'because the strongest Act of Parliament that could be framed would not compel readers into their service.' It is equally astonishing

Spenser.

to find Dryden speaking of Spenser's 'ill choice of stanza,' and saying of the *Faerie Queene* that if completed it might have been more of a piece, but it could not be perfect, because its model was not true: an example followed up in the next century by a 'person of quality,' who translated a book of the *Faerie Queene* out of its 'obsolete language and manner of verse' into heroic couplets. I pass over the

Gray.

crowd of illustrations, such as the fate of Gray at the hands

Keats.

of Dr. Johnson, of Keats at the hands of monthly and

Waverley Novels.

quarterly reviewers, or of the various Waverley Novels capriciously selected by different critics as examples of literary suicide. But we have not yet had time to forget how Jeffrey —one of the greatest names in criticism—set in motion the whole machinery of reviewing in order to put down Words-

Words-worth.

worth. Wordsworth's most elaborate poem he describes as a 'tissue of moral and devotional ravings,' a 'hubbub of strained raptures and fantastical sublimities': his 'effusions on . . . the physiognomy of external nature' he characterises as 'eminently fantastic, obscure, and affected.' Then, to find a climax, he compares different species of Wordsworth's poetry to the various stages of intoxication : his Odes are 'glorious delirium' and 'incoherent rapture,' his Lyrical Ballads a 'vein of pretty deliration,' his *White Doe* is ' low and maudlin imbecility.' Not a whit the less has the influence of Wordsworth deepened and solidified ; and if all are not yet prepared to accept him as the apostle of a new religion, yet he has tacitly secured his place in the inner circle of English poets. In fine, the work of modern criticism is seriously blocked by the perpetual necessity of revising and reversing what this same Jeffrey calls the ' impartial and irreversible sentences' of criticism in the past. And as a set-off in the opposite scale only one considerable achievement is to be noted : that journalism afforded a medium for Macaulay to quench the light of Robert Montgomery, which, on Macaulay's own showing, journalism had puffed into a flame. *Robert Mont- gomery.*

  It is the same with the great literary questions that have from time to time arisen, the pitched battles of criticism : as Goldsmith says, there never has been an unbeaten path trodden by the poet that the critic has not endeavoured to recall him by calling his attempt an innovation. Criticism set its face steadily from the first against blank verse in English poetry. The interlocutors in Dryden's *Essay on the Drama* agree that it is vain to strive against the stream of the people's inclination, won over as they have been by Shakespeare, Ben Jonson, Beaumont and Fletcher ; but, as they go on to discuss the rights of the matter, the most remarkable thing to a modern reader is that the defence of blank verse is made to rest only on the colloquial character of dramatic poetry, and neither party seems to conceive the possibility of non-dramatic poetry other than in rhyme. Before Dryden's *Essay on Satire* the *Paradise Lost* had made its appearance ; but so impossible an idea is literary novelty to the ' father of English criticism ' that Dryden in this Essay *Defeat of criticism in the great literary questions.* *Blank verse.*

refuses to believe Milton's own account of the matter, saying that, whatever reasons Milton may allege for departing from rhyme, 'his own particular reason is plainly this, that rhyme was not his talent, he has neither the ease of doing it nor the graces of it.' To one so steeped in French fashions as Rymer, poetry that lacks rhyme seems to lack everything; many of Shakespeare's scenes might, he says, do better without words at all, or at most the words set off the action like the drone of a bagpipe. Voltaire estimates blank verse at about the same rate, and having to translate some of Shakespeare's for purposes of exact comparison, he remarks that blank verse costs nothing but the trouble of dictating, that it is not more difficult to write than a letter. Dr. Johnson finds a theoretic argument in the unmusical character of English poetry to prove the impossibility of its ever adapting itself to the conditions of blank verse, and is confident enough to prophesy: 'poetry may subsist without rhyme, but English poetry will not often please.' Even Byron is found only one degree more tolerant than Dryden: he has the grace to except Milton from his dictum that no one ever wrote blank verse who could rhyme. Thus critical taste, critical theory, and critical prophecy were unanimous against blank verse as an English measure: for all that it has become the leading medium of English poetry, and a doubter of to-day would be more likely to doubt the permanence of *The 'three* English rhyme than of English blank verse. As to the *unities':* famous 'three unities,' not only the principles themselves, but even the refutation of them has now become obsolete. Yet this stickling for the unities has been merely the chief amongst many examples of the proneness the critical mind has exhibited towards limiting literary appreciation and pro- *and limita-* duction by single standards of taste. The same tone of *tions by* mind that contended for the classical unities had in an *still nar-* *rower* earlier generation contended for the classical languages as *classical* *standards.* the sole vehicle of literary expression, and the modern languages of Europe had to assert their rights by hard fighting. In Latin literature itself a more successful attempt has been made to limit taste by the writers of a single period, the Augustan age, and so construct a list of Latin poets which omits Lucretius. And for a short period of the Renaissance movement the limitation was carried further to a single one of the Augustan writers, and 'Ciceronianism' struggled hard against the freedom of style it chose to nickname 'Apuleianism,' till it fell itself before the laughter of Erasmus. It *Criticism* would seem almost to be a radical law of the critical tem- *failing to* perament that admiration for the past paralyses faith in the *distinguish* future ; while criticism proves totally unable to distinguish *the permanent* between what has been essential in the greatness of its idols *and transitory.* and what has been as purely accidental as, to use Scott's illustration, the shape of the drinking-glass is to the flavour of the wine it contains. And if criticism has thus failed in distinguishing what is permanent in past literature, it has proved equally mistaken in what it has assumed to be accidental and transitory. Early commentators on Shakespeare, whatever scruples they may have had upon other points, had no misgivings in condemning the irregularities of his English and correcting his grammar. This was described as obsolete by Dryden half a century after the poet's death; while it is delicious to hear Steevens, in the Advertisement to his edition of 1766, mentioning that 'some have been of opinion that even a particular syntax prevailed in the time of Shakespeare'—a novel suggestion he promptly rejects. If the two could have lived each a century later, Dryden would have found Malone laying down that Shakespeare had been the great purifyer and refiner of our language, and Steevens would have seen Shakespeare's grammar studied with the same minuteness and reduced to the same regular form as the grammar of his commentators and readers ; while one of the most distinguished of our modern grammarians, instituting a comparison between Elizabethan and nineteenth century English, fancies the representative of the old-fashioned tongue characterising current speech in the words of Sebastian :

> Surely
> It is a sleepy language!

Critical works where inductive retain their force, where judicial have become obsolete. The critics may themselves be called as chief witnesses against themselves. Those parts of their works in which they apply themselves to analysing and interpreting their authors survive in their full force : where they judge, find fault, and attempt to regulate, they inevitably become obsolete. Aristotle, the founder of all criticism, is for the most part inductive in his method, describing poetry as it existed in his day, distinguishing its different classes and elements, and tabulating its usages : accordingly Aristotle's treatise, though more than two thousand years old, remains the text-book of the Greek Drama. In some places, however, he diverges from his main purpose, as in the final chapter, in which he raises the question whether Epic or Tragic is more excellent, or where he promises a special treatise to discuss whether Tragedy is yet perfect : here he has for modern readers only the interest of curiosity. Dr. Johnson's analysis of 'metaphysical poetry,' Addison's development of the leading effects in *Paradise Lost*, remain as true and forcible to-day as when they were written : Addison constructing an order of merit for English poets with Cowley and Sprat at the head, Dr. Johnson lecturing Shakespeare and Milton as to how they ought to have written—these are to us only odd anachronisms. It is like a contest with atomic force, this attempt at using ideas drawn from the past to mould and limit productive power in the present and future. The critic peers into the dimness of history, and is found to have been blind to what was by his side : Boileau strives to erect a throne of Comedy for Terence, and never suspects that a truer king was at hand in his own personal friend Molière. It is in vain for critics to denounce, their denunciation recoils on themselves: the sentence of Rymer that the soul of modern Drama was a brutish and not a reasonable soul, or of Voltaire, that Shakespeare's Tragedy would not be tolerated by the lowest French mob, can harm none but Rymer and Voltaire. If the critics venture to prophesy, the sequel is the only refutation of them needed ; if they give reasons, the reasons survive only to explain how the critics were led astray; if they lay down laws, literary greatness in the next generation is found to vary directly with the boldness with which authors violate the laws. If they assume a judicial attitude, the judgment-seat becomes converted into a pillory for the judge, and a comic side to literary history is furnished by the mockery with which time preserves the proportions of things, as seen by past criticism, to be laid side by side with the true perspective revealed by actual history. In such wise it has preserved to us the list of ' poets laureate ' who preceded Southey : Shadwell, Tate, Rowe, Eusden, Cibber, Whitehead, Warton, Pye. It reveals Dryden sighing that Spenser could only have read the rules of Bossu, or smitten with a doubt whether he might not after all excuse Milton's use of blank verse ' by the example of Hannibal Caro ' ; Rymer preferring Ben Jonson's *Catiline* to all the tragedies of the Elizabethan age, and declaring Waller's *Poem on the Navy Royal* beyond all modern poetry in any language ; Voltaire wondering that the extravagances of Shakespeare could be tolerated by a nation that had seen Addison's *Cato* ; Pope assigning three-score years and ten as the limit of posthumous life to ' moderns ' in poetry, and celebrating the trio who had rescued from the ' uncivilised ' Elizabethan poetry the ' fundamental laws of wit.' These three are Buckingham, Roscommon, and Walsh : as to the last of whom if we search amongst contemporary authorities to discover who he was, we at last come upon his works described in the *Rambler* as ' pages of inanity.'

But in the conflict between judicial criticism and science

the most important point is to note how the critics' own
ideas of criticism are found to be gradually slipping away
from them. Between the Renaissance and the present day
criticism, as judged by the methods actually followed by
critics, has slowly changed from the form of laying down
laws to authors into the form of receiving laws from authors.
The process of change falls into five stages. In its first
stage the conception of criticism was bounded by the notion
of comparing whatever was produced with the masterpieces
and trying it by the ideas of Greek and Roman literature.
Boileau objected to Corneille's tragedies, not because they
did not excite admiration, but because admiration was not
one of the tragical passions as laid down by Aristotle, To
Rymer's mind it was clearly a case of classical standards or
no standards, and he describes his opponents as 'a kind of
stage-quacks and empirics in poetry who have got a receipt
to please.' And there is a degree of *naïveté* in the way in
which Bossu betrays his utter unconsciousness of the possibility that there should be more than one kind of excellence,
where, in a passage in which he is admitting that the
moderns have as much spirit and as lucky fancies as the
ancients, he nevertheless calls it 'a piece of injustice to pretend that our new rules destroy the fancies of the old
masters, and that they must condemn all their works who
could not foresee all our humours.' Criticism in this spirit
is notably illustrated by the Corneille incident in the history
of the French Academy. The fashionable literary world,
led by a Scudéry, solemnly impeach Corneille of originality,
and Richelieu insists on the Academy pronouncing judgment; which they at last do, unwillingly enough, since, as
Boileau admitted, all France was against them. The only
one that in the whole incident retained his sense of humour
was the victim himself; who, early in the struggle, being
confronted by critics recognising no merit but that of
obedience to rules, set himself to write his *Clitandre* as a

play which should obey all the rules of Drama and yet have
nothing in it: 'in which,' he said, 'I have absolutely succeeded.'—But this reign of simple faith began to be dis- 2. *Recognition of
modern as
illegitimate
merit.*
turbed by sceptical doubts: it became impossible entirely to
ignore merit outside the pale of classical conformity.   Thus
we get a Dennis unable to conceal his admiration for the
daring of Milton, as a man who knew the rules of Aristotle,
'no man better,' and yet violated them.   Literature of the
modern type gets discussed as it were under protest.   Dr.
Johnson, when he praises Addison's *Cato* for adhering to
Aristotle's principles 'with a *scrupulousness* almost unex-
ampled on the English stage,' is reflecting the constant
assumption throughout this transitional stage, that departure
from classical models is the result of carelessness, and that
beauties in such offending writers are lucky hits.   The spirit
of this period is distinctly brought out by Dr. Johnson where
he 'readily allows' that the union in one composition of
serious and ludicrous is 'contrary to the rules of criticism,'
but, he adds, 'there is always an appeal open from criticism
to nature.'—Once admitted to examination the force of 3. *Modern
standards
of judging
side by
side with
ancient.*
modern literature could not fail to assert its equality with the
literature of the ancients, and we pass into a third stage of
criticism when critics grasp the conception that there may
be more than one set of rules by which authors may be
judged.   The new notion made its appearance early in the
country which was the main stronghold of the opposite view.
Perrault in 1687 instituted his 'Parallels' between the
ancients and the moderns to the advantage of the latter;
and the question was put in its naked simplicity by Fon-
tenelle, the 'Nestor of literature,' when he made it depend
upon another question, 'whether the trees that used to grow
in our woods were larger than those which grow now.'
Later, and with less distinctness, English criticism followed
the lead.   Pope, with his happy indifference to consistency,
after illustrating the first stage where he advises to write 'as

if the Stagirite o'erlooked each line,' and where he contends that if the classical authors indulge in a licence that licence becomes a law to us, elsewhere lays down that to apply ancient rules in the treatment of modern literature is to try by the laws of one country a man belonging to another. In one notable instance the genius of Dr. Johnson rises superior to the prejudices of his age, and he vindicates in his treatment of Shakespeare the conception of a school of Drama in which the unities of time and place do not apply. But he does it with trembling: 'I am almost frightened at my own temerity; and when I estimate the fame and the strength of those who maintain the contrary opinion, am

4. Concep-tion of criticism as judging begins to waver;

ready to sink down in reverential silence.'—Criticism had set out with judging by one set of laws, it had come to judge by two: the change began to shake the notion of *judging* as the function of criticism, and the eyes of critics came to be turned more to the idea of literary beauty itself, as the end for which the laws of literary composition were merely means. Addison is the great name connected with this further transitional stage. We find Addison not only arguing negatively that 'there is sometimes a greater judgment shown in deviating from the rules of art than in ad-hering to them,' but even laying down as a positive theory

changing to the search for beau-ties;

that the true function of a critic is 'to discover the concealed beauties of a writer'; while the practical illustration of his theory which he gave in the case of the *Paradise Lost* is supposed to have revolutionised the opinion of the fashion-able reading-public.—Addison was removed by a very little

5, and finally to investiga-tion of laws in litera-ture as it stands.

from the final stage of criticism, the conception of which is perhaps most fully brought out by Gervinus, where he de-clares his purpose of treating Shakespeare as the 'revealing genius' of his department of art and of its laws. Thus slowly and by gradual stages has the conception of criticism been changing in the direction of induction: starting from judgment by the laws of the ancient classics as standards beyond which there is no appeal, passing through the transitional stage of greater and greater toleration for intrinsic worth though of a modern type, to arrive at the recognition of modern standards of judgment side by side with ancient; again passing through a further transitional stage of discrediting judgment altogether as the purpose of criticism in favour of the search for intrinsic worth in literature as it stands, till the final conception is reached of analysing literature as it stands for the purpose of discovering its laws in itself. The later stages do not universally prevail yet. But the earlier stages have at all events become obsolete; and there is no reader who will not acquiesce cheerfully in one of the details Addison gives out for his ideal theatre, by which Rymer's tragedy *Edgar* was to be cut up into snow to make the Storm Scene in Shakespeare's *Lear*.

It may be well to recall the exact purpose to which the *Separateness of the two criticisms* present argument is intended to lead. The purpose is not to attack journalism and kindred branches of criticism in the interests of inductive treatment. It would be false to the principles of induction not to recognise that the criticism of taste has long since established its position as a fertile branch of literature. Even in an inductive system journalism would still have place as a medium for fragmentary and tentative treatment. Moreover it may be admitted that induction in its formal completeness of system can never be applied in practical life; and in the intellectual pursuits of real life trained literary taste may be a valuable acquisition. What is here attacked is the mistake which has identified the criticism of taste and valuation with the conception of criticism as a whole; the intrusion of methods belonging to journalism into treatment that claims to be systematic. So far from being a *Criticism of taste belongs to creative literature.* standard of method in the treatment of literature, criticism of the reviewer's order is outside science altogether. It finds its proper place on the creative side of literature, as a branch in which literature itself has come to be taken as a theme for literary writing; it thus belongs to the literature treated, not to the scientific treatment of it.   Reviews so placed may be regarded almost as the lyrics of prose: like lyric poems they have their completeness in themselves, and their interest lies, not in their being parts of some whole, but in their flashing the subjectivity of a writer on to a variety of isolated topics; they thus have value, not as fragments of literary science, but as fragments of Addison, of Jeffrey, of Macaulay. Nor is the bearing of the present argument that commentators should set themselves to eulogise the authors they treat instead of condemning them (though this would certainly be the safer of two errors).   The treatment aimed at is one independent of praise or blame, one that has nothing to do with merit, relative or absolute.   The contention is for a branch of criticism separate from the criticism of taste; a branch that, in harmony with the spirit of other modern sciences, reviews the phenomena of literature as they actually stand, enquiring into and endeavouring to systematise the laws and principles by which they are moulded and produce their effects. Scientific criticism and the criticism of taste have distinct spheres: and the whole of literary history shows that the failure to keep the two separate ⁻esults only in mutual confusion.

as the lyrics of prose.

Our present purpose is with inductive criticism.   What, by the analogy of other sciences, is implied in the inductive treatment of literature?

Application of induction to literary subject-matter.

The inductive sciences occupy themselves directly with facts, that is, with phenomena translated by observation into the form of facts; and soundness of inductive theory is measured by the closeness with which it will bear confronting with the facts.   In the case of literature and art the facts are to be looked for in the literary and artistic productions themselves: the dramas, epics, pictures, statues, pillars, capitals, symphonies, operas—the details of these are the phenomena which the critical observer translates into facts.

A picture is a title for a bundle of facts : that the painter has united so many figures in such and such groupings, that he has given such and such varieties of colouring, and such and such arrangement of light and shade. Similarly the *Iliad* is a short name implying a large number of facts characterising the poem : that its principal personages are Agamemnon and Achilles, that these personages are represented as displaying certain qualities, doing certain deeds, and standing in certain relations to one another.

Here, however, arises that which has been perhaps the greatest stumbling-block in the way of securing inductive treatment for literature. Science deals only with ascertained facts : but the details of literature and art are open to the most diverse interpretation. They leave conflicting impressions on different observers, impressions both subjective and variable in themselves, and open to all manner of distracting influences, not excepting that of criticism itself. Where in the treatment of literature is to be found the positiveness of subject-matter which is the first condition of science ? *Difficulty · the want of positiveness in literary impressions*

In the first place it may be pointed out that this want of certainty in literary interpretation is not a difficulty of a kind peculiar to literature. The same object of terror will affect the members of a crowd in a hundred different ways, from presence of mind to hysteria ; yet this has not prevented the science of psychology from inductively discussing fear. Logic proposes to scientifically analyse the reasoning processes in the face of the infinite degrees of susceptibility different minds show to proof and persuasion. It has become proverbial that taste in art is incapable of being settled by discussion, yet the art of music has found exact treatment in the science of harmony. In the case of these well-established sciences it has been found possible to separate the variable element from that which is the subject-matter of the science : such a science as psychology really covers two distinct branches of thought, the psychology that discusses formally *The difficulty not confined to literature.*

the elements of the human mind, and another psychology, not yet systematised, that deals with the distribution of these elements amongst different individuals. It need then be no barrier to inductive treatment that in the case of literature and art the will and consciousness act as disturbing forces, refracting what may be called natural effects into innumerable effects on individual students. It only becomes a question of practical procedure, in what way the interfering variability is to be eliminated.

The vari-
able ele-
ment to be
eliminated
by reference
not to taste;

It is precisely at this point that *à priori* criticism and induction part company. The *à priori* critic gets rid of uncertainty in literary interpretation by confining his attention to effects produced upon the best minds : he sets up *taste* as a standard by which to try impressions of literature which he is willing to consider. The inductive critic cannot have recourse to any such arbitrary means of limiting his materials; for his doubts he knows no court of appeal ex-

but to the
objective
details of
the litera-
ture itself.

cept the appeal to the literary works themselves. The astronomer, from the vast distance of the objects he observes, finds the same phenomenon producing different results on different observers, and he has thus regularly to allow for personal errors : but he deals with such discrepancies only by fresh observations on the stars themselves, and it never occurs to him that he can get rid of a variation by abstract argument or deference to a greater observer. In the same way the inductive critic of literature must settle his doubts by referring them to the literary productions themselves; to him the question is not of the nobler view or the view in best taste, but simply what view fits in best with the details as they stand in actual fact. He quite recognises that it is not the objective details but the subjective impressions they produce that make literary effect, but the objective details are the *limit* on the variability of the subjective impressions. The character of Macbeth impresses two readers differently : how is the difference to be settled? The *à priori* critic contends that his conception is the loftier; that a hero should be heroic; that moreover the tradition of the stage and the greatest names in the criticism of the past bear him out; or, finally, falls back upon good taste, which closes the discussion.   The inductive critic simply puts together all the sayings and doings of Macbeth himself, all that others in the play say and appear to feel about him, and whatever view of the character is consistent with these and similar facts of the play, that view he selects; while to vary from it for any external consideration would seem to him as futile as for an astronomer to make a star rise an hour earlier to tally with the movements of another star.

We thus arrive at a foundation axiom of inductive literary criticism: *Interpretation in literature is of the nature of a scientific hypothesis, the truth of which is tested by the degree of completeness with which it explains the details of the literary work as they actually stand.*   That will be the true meaning of a passage, not which is the most worthy, but which most nearly explains the words as they are; that will be the true reading of a character which, however involved in expression or tame in effect, accounts for and reconciles all that is represented of the personage.   The inductive critic will interpret a complex situation, not by fastening attention on its striking elements and ignoring others as oversights and blemishes, but by putting together with business-like exactitude all that the author has given, weighing, balancing, and standing by the product.   He will not consider that he has solved the action of a drama by some leading plot, or some central idea powerfully suggested in different parts, but will investigate patiently until he can find a scheme which will give point to the inferior as well as to the leading scenes, and in connection with which all the details are harmonised in their proper proportions.   In this way he will be raising a superstructure of exposition that rests, not on authority however high, but upon a basis of indisputable fact.

Foundation axiom of the inductive criticism · Interpretation of the nature of an hypothesis.

Practical objection: Did the authors intend these interpretations? In actual operation I have often found that such positive analysis raises in the popular mind a very practical objection : that the scientific interpretation seems to discover in literary works much more in the way of purpose and design than the authors themselves can be supposed to have dreamed of. Would not Chaucer and Shakespeare, it is asked, if they could come to life now, be greatly astonished to hear themselves lectured upon? to find critics knowing their purposes better than they had known them themselves, and discovering in their works laws never suspected till after they were dead, and which they themselves perhaps would need some effort to understand? Deep designs are traced in Shakespeare's plots, and elaborate combinations in his characters and passions: is the student asked to believe that Shakespeare really *intended* these complicated effects?

Answer: changed meaning of 'design' in science. The difficulty rests largely upon a confusion in words. Such words as 'purpose,' 'intention,' have a different sense when used in ordinary parlance from that which they bear when applied in criticism and science. In ordinary parlance a man's 'purpose' means his conscious purpose, of which he is the best judge ; in science the 'purpose' of a thing is the purpose it actually serves, and is discoverable only by analysis. Thus science discovers that the 'purpose' of earthworms is to break up the soil, the 'design' of colouring in flowers is to attract insects, though the flower is not credited with foresight nor the worm with disinterestedness. In this usage alone can the words 'purpose,' 'intention,' be properly applied to literature and art: science knows no kind of evidence in the matter of creative purpose so weighty as the thing it has actually produced. This has been well put by Ulrici :

> The *language* of the artist is poetry, music, drawing, colouring : there is no other form in which he can express himself with equal depth and clearness. Who would ask a philosopher to paint his ideas in colours? It would be equally absurd to think that because a poet cannot say with perfect philosophic certainty in the form of reflection and pure thought what it was that he wished and intended to produce,

that he never thought at all, but let his imagination improvise at random.

Nothing is more common than for analysis to discover design in what, so far as consciousness is concerned, has been purely instinctive. Thus physiology ascertains that bread contains all the necessary elements of food except one, which omission happens to be supplied by butter : this may be accepted as an explanation of our 'purpose' in eating butter with bread, without the explanation being taken to imply that all who have ever fed on bread and butter have consciously *intended* to combine the nitrogenous and oleaginous elements of food. It is the natural order of things that the practical must precede the analytic. Bees by instinct construct hexagonal cells, and long afterwards mensuration shows that the hexagon is the most economic shape for such stowage ; individual states must rise and fall first before the sciences of history and politics can come to explain the how and why of their mutations. Similarly it is in accordance with the order of things that Shakespeare should produce dramas by the practical processes of art-creation, and that it should be left for others, his critics succeeding him at long intervals, to discover by analysis his 'purposes' and the laws which underlie his effects. The poet, if he could come to life now, would not feel more surprise at this analysis of his 'motives' and unfolding of his unconscious 'design' than he would feel on hearing that the beating of his heart—to him a thing natural enough, and needing no explanation— had been discovered to have a distinct purpose he could never have dreamed of in propelling the circulation of his blood, a thing of which he had never heard.

Three points of contrast between judicial and inductive criticism.

There are three leading ideas in relation to which inductive and judicial criticism are in absolute antagonism : to bring out these contrasts will be the most effective way of describing the inductive treatment.

The first of these ideas is order of merit, together with the

1.
*Compari-
sons of
merit:
these out-
side science.*
kindred notions of partisanship and hostility applied to individual authors and works.   The minds of ordinary readers
are saturated with this class of ideas; they are the weeds of
taste, choking the soil, and leaving no room for the purer
forms of literary appreciation. Favoured by the fatal blunder
of modern education, which considers every other mental
power to stand in need of training, but leaves taste and
imagination to shift for themselves, literary taste has largely
become confused with a spurious form of it: the mere taste
for competition, comparison of likes and dislikes, gossip
applied to art and called criticism. Of course such likes and
dislikes must always exist, and journalism is consecrated to
the office of giving them shape and literary expression;
though it should be led by experience, if by nothing else, to
exercise its functions with a double reserve, recognising that
the judicial attitude of mind is a limit on appreciation, and
that the process of testing will itself be tried by the test of
vitality.   But such preferences and comparisons of merit
must be kept rigidly outside the sphere of science. Science
knows nothing of competitive examination: a geologist is
not heard extolling old red sandstone as a model rock-
formation, or making sarcastic comments on the glacial
epoch. Induction need not disturb the freedom with which
we attach ourselves to whatever attracts our individual dis-
positions: individual partisanship for the wooded snugness
of the Rhine or the bold and bracing Alps is unaffected by
the adoption of exact methods in physical geography. What
is to be avoided is the confusion of two different kinds of
interest attaching to the same object.   In the study of the
stars and the rocks, which can inspire little or no personal
interest, it is easy to keep science pure; to keep it to 'dry
light,' as Heraclitus calls it, intelligence unclouded by the
humours of individual sentiment, as Bacon interprets. But
when science comes to be applied to objects which can excite
emotion and inspire affection, then confusion arises, and the

scientific student of political economy finds his treatment of
pauperism disturbed by the philanthropy which belongs to
him as a man. Still more in so emotional an atmosphere as
the study of beauty, the student must use effort to separate
the *beauty* of an object, which is a thing of art and perfectly
analysable, from his personal *interest* in it, which is as distinctly external to the analysis of beauty as his love for his
dog is external to the science of zoology. The possibility of
thus separating interest and perception of beauty without
diminishing either may be sufficiently seen in the case of
music—an art which has been already reduced to scientific
form. Music is as much as any art a thing of tastes and
preferences; besides partialities for particular masters one
student will be peculiarly affected by melody, another is all
for dramatic effect, others have a special taste for the fugue
or the sonata. No one can object to such preferences, but
the science of music knows nothing about them; its exposition deals with modes of treatment or habits of orchestration
distinguishing composers, irrespective of the private partialities
they excite. Mozart and Wagner are analysed as two items
in the sum of facts which make up music; and if a particular
expositor shows by a turn in the sentence that he has a leaning to one or the other, the slip may do no harm, but for the
moment science has been dropped.

There is, however, a sort of difference between authors and *Inductive*
works, the constant recognition of which would more than *treatment concerned*
make up to cultured pleasure for discarding comparisons of *with dif-*
merit. Inductive treatment is concerned with *differences of* *ferences of kind, not of*
kind as distinguished from differences of degree. Elementary *degree.*
as this distinction is, the power of firmly grasping it is no
slight evidence of a trained mind: the power, that is, of clearly
seeing that two things are different, without being at the same
time impelled to rank one above the other. The confusion
of the two is a constant obstacle in the way of literary appreciation. It has been said, by way of comparison between two

great novelists, that George Eliot constructs characters, but
Charlotte Brontë creates them.   The description (assuming
it to be true) ought to shed a flood of interest upon both
authoresses; by perpetually throwing on the two modes of
treatment the clear light of contrast it ought to intensify our
appreciation of both.   As a fact, however, the description is
usually quoted to suggest a preference for Charlotte Brontë
on the supposed ground that creation is 'higher' than construction; and the usual consequences of preferences are
threatened—the gradual closing of our susceptibilities to those
qualities in the less liked of the two which do not resemble
the qualities of the favourite.   Yet why should we not be
content to accept such a description (if true) as constituting
a difference of kind, and proceed to recognise 'construction'
and 'creation' as two parallel modes of treatment, totally
distinct from one another in the way in which a fern is distinct from a flower, a distinction allowing no room for preferences because there is no common ground on which to compare ?   This separateness once granted, the mind, instead of
having to choose between the two, would have scope for
taking in to the full the detailed effects flowing from both
modes of treatment, and the area of mental pleasure would be
enlarged.   The great blunders of criticism in the past, which
are now universally admitted, rest on this inability to recognise
differences of kind in literature.   The Restoration poets had
a mission to bring the heroic couplet to perfection: poetry
not in their favourite measure they treated, not as different,
but as bad, and rewrote or ignored Spenser and Milton. And
generations of literary history have been wasted in discussing
whether the Greek dramatists or Shakespeare were the higher :
now every one recognises that they constitute two schools
different in kind that cannot be compared.

Distinc-
tions of
kind a pri-   It is hardly going too far to assert that this sensitiveness to
mary ele-
ment in ap- differences of kind as distinguished from differences of degree
preciation. is the first condition of literary appreciation.   Nothing can be

more essential to art-perception than receptiveness, and receptiveness implies a change in the receptive attitude of mind with each variety of art. To illustrate by an extreme case. Imagine a spectator perfectly familiar with the Drama, but to whom the existence of the Opera was unknown, and suppose him to have wandered into an opera-house, mistaking it for a theatre. At first the mistake under which he was labouring would distort every effect : the elaborate overture would seem to him a great 'waste' of power in what was a mere accessory ; the opening recitative would strike him as 'unnaturally' delivered, and he would complain of the orchestral accompaniment as a 'distraction' ; while at the first aria he would think the actor gone mad. As, however, arias, terzettos, recitatives succeeded one another, he must at last catch the idea that the music was an essential element in the exhibition, and that he was seeing, not a drama, but a drama translated into a different kind of art. The catching of this idea would at once make all the objectionable elements fall into their proper places. No longer distracted by the thought of the ordinary Drama, his mind would have leisure to catch the special effects of the Opera : he would feel how powerfully a change of passion could move him when magnified with all the range of expression an orchestra affords, and he would acknowledge a dramatic touch as the diabolic spirit of the conspirator found vent in a double D. The illustration is extreme to the extent of absurdity : but it brings out how expectation plays an important part in appreciation, and how the expectation has to be adapted to that on which it is exercised. The receptive attitude is a sort of mental focus which needs adjusting afresh to each variety of art if its effects are to be clearly caught ; and to disturb attention when engaged on one species of literature by the thought of another is as unreasonable as to insist on one microscopic object appearing definite when looked at with a focus adjusted to another object. This will be acknowledged in reference to the great

Each author a separate species.

divisions of art : but does it not apply to the species as well as the genera, indeed to each individual author? Wordsworth has laid down that each fresh poet is to be tried by fresh canons of taste : this is only another way of saying that the differences between poets are differences of kind, that each author is a ' school' by himself, and can be appreciated only by a receptive attitude formed by adjustment to himself alone. In a scientific treatment of literature, at all events, an ele-

Second axiom of inductive criticism: its function in distinguishing literary species.

mentary axiom must be : *That inductive criticism is mainly occupied in distinguishing literary species.* And on this view it will clearly appear how such notions as order of merit become disturbing forces in literary appreciation : unconsciously they apply the *qualitative* standard of the favourite works to works which must necessarily be explained by a different standard. They are defended on the ground of pleasure, but they defeat their own object: no element in pleasure is greater than variety, and comparisons of merit, with every other form of the judicial spirit, are in reality arrangements for appreciating the smallest number of varieties.

II.
The ' laws of art': confusion between law external and scientific.

The second is the most important of the three ideas, both for its effect in the past and for the sharpness with which it brings judicial and inductive criticism into contrast. It is the idea that there exist ' laws ' of art, in the same sense in which we speak of laws in morality or the laws of some particular state—great principles which have been laid down, and which are binding on the artist as the laws of God or his country are binding on the man ; that by these, and by lesser principles deduced from these, the artist's work is to be tried, and praise or blame awarded accordingly. Great part of formal criticism runs on these lines; while, next in importance to comparisons of merit, the popular mind considers literary taste to consist in a keen sensitiveness to the ' faults ' and ' flaws ' of literary workmanship.

This attitude to art illustrates the enormous misleading

power of the metaphors that lie concealed in words. The
word ' law,' justly applicable in one of its senses to art, has
in practice carried with it the associations of its other sense ;
and the mistake of metaphor has been sufficient to distort
criticism until, as Goldsmith remarks, rules have become the
greatest of all the misfortunes which have befallen the commonwealth of letters. Every expositor has had to point out
the widespread confusion between the two senses of this
term. Laws in the moral and political world are external
obligations, restraints of the will; they exist where the will
of a ruler or of the community is applied to the individual
will. In science, on the other hand, law has to do not with
what ought to be, but with what is; scientific laws are facts
reduced to formulæ, statements of the habits of things, so to
speak. The laws of the stars in the first sense could only
mean some creative fiat, such as ' Let there be lights in the
firmament of heaven ' ; in the scientific sense laws of the stars
are summaries of their customary movements. In the act of
getting drunk I am violating God's moral law, I am obeying
his law of alcoholic action. So scientific laws, in the case of
art and literature, will mean descriptions of the practice of
artists or the characteristics of their works, when these will go
into the form of general propositions as distinguished from
disconnected details. The key to the distinction is the notion
of external authority. There cannot be laws in the moral and
political sense without a ruler or legislative authority; in
scientific laws the law-giver and the law-obeyer are one and
the same, and for the laws of vegetation science looks no
further than the facts of the vegetable world. In literature *The ' laws*
and art the term ' law ' applies only in the scientific sense; *of art' are*
scientific
the laws of the Shakespearean Drama are not laws imposed *laws.*
by some external authority upon Shakespeare, but laws of
dramatic practice derived from the analysis of his actual
works. Laws of literature, in the sense of external obligations
limiting an author, there are none: if he were voluntarily to

bind himself by such external laws, he would be so far cur-
tailing art; it is hardly a paradox to say the art is legitimate

only when it does not obey laws.   What applies to the term
'law' applies similarly to the term 'fault.'   The term is
likely always to be used from its extreme convenience in art-
training; but it must be understood strictly as a term of education and discipline.   In inductive criticism, as in the other
inductive sciences, the word 'fault' has no meaning.   If an
artist acts contrary to the practice of all other artists, the
result is either that he produces no art-effect at all, in which
case there is nothing for criticism to register and analyse, or
else he produces a new effect, and is thus extending, not
breaking, the laws of art.   The great clash of horns in
Beethoven's Heroic Symphony was at first denounced as a
gross fault, a violation of the plainest laws of harmony; now,
instead of a 'fault,' it is spoken of as a 'unique effect,' and
in the difference between the two descriptions lies the whole
difference between the conceptions of judicial and inductive
criticism.   Again and again in the past this notion of faults
has led criticism on to wrong tracks, from which it has had
to retrace its steps on finding the supposed faults to be in
reality new laws.   Immense energy was wasted in denouncing
Shakespeare's 'fault' of uniting serious with light matter in
the same play as a violation of fundamental dramatic laws;
experience showed this mixture of passions to be the source
of powerful art-effects hitherto shut out of the Drama, and the
'fault' became one of the distinguishing 'laws' in the most
famous branch of modern literature.   It is necessary then to
insist upon the strict scientific sense of the term 'law' as
used of literature and art; and the purging of criticism from
the confusion attaching to this word is an essential step in its
elevation to the inductive standard.   It is a step, moreover,
in which it has been preceded by other branches of thought.
At one time the practice of commerce and the science of
economy suffered under the same confusion: the battle of

'free trade' has been fought, the battle of 'free art' is still going on. In time it will be recognised that the practice of artists, like the operations of business, must be left to its natural working, and the attempt to impose external canons of taste on artists will appear as futile as the attempt to effect by legislation the regulation of prices.

Objections may possibly be taken to this train of argument on very high grounds, as if the protest against the notion of law-obeying in art were a sort of antinomianism. Literature, it may be said, has a moral purpose, to elevate and refine, and no duty can be higher than that of pointing out what in it is elevating and refining, and jealously watching against any lowering of its standard. Such contention may readily be granted, and yet may amount to no more than this: that there are ways of dealing with literature which are more important than inductive criticism, but which are none the less outside it. Jeremy Collier did infinite service to our Restoration Drama, but his was not the service of a scientific critic. The same things take different ranks as they are tried by the standards of science or morals. An enervating climate may have the effect of enfeebling the moral character, but this does not make the geographer's interest in the tropical zone one whit the less. Economy concerns itself simply with the fact that a certain subsidence of profits in a particular trade will drive away capital to other trades. But the details of human experience that are latent in such a proposition: the chilling effects of unsuccess and the dim colour it gives to the outlook into the universe, the sifting of character and separation between the enterprising and the simple, the hard thoughts as to the mysterious dispensations of human prosperity, the sheer misery of a wage-class looking on plenty and feeling starvation—this human drama of failing profits may be vastly more important than the whole science of economy, but economy none the less entirely and rightly ignores it.

To some, I know, it appears that literature is a sphere in

Objection as to the moral purpose of literature:

this outside inductive treatment, though intrinsically more important.

Objection: Art as an arbitrary product not subject to law. which the strict sense of the word 'law' has no application: that such laws belong to nature, not to art. The essence, it is contended, of the natural sciences is the certainty of the facts with which they deal. Art, on the contrary, is creative; it does not come into the category of objective phenomena at all, but is the product of some artist's will, and therefore purely arbitrary. If in a compilation of observations in natural history for scientific use it became known that the compiler had at times drawn upon his imagination for his details, the whole compilation would become useless; and any scientific theories based upon it would be discredited. But the artist bases his work wholly on imagination, and caprice is a leading art-beauty: how, it is asked, can so arbitrary a subject-matter be reduced to the form of positive laws?

Third axiom of inductive criticism: art a part of nature. In view of any such objections, it may be well to set up a third axiom of inductive criticism: *That art is a part of nature.* Nature, it is true, is the vaguest of words: but this is a vagueness common to the objection and the answer. The objection rests really on a false antithesis, of which one term is 'nature,' while it is not clear what is the other term; the axiom set up in answer implies that there is no real distinction between 'nature' and the other phenomena which are the subject of human enquiry. The distinction is supposed to rest upon the degree to which arbitrary elements of the mind, such as imagination, will, caprice, enter into such *Other arbitrary products subject to inductive treatment.* a thing as art-production. But there are other things in which the human will plays as much part as it does in art, and which have nevertheless proved compatible with inductive treatment. Those who hold that 'thought is free' do not reject psychology as an inductive science; actual politics are made up of struggles of will, exercises of arbitrary power, and the like, and yet there is a political science. If there is an inductive science of politics, men's voluntary actions in the pursuit of public life, and an inductive science of economy, men's voluntary actions in pursuit of wealth, why should there not be an inductive science of art, men's voluntary actions in pursuit of the beautiful? The whole of human action, as well as the whole of external nature, comes within the jurisdiction of science; so far from the productions of the will and imagination being exempted from scientific treatment, will and imagination themselves form chapters in psychology, and caprice has been analysed.

It remains to notice the third of the three ideas in relation to which the two kinds of criticism are in complete contrast with one another. It is a vague notion, which no objector would formulate, but which as a fact does underlie judicial criticism, and insensibly accompanies its testing and assaying. It is the idea that the foundations of literary form have reached their final settlement, the past being tacitly taken as a standard for the present and future, or the present as a standard for the past. Thus in the treatment of new literature the idea manifests itself in a secret antagonism to variations from received models; at the very least, new forms are called upon to justify themselves, and so the judicial critic brings his least receptive attitude to the new effects which need receptiveness most. In opposition to this tacit assumption, inductive criticism starts with a distinct counter-axiom of the utmost importance: *That literature is a thing of development.* This axiom implies that the critic must come to literature as to that in which he is expecting to find unlimited change and variety; he must keep before him the fact that production must always be far ahead of criticism and analysis, and must have carried its conquering invention into fresh regions before science, like settled government in the wake of the pioneer, follows to explain the new effects by new principles. No doubt in name literary development is recognised in all criticism; yet in its treatment both of old literature and new the *à priori* criticism is false to development in the scientific sense of the term. Such systems are apt to begin by laying down that 'the object of literature is so and

III.
Testing by fixed standards inconsistent with inductive treatment.

Fourth axiom of inductive criticism: literature a thing of development.

Ignoring of development in new literature:

'purpose' in literature continually modifying.

Development in past literature confused with improvement.

so,' or that 'the purpose of the Drama is to pourtray human nature'; they then proceed to test actual literature and dramas by the degree in which they carry out these fundamental principles. Such procedure is the opposite of the inductive method, and is a practical denial of development in literature. Assuming that the object of existing literature were correctly described, such a formula could not bind the literature of the future. Assuming that there was ever a branch of art which could be reduced to one simple purpose, yet the inherent tendency of the human mind and its productions to develop would bring it about that what were at first means towards this purpose would in time become ends in themselves side by side with the main purpose, giving us in addition to the simple species a modified variety of it; external influences, again, would mingle with the native characteristics of the original species, and produce new species compound in their purposes and effects. The real literature would be ever obeying the first principle of development and changing from simple to complex, while the criticism that tried it by the original standard would be at each step removed one degree further from the only standard by which the literature could be explained. And if judicial criticism fails in providing for development in the future and present, it is equally unfortunate in giving a false twist to development when looked for in the past. The critic of comparative standards is apt to treat early stages of literature as elementary, tacitly assuming his own age as a standard *up to* which previous periods have developed. Thus his treatment of the past becomes often an assessment of the degrees in which past periods have approximated to his own, advancing from literary pot-hooks to his own running facility. The clearness of an ancient writer he values at fifty per cent. as compared with modern standards, his concatenation of sentences is put down as only forty-five. But what if a certain degree of mistiness be an essential element in the phase of literary development to which the particular writer belongs, so that in him modern clearness would become, in judicial phrase, a fault? What if Plato's concatenation of sentences would simply spoil the flavour of Herodotus's story-telling, if Jeremy Taylor's prolixity and Milton's bi-lingual prose be simply the fittest of all dresses for the thought of their age and individual genius? In fact, the critic of fixed standards confuses development with *improvement* : a parallel mistake in natural history would be to understand the statement that man is higher in the scale of development than the butterfly as implying that a butterfly was God's failure in the attempt to make man. The inductive critic will accord to the early forms of his art the same independence he accords to later forms. Development will not mean to him education for a future stage, but the perpetual branching out of literary activity into ever fresh varieties, different in kind from one another, and each to be studied by standards of its own : the 'individuality' of authors is the expression in literary parlance which corresponds to the perpetual 'differentiation' of new species in science. Alike, then, in his attitude to the past and the future, the inductive critic will eschew the temptation to judgment by fixed standards, which in reality means opposing lifeless rules to the ever-living variety of nature. He will leave a dead judicial criticism to bury its dead authors and to pen for them judicious epitaphs, and will himself approach literature filled equally with reverence for the unbroken vitality of its past and faith in its exhaustless future.

To gather up our results. Induction, as the most uni- *Summary.* versal of scientific methods, may be presumed to apply wherever there is a subject-matter reducible to the form of fact ; such a subject-matter will be found in literature where its effects are interpreted, not arbitrarily, but with strict reference to the details of the literary works as they actually stand. There is thus an inductive literary criticism, akin in spirit and methods to the other inductive sciences, and distinct from other branches of criticism, such as the criticism of taste. This inductive criticism will entirely free itself from the judicial spirit and its comparisons of merit, which is found to have been leading criticism during half its history on to false tracks from which it has taken the other half to retrace its steps. On the contrary, inductive criticism will examine literature in the spirit of pure investigation: looking for the laws of art in the practice of artists, and treating art, like the rest of nature, as a thing of continuous development, which may thus be expected to fall, with each author and school, into varieties distinct in kind from one another, and each of which can be fully grasped only when examined with an attitude of mind adapted to the special variety without interference from without.

To illustrate the criticism thus described in its application to Shakespeare is the purpose of the present work.

The scope of the book is limited to the consideration of Shakespeare in his character as the great master of the Romantic Drama; and its treatment of his dramatic art divides itself into two parts. The first applies the inductive method in a series of Studies devoted to particular plays, and to single important features of dramatic art which these plays illustrate. One of the purposes of this first part is to bring out how the inductive method, besides its scientific interest, has the further recommendation of assisting more than any other treatment to enlarge our appreciation of the author and of his achievements. The second part will use the materials collected in the first part to present, in the form of a brief survey, Dramatic Criticism as an inductive science: enumerating, so far as its materials admit, the leading topics which such a science would treat, and arranging these topics in the logical connection which scientific method requires.

PART FIRST.

SHAKESPEARE

CONSIDERED AS A

DRAMATIC ARTIST

IN TEN STUDIES.

I.

THE TWO STORIES SHAKESPEARE BORROWS FOR HIS MERCHANT OF VENICE.

A Study in the Raw Material of the Romantic Drama.

THE starting-point in the treatment of any work of literature is its position in literary history: the recognition of this gives the attitude of mind which is most favourable for extracting from the work its full effect. The division of the universal Drama to which Shakespeare belongs is known as the 'Romantic Drama,' one of its chief distinctions being that it uses the stories of Romance, together with histories treated as story-books, as the sources from which the matter of the plays is taken; Romances are the *raw material* out of which the Shakespearean Drama is manufactured. This very fact serves to illustrate the elevation of the Elizabethan Drama in the scale of literary development: just as the weaver uses as his raw material that which is the finished product of the spinner, so Shakespeare and his contemporaries start in their art of dramatising from Story which is already a form of art. In the exhibition, then, of Shakespeare as an Artist, it is natural to begin with the raw material which he worked up into finished masterpieces. For illustration of this no play could be more suitable than *The Merchant of Venice*, in which two tales, already familiar in the story form, have been woven together into a single plot: the Story of the Cruel Jew, who entered into a bond with his enemy of which the forfeit was to be a pound of this

CHAP. I. enemy's own flesh, and the Story of the Heiress and the Caskets. The present study will deal with the stories themselves, considering them as if with the eye of a dramatic artist to catch the points in which they lend themselves to dramatic effect; the next will show how Shakespeare improves the stories in the telling, increasing their dramatic force by the very process of working them up; a third study will point out how, not content with two stories, he has added others in the development of his plot, making it more complex only in reality to make it more simple.

Story of the Jew. In the Story of the Jew the main point is its special capability for bringing out the idea of *Nemesis*, one of the simplest and most universal of dramatic motives. Described *Nemesis as a dramatic idea.* broadly, Nemesis is retribution as it appears in the world of art. In reality the term covers two distinct conceptions: in ancient thought Nemesis was an artistic bond between excess and reaction, in modern thought it is an artistic bond between sin and retribution. The distinction is part of the general difference between Greek and modern views of life. *Ancient conception : artistic connection between excess and reaction.* The Greeks may be said to be the most artistic nation of mankind, in the sense that art covered so large a proportion of their whole personality: it is not surprising to find that they projected their sense of art into morals. Aristotle was a moral philosopher, but his system of ethics reads as an artistically devised pattern, in which every virtue is removed at equal distances from vices of excess and defect balancing it on opposite sides. The Greek word for law signifies proportion and distribution, *nomos*; and it is only another form of it that expresses *Nemesis* as the power punishing violations of proportion in things human. Distinct from Justice, which was occupied with crime, Nemesis was a companion deity to Fortune; and as Fortune went through the world distributing the good things of life heedlessly without regard to merit, so Nemesis followed in her steps, and, equally without regard to merit, delighted in cutting down the

prosperity that was high enough to attract her attention. Polycrates is the typical victim of such Nemesis : cast off by his
firmest ally for no offence but an unbroken career of good
luck, in the reaction from which his ally feared to be involved; essaying as a forlorn hope to propitiate by voluntarily
throwing in the sea his richest crown-jewel ; recognising
when this was restored by fishermen that heaven had refused
his sacrifice, and abandoning himself to his fate in despair.
But Nemesis, to the moral sense of antiquity, could go even
beyond visitation on innocent prosperity, and goodness itself
could be carried to a degree that invited divine reaction.
Heroes like Lycurgus and Pentheus perished for excess of
temperance; and the ancient Drama startles the modern
reader with an Hippolytus, whose passionate purity brought
down on him a destruction prophesied beforehand by those
to whom religious duty suggested moderate indulgence in
lust.

Such malignant correction of human inequalities is not *Modern*
a function to harmonise with modern conceptions of Deity. *conception*
Yet the Greek notion of Nemesis has an element of per- *artistic*
manency in it, for it represents a principle underlying human *connection*
between sin
life. It suggests a sort of elasticity in human experience, a *and retri-*
bution.
tendency to rebound from a strain ; this is the equilibrium of
the moral world, the force which resists departure from the
normal, becoming greater in proportion as departure from
the normal is wider. Thus in commercial speculation there
is a safe medium certain to bring profit in the long run; in
social ambition there is a certain rise though slow : if a man
hurries to be rich, or seeks to rise in public life by leaps and
bounds, the spectator becomes aware of a secret force that
has been set in motion, as when the equilibrium of physical
bodies has been disturbed, which force threatens to drag the
aspirant down to the point from which he started, or to
debase him lower in proportion to the height at which he
rashly aimed. Such a force is 'risk,' and it may remain risk,

but if it be crowned with the expected fall the whole is recognised as 'Nemesis.' This Nemesis is deeply embedded in the popular mind and repeatedly crops up in its proverbial wisdom. Proverbs like 'Grasp all, lose all,' 'When things come to the worst they are sure to mend,' exactly express moral equilibrium, and the 'golden mean' is its proverbial formula. The saying 'too much of a good thing' suggests that the Nemesis on departures from the golden mean applies to good things as well as bad; while the principle is made to apply even to the observation of the golden mean itself in the proverb 'Nothing venture, nothing have.' Nevertheless, this side of the whole notion has in modern usage fallen into the background in comparison with another aspect of Nemesis. The grand distinction of modern thought is the predominance in it of moral ideas: they colour even its imagination; and if the Greeks carried their art-sense into morals, modern instincts have carried morals into art. In particular the speculations raised by Christianity have cast the shadow of Sin over the whole universe. It has been said that the conception of Sin is unknown to the ancients, and that the word has no real equivalent in Latin or Classical Greek. The modern mind is haunted by it. Notions of Sin have invaded art, and Nemesis shows their influence: vague conceptions of some supernatural vindication of artistic proportion in life have now crystallised into the interest of watching morals and art united in their treatment of Sin. The link between Sin and its retribution becomes a form of art-pleasure; and no dramatic effect is more potent in modern Drama than that which emphasises the principle that whatsoever a man soweth that shall he also reap.

Dramatic Nemesis latent in the Story of the Jew   Now for this dramatic effect of Nemesis it would be difficult to find a story promising more scope than the Story of the Cruel Jew. It will be seen at once to contain a double nemesis, attaching to the Jew himself and to his

victim. The two moreover represent the different conceptions
of Nemesis in the ancient and modern world; Antonio's
excess of moral confidence suffers a nemesis of reaction in
his humiliation, and Shylock's sin of judicial murder finds a
nemesis of retribution in his ruin by process of law.   The
nemesis, it will be observed, is not merely two-fold, but
double in the way that a double flower is distinct from two
flowers : it is a nemesis *on* a nemesis ; the nemesis which
visits Antonio's fault is the crime for which Shylock suffers
his nemesis.   Again, in that which gives artistic character
to the reaction and the retribution the two nemeses differ.
Let St. Paul put the difference for us : ' Some men's sins
are evident, going before unto judgment; and some they
follow after.' So in cases like that of Shylock the nemesis
is interesting from its very obviousness and the impatience
with which we look for it; in the case of Antonio the
nemesis is striking for the very opposite reason, that he of
all men seemed most secure against it.

Antonio must be understood as a perfect character : for *Antonio*
we must read the play in the light of its age, and intolerance *perfection and self-*
was a mediæval virtue. But there is no single good quality *sufficiency,*
that does not carry with it its special temptation, and the *the Nemesis of Sur-*
sum of them all, or perfection, has its shadow in self- *prise.*
sufficiency. It is so with Antonio. Of all national types
of character the Roman is the most self-sufficient, alike
incorruptible by temptation and independent of the softer
influences of life : we find that ' Roman honour' is the iii. ii. 297.
idea which Antonio's friends are accustomed to associate
with him. Further the dramatist contrives to exhibit Antonio
to us in circumstances calculated to bring out this drawback to his perfection. In the opening scene we see the
dignified merchant-prince suffering under the infliction of
frivolous visitors, to which his friendship with the young
nobleman exposes him : his tone throughout the interview is
that of the barest toleration, and suggests that his courtesies

CHAP. I.   are felt rather as what is due to himself than what is due
            to those on whom they are bestowed. When Salarino makes
l. i. 60-64. flattering excuses for taking his leave, Antonio replies, first
            with conventional compliment,

> Your worth is very dear in my regard,

and then with blunt plainness, as if Salarino were not worth
the trouble of keeping up polite fiction:

> I take it, your own business calls on you
> And you embrace the occasion to depart.

l. i. 8.   The visitors, trying to find explanation for Antonio's serious-
            ness, suggest that he is thinking of his vast commercial
            speculations; Antonio draws himself up:

l. i. 41.
> Believe me, no: I thank my fortune for it,
> My ventures are not in one bottom trusted,
> Nor to one place; nor is my whole estate
> Upon the fortune of this present year:
> Therefore my merchandise makes me not sad.

Antonio is saying in his prosperity that *he* shall never be
moved. But the great temptation to self-sufficiency lies in
his contact, not with social inferiors, but with a moral outcast such as Shylock: confident that the moral gulf between
the two can never be bridged over, Antonio has violated
dignity as well as mercy in the gross insults he has heaped
upon the Jew whenever they have met. In the Bond Scene
l. iii. 99 &c. we see him unable to restrain his insults at the very moment
            in which he is soliciting a favour from his enemy; the effect
l. iii. 107- reaches a climax as Shylock gathers up the situation in a
130.   single speech, reviewing the insults and taunting his op-
            pressor with the solicited obligation:

> Well then, it now appears you need my help:
> Go to, then; you come to me, and you say,
> 'Shylock, we would have moneys': you say so;
> You, that did void your rheum upon my beard
> And foot me as you spurn a stranger cur
> Over your threshold: moneys is your suit.

There is such a foundation of justice for these taunts that

for a moment our sympathies are transferred to Shylock's
side. But Antonio, so far from taking warning, is betrayed
beyond all bounds in his defiance; and in the challenge
to fate with which he replies we catch the tone of infatuated
confidence, the *hybris* in which Greek superstition saw the
signal for the descent of Nemesis.

> I am as like to call thee so again,   i. iii. 131.
> To spit on thee again, to spurn thee too.
> If thou wilt lend this money, lend it not
> As to thy friends . . .   . . .
> *But lend it rather to thine enemy,*
> *Who, if he break, thou may'st with better face*
> *Exact the penalty.*

To this challenge of self-sufficiency the sequel of the story
is the answering Nemesis: the merchant becomes a bankrupt, the first citizen of Venice a prisoner at the bar, the
morally perfect man holds his life and his all at the mercy of
the reprobate he thought he might safely insult.

So Nemesis has surprised Antonio in spite of his perfect- *Shylock*
ness: but the malice of Shylock is such as is perpetually *malignant*
crying for retribution, and the retribution is delayed only *justice, the*
that it may descend with accumulated force. In the case of *Nemesis of*
this second nemesis the Story of the Jew exhibits dramatic *Measure.*
capability in the opportunity it affords for the sin and the
retribution to be included within the same scene. Portia's *iv. i.*
happy thought is a turning-point in the Trial Scene on the
two sides of which we have the Jew's triumph and the Jew's
retribution; the two sides are bound together by the principle of measure for measure, and for each detail of vindic-
tiveness that is developed in the first half of the scene there
is a corresponding item of nemesis in the sequel. To begin *Charter v.*
with, Shylock appeals to the charter of the city. It is one of *statute.*
the distinctions between written and unwritten law that no *iv. i. 38;*
flagrant injustice can arise out of the latter. If the analogy *compare*
of former precedents would seem to threaten such an *102, 219.*
injustice, it is easy in a new case to meet the special

E

CHAP. I. emergency by establishing a new precedent; where, however, the letter of the written law involves a wrong, however great, it must, nevertheless, be exactly enforced. Shylock takes his stand upon written law; indeed upon the strictest of all compare iii. iii. 26– 31. kinds of written law, for the charter of the city would seem to be the instrument regulating the relations between citizens and aliens—an absolute necessity for a free port—which could not be superseded without international negotiations. But what is the result? As plaintiff in the cause Shylock would, in the natural course of justice, leave the court, when judgment had been given against him, with no further mortification than the loss of his suit. He is about to do so when he is recalled:

It is enacted in the laws of Venice, &c.

iv. i. 314. Unwittingly, he has, by the action he has taken, entangled himself with an old statute law, forgotten by all except the learned Bellario, which, going far beyond natural law, made the mere attempt upon a citizen's life by an alien punishable to the same extent as murder. Shylock had chosen the letter of the law, and by the letter of the law he is to suffer. *Humour v. quibble.* Again, every one must feel that the plea on which Portia upsets the bond is in reality the merest quibble. It is appropriate enough in the mouth of a bright girl playing the lawyer, but no court of justice could seriously entertain it for a moment: by every principle of interpretation a bond that could justify the cutting of human flesh must also justify the shedding of blood, which is necessarily implied in such cutting. But, to balance this, we have Shylock in the earlier part of the scene refusing to listen to arguments of justice, iv. i. 40– 62. and taking his stand upon his 'humour': if he has a whim, he pleads, for giving ten thousand ducats to have a rat poisoned, who shall prevent him? The suitor who rests his cause on a whim cannot complain if it is upset by a quibble. Similarly, throughout the scene, every point in Shylock's

justice of malice meets its answer in the justice of nemesis.
He is offered double the amount of his loan :

> If every ducat in six thousand ducats
> Were in six parts, and every part a ducat,

he answers, he would not accept them in lieu of his bond. iv. 1. 318, 336.
The wheel of Nemesis goes round, and Shylock would
gladly accept not only this offer but even the bare principal;
but he is denied, on the ground that he has refused it in open
court.   They try to bend him to thoughts of mercy :

> How shalt thou hope for mercy, rendering none ?

He dares to reply :

> What judgement shall I dread, doing no wrong ?

The wheel of Nemesis goes round, and Shylock's life and all
lie at the mercy of the victim to whom he had refused mercy
and the judge to whose appeal for mercy he would not
listen.   In the flow of his success, when every point is
being given in his favour, he breaks out into unseemly
exultation :

> A Daniel come to judgement ! yea, a Daniel !

The ebb comes, and his enemies catch up the cry and turn
it against him :

> A Daniel, still say I, a second Daniel !
> I thank thee, Jew, for *teaching* me that word.

Such then is the Story of the ' Jew, and so it exhibits
nemesis clashing with nemesis, the nemesis of surprise with
the nemesis of equality and intense satisfaction.

In the Caskets Story, which Shakespeare has associated
with the Story of the Jew, the dramatic capabilities are of a
totally different kind.   In the artist's armoury one of the
most effective weapons is Idealisation : inexplicable touches
throwing an attractiveness over the repulsive, uncovering
the truth and beauty which lie hidden in the commonplace,
and showing how much can be brought out of how little

with how little change.   A story will be excellent material,
then, for dramatic handling which contains at once some
experience of ordinary life, and also the surroundings which
can be made to exhibit this experience in a glorified form :
the more commonplace the experience, the greater the
triumph of art if it can be idealised.   The point of the
Caskets Story to the eye of an artist in Drama is the opportunity it affords for such an idealisation of the commonest
problem in everyday experience—what may be called the
Problem of Judgment by Appearances.

In the choice between alternatives there are three ways in
which judgment may be exercised.   The first mode, if it can be
called judgment at all, is to accept the decision of chance—to
cast lots, or merely to drift into a decision.   An opposite to
this is purely rational choice.   But rational choice, if strictly
interpreted as a logical process, involves great complications.
If a man would choose according to the methods of strict
reason, he must, first of all, purge himself of all passion, for
passion and reason are antagonistic.   Next, he must examine
himself as to the possibility of latent prejudice ; and as
prejudice may be unconsciously inherited, he must include in
the sphere of his examination ancestral and national bias.
Then, he must accumulate all the evidence that can possibly
bear upon the question in hand, and foresee every eventuality
that can result from either alternative.   When he has all the
materials of choice before him, he must proceed to balance
them against one another, seeing first that the mental
faculties employed in the process have been equally developed by training.   All such preliminary conditions having
been satisfied, he may venture to enquire on which side the
balance dips, maintaining his suspense so long as the dip
is undecided.   And when a man has done all this he has
attained only that degree of approach to strictly rational
choice which his imperfect nature admits.   Such pure
reason has no place in real life : judgment in practical affairs

is something between chance and this strict reason; it
attempts to use the machinery of rational choice, but only so
far as practical considerations proper to the matter in hand
allow. This medium choice is what I am here calling Judgment by Appearances, for it is clear that the antithesis
between appearance and reality will obtain so long as the
materials of choice are scientifically incomplete; the term
will apply with more and more appropriateness as the
divergence from perfect conditions of choice is greater.

Judgment by Appearances so defined is the only method *This ideal-*
of judgment proper to practical life, and accordingly an *ised · a*
maximum
exalted exhibition of it must furnish a keen dramatic interest. *in the issue,*
How is such a process to be glorified? Clearly Judgment by
Appearances will reach the ideal stage when there is the
maximum of importance in the issue to be decided and the
minimum of evidence by which to decide it. These two
conditions are satisfied in the Caskets Story. In questions
touching the individual life, that of marriage has this unique
importance, that it is bound up with wide consequences which
extend beyond the individual himself to his posterity. With
the suitors of Portia the question is of marriage with the
woman who is presented as supreme of her age in beauty, in
wealth and in character; moreover, the other alternative is ii. i. 40,
a vow of perpetual celibacy. So the question at issue in the &c.
Caskets Story concerns the most important act of life in the
most important form in which it can be imagined to present
itself. When we turn to the evidence on which this question *and a*
is to be decided we find that of rational evidence there is ab- *minimum*
in the evi-
solutely none. The choice is to be made between three *dence.*
caskets distinguished by their metals and by the accompany-
ing inscriptions:

> Who chooseth me shall gain what many men desire.   ii. vii. 5–9.
> Who chooseth me shall get as much as he deserves.
> Who chooseth me must give and hazard all he hath.

However individual fancies may incline, it is manifestly im-

CHAP. I. possible to set up any train of *reasoning* which should discover a ground of preference amongst the three. And it is worth noting, as an example of Shakespeare's nicety in detail, that the successful chooser reads in the scroll which announces his victory,

iii. ii. 132.
> You that choose not by the view,
> Chance *as* fair, and choose *as* true:

Shakespeare does not say '*more* fair,' '*more* true.' This equal balancing of the alternatives will appear still clearer
i. ii. 30–36. when we recollect that it is an intentional puzzle with which we are dealing, and accordingly that even if ingenuity could discover a preponderance of reason in favour of any one of the three, there would be the chance that this preponderance had been anticipated by the father who set the puzzle. The case becomes like that of children bidden to guess in which hand a sweetmeat is concealed. They are inclined to say the right hand, but hesitate whether that answer may not have been foreseen and the sweetmeat put in the left hand; and if on this ground they are tempted to be sharp and guess the left hand, there is the possibility that this sharpness may have been anticipated, and the sweetmeat kept after all in the right hand. If then the Caskets Story places before us three suitors, going through three trains of intricate reasoning for guidance in a matter on which their whole future depends, whereas we, the spectators, can see that from the nature of the case no reasoning can possibly avail them, we have clearly the Problem of Judgment by Appearances drawn out in its ideal form ; and our sympathies are attracted by the sight of a process, belonging to our everyday experience, yet developed before us in all the force artistic setting can bestow.

Solution of the problem: the characters of the But is this all? Does Shakespeare display before us the problem, yet give no help towards its solution? The key to the suitors' fates is not to be found in the trains of reasoning they go through. As if to warn us against looking for it in

this direction, Shakespeare contrives that we never hear the CHAP. I.
reasonings of the successful suitor. By a natural touch *choosers*
Portia, who has chosen Bassanio in her heart, is re- *determine*
their fates.
presented as unable to bear the suspense of hearing him iii. ii, from
deliberate, and calls for music to drown his meditations; it is 43; esp. 61.
only the conclusion to which he has come that we catch as
the music closes. The particular song selected on this
occasion points dimly in the direction in which we are to
look for the true solution of the problem:

> Tell me where is fancy bred,   iii. ii. 63.
> Or in the heart or in the head?

'Fancy' in Shakespearean English means 'love'; and the
discussion, whether love belongs to the head or the heart, is
no inappropriate accompaniment to a reality which consists
in this—that the success in love of the suitors, which they
are seeking to compass by their reasonings, is in fact being
decided by their characters.

To compare the characters of the three suitors, it will be
enough to note the different form that pride takes in each.
The first suitor is a prince of a barbarian race, who has ii. i, vii.
thus never known equals, but has been taught to consider
himself half divine; as if made of different clay from the rest
of mankind he instinctively shrinks from 'lead.' Yet modesty ii. vii. 20.
mingles with his pride, and though he feels truly that, so far ii vii. 24-
as the estimation of him by others is concerned, he might 30.
rely upon 'desert,' yet he doubts if desert extends as far as
Portia. What seizes his attention is the words, 'what many ii. vii, from
men desire'; and he rises to a flight of eloquence in pictur- 36.
ing wildernesses and deserts become thoroughfares by the
multitude of suitors flocking to Belmont. But he is all the
while betraying a secret of which he was himself unconscious: he has been led to seek the hand of Portia, not
by true love, but by the feeling that what all the world is
seeking the Prince of Morocco must not be slow to claim.
Very different is the pride of Arragon. He has no regal ii. ix.

CHAP. I.

compare
ii. ix. 47-9. position, but rather appears to be one who has fallen in social rank; he makes up for such a fall by intense pride of family, and is one of those who complacently thank heaven that they are not as other men. The 'many men' which had attracted Morocco repels Arragon:

ii. ix. 31.

> I will not choose what many men desire,
> Because I will not jump with common spirits,
> And rank me with the barbarous multitudes.

ii. ix, from
36. He is caught by the bait of 'desert.' It is true he almost deceives us with the lofty tone in which he reflects how the world would benefit if dignities and offices were in all cases purchased by the merit of the wearer; yet there peeps through his sententiousness his real conception of merit—the sole merit of family descent. His ideal is that the 'true seed of honour' should be 'picked from the chaff and ruin of the times,' and wrest greatness from the 'low peasantry' who had risen to it. He accordingly rests his fate upon desert: and he finds in the casket of his choice a fool's head. Of

iii. ii, from
73.
compare
i. ii. 124. Bassanio's soliloquy we hear enough to catch that his pride is the pride of the soldier, who will yield to none the post of danger, and how he is thus attracted by the 'threatening' of the leaden casket:

> thou meagre lead,
> Which rather threatenest than dost promise aught,
> Thy paleness moves me more than eloquence.

Moreover, he is a lover, and the threatening is a challenge to show what he will risk for love: his true heart finds its natural satisfaction in 'giving and hazarding' his all. This is the pride that is worthy of Portia; and thus the ingenious puzzle of the 'inspired' father has succeeded in piercing through the outer defence of specious reasoning, and carrying its repulsion and attraction to the inmost characters

*General
principle:
character
as an ele-
ment in
judgment.* of the suitors.

Such, then, is Shakespeare's treatment of the Problem of Judgment by Appearances: while he draws out the problem itself to its fullest extent in displaying the suitors elaborating

trains of argument for a momentous decision in which we
see that reason can be of no avail, he suggests for the
solution that, besides reason, there is in such judgments
another element, character, and that in those crises in which
reason is most fettered, character is most potent. An important solution this is; for what is character? A man's
character is the shadow of his past life; it is the grand
resultant of all the forces from within and from without that
have been operating upon him since he became a conscious
agent. Character is the sandy footprint of the commonplace hardened into the stone of habit; it is the complexity
of daily tempers, judgments, restraints, impulses, all focussed
into one master-passion acting with the rapidity of an
instinct. To lay down then, that where reason fails as an
element in judgment, character comes to its aid, is to bind
together the exceptional and the ordinary in life. In most of
the affairs of life men have scope for the exercise of
commonplace qualities, but emergencies do come where
this is denied them; in these cases, while they think, like
the three suitors, that they are moving voluntarily in the
direction in which they are judging fit at the moment, in
reality the weight of their past lives is forcing them in the
direction in which their judgment has been accustomed
to take them. Thus in the moral, as in the physical world,
nothing is ever lost: not a ripple on the surface of conduct
but goes on widening to the outermost limit of experience.
Shakespeare's contribution to the question of practical
judgment is that by the long exercise of commonplace
qualities we are building up a character which, though
unconsciously, is the determining force in the emergencies
in which commonplace qualities are impossible.

II.

How Shakespeare Improves the Stories
in the Telling.

A Study in Dramatic Workmanship.

Chap. II.

Two points of Drama-tic Mechan-ism.

IN treating the Story as the raw material of the Romantic Drama it has already been shown, in the case of the stories utilised for *The Merchant of Venice*, what natural capacities these exhibit for dramatic effect. The next step is to show how the artist increases their dramatic force in the process of working them up. Two points will be illustrated in the present study: first, how Shakespeare meets the difficulties of a story and reduces them to a minimum; secondly, how he improves the two tales by weaving them together so that they assist one another's effect.

Reduction of diffi-culties spe-cially im-portant in Drama.

The avoidance or reduction of difficulties in a story is an obvious element in any kind of artistic handling; it is of special importance in Drama in proportion as we are more sensitive to improbabilities in what is supposed to take place before our eyes than in what we merely hear of by narrative. This branch of art could not be better illustrated than in the Story of the Jew: never perhaps has an artist had to deal with materials so bristling with difficulties of the greatest magnitude, and never, it may be added, have they been met with greater ingenuity. The host of improbabilities gathering about such a detail as the pound of flesh must strike every mind. There is, however, preliminary to these, another difficulty of more general application: the difficulty of painting a character bad enough to be the hero of the

First diffi-culty: monstros-ity of the

story. It might be thought that to paint excess of badness Chap. II.
is comparatively easy, as needing but a coarse brush. On the *Jew's cha-*
contrary, there are few severer tests of creative power than *racter.*
the treatment of monstrosity. To be told that there is
villainy in the world and tacitly to accept the statement may
be easy; it is another thing to be brought into close contact
with the villains, to hear them converse, to watch their actions
and occasionally to be taken into their confidence. We realise
in Drama through our sympathy and our experience: in real
life we have not been accustomed to come across monsters
and are unfamiliar with their behaviour; in proportion then
as the badness of a character is exaggerated it is carried outside the sphere of our experience, the naturalness of the
scene is interrupted and its human interest tends to decline.
So, in the case of the story under consideration, the dramatist
is confronted with this dilemma: he must make the character
of Shylock absolutely bad, or the incident of the bond will
appear unreal; he must not make the character extra-
ordinarily bad, or there is danger of the whole scene appearing unreal.

Shakespeare meets a difficulty of this kind by a double *Its re-*
treatment. On the one hand, he puts no limits to the *pulsiveness*
counter-
blackness of the character itself; on the other hand, he *acted by*
provides against repulsiveness by giving it a special attraction *sympathy*
with his
of another kind. In the present case, while painting Shylock *wrongs.*
as a monster, he secures for him a hold upon our sympathy
by representing him as a victim of intolerable ill-treatment
and injustice. The effect resembles the popular sympathy
with criminals. The men themselves and their crimes are
highly repulsive; but if some slight irregularity occurs in the
process of bringing them to justice—if a counsel shows
himself unduly eager, or a judge appears for a moment one-
sided, a host of volunteer advocates espouse their cause.
These are actuated no doubt by sensitiveness to purity of
justice; but their protests have a ring that closely resembles

CHAP. II. sympathy with the criminals themselves, whom they not
unfrequently end by believing to be innocent and injured.

e.g. in iii. In the same way Shakespeare shows no moderation
i, iii; iv. in the touches of bloodthirstiness, of brutality, of sordid
i; ii. 5. meanness he heaps together in the character of Shylock;
but he takes equal pains to rouse our indignation at the
e.g. iii. i; treatment he is made to suffer. Personages such as Gratiano,
iv. i, &c. Salanio, Salarino, Tubal, serve to keep before us the mediæval feud between Jew and Gentile, and the persecuting
insolence with which the fashionable youth met the money-
i. iii.¹ 107– lenders who ministered to their necessities. Antonio
138. himself has stepped out of his natural character in the
iii. i. 57, grossness of his insults to his enemy. Shylock has been
133; injured in pocket as well as in sentiment, Antonio using his
iii iii. 22; wealth to disturb the money-market and defeat the schemes
and i. iii. of the Jew; according to Shylock Antonio has hindered
45. him of half-a-million, and were he out of Venice the usurer
could make what merchandise he would. Finally, our sense
of deliverance in the Trial Scene cannot hinder a touch
of compunction for the crushed plaintiff, as he appeals
against the hard justice meted out to him :—the loss of his
property, the acceptance of his life as an act of grace, the
abandonment of his religion and race, which implies the
abandonment of the profession by which he makes his living.

iv. i. 374
> Nay, take my life and all; pardon not that:
> You take my house when you do take the prop
> That doth sustain my house; you take my life
> When you do take the means whereby I live.

By thus making us resent the harsh fate dealt to Shylock the
dramatist recovers in our minds the fellow-feeling we have
Dramatic lost in contemplating the Jew himself. A name for such
Hedging. double treatment might be 'Dramatic Hedging': as the better
covers a possible loss by a second bet on the opposite side,
so, when the necessities of a story involve the creation of a
monster, the dramatic artist 'hedges' against loss of attrac-

tiveness by finding for the character human interest in some Chap. II.
other direction.   So successful has Shakespeare been in
the present instance that a respectable minority of readers
rise from the play partisans of Shylock.

We pass on to the crop of difficulties besetting the pound *Difficulties*
of flesh as a detail in the bond.   That such a bond should be *connected*
proposed, that when proposed it should be accepted, that it *pound of*
should be seriously entertained by a court of justice, that if *flesh.*
entertained at all it should be upset on so frivolous a pretext
as the omission of reference to the shedding of blood : these
form a series of impossible circumstances that any dramatist
might despair of presenting with even an approach to
naturalness.   Yet if we follow the course of the story as
moulded by Shakespeare we shall find all these impossibilities
one after another evaded.

At the end of the first scene Antonio had bidden Bassanio *Proposal of*
go forth and try what his credit could do in Venice.   Armed *the bond.*
with this blank commission Bassanio hurries into the city. i. i. 179.
As a gay young nobleman he knows nothing of the commercial world except the money-lenders ; and now proceeds
to the best-known of them, apparently unaware of what any
gossip on the Rialto could have told him, the unfortunate compare
relations between this Shylock and his friend Antonio.   At i. iii. 1-40.
the opening of the Bond Scene we find Bassanio and Shylock
in conversation, Bassanio impatient and irritated to find that
the famous security he has to offer seems to make so little
impression on the usurer.   At this juncture Antonio himself i. iii. 41.
falls [1] in with them, sees at a glance to what his rash friend

---

[1] No commentator has succeeded in making intelligible the line
  How like a fawning publican he looks !   i. iii. 42.
as it stands in the text at the opening of Shylock's soliloquy.   The
expression 'fawning publican' is so totally the opposite of all the
qualities of Antonio that it could have no force even in the mouth of
a satirist.   It is impossible not to be attracted by the simple change in
the text that would not only get over this difficulty, but add a new
effect to the scene : the change of assigning this single line to Antonio,

has committed him, but is too proud to draw back in sight
of his enemy.   Already a minor difficulty is surmounted, as
to how Antonio comes to be in the position of asking an
obligation of Shylock.   Antonio is as impatient as dignity
will permit to bring an awkward business to a conclusion.
Shylock, on the contrary, to whom the interview itself is a
triumph, in which his persecutor is appearing before him in
the position of a client, casts about to prolong the conversation to as great a length as possible.   Any topic would serve
his purpose ; but what topic more natural than the question
at the root of the feud between the two, the question of lend-
ing money on interest?   It is here we reach the very heart
of our problem, how the first mention of the pound of flesh
is made without a shock of unreality sufficient to ruin the
whole scene.   Had Shylock asked for a forfeiture of a
million per cent., or in any other way thrown into a commercial form his purpose of ruining Antonio, the old feud
and the present opportunity would be explanation sufficient :
the real difficulty is the total incongruity between such an
idea as a pound of human flesh and commercial transactions

The pro-
posal led
up to by the of any kind.   This difficulty Shakespeare has met by one of
his greatest triumphs of mechanical ingenuity : his leading

reserving, of course, the rest of the speech for Shylock.   The passage
would then read thus [the stage direction is my own] :

Enter ANTONIO.

Bass.   This is Signior Antonio.
Ant.   [*Aside*].   How like a fawning publican he looks—
          [BASSANIO *whispers* ANTONIO *and brings him to* SHYLOCK.
Shy.   [*Aside*].   I hate him, for he is a Christian,
          But more, &c.

Both the terms 'fawning' and 'publican' are literally applicable to
Shylock, and are just what Antonio would be likely to say of him.   It
is again a natural effect for the two foes on meeting for the first time in
the play to exchange scowling defiance.   Antonio's defiance is cut short
at the first line by Bassanio's running up to him, explaining what he has
done, and bringing Antonio up to where Shylock is standing ; the time
occupied in doing this gives Shylock scope for his longer soliloquy.

up to the proposal of the bond by the discussion on interest. CHAP. II.
The effect of this device a modern reader is in danger of *discourse*
losing : we are so familiar with the idea of interest at the *on interest.*
present day that we are apt to forget what the difficulty was i. iii, from
to the ancient and mediæval mind, which for so many gene-
69.
rations kept the practice of taking interest outside the pale
of social decency. This prejudice was one of the confusions
arising out of the use of a metal currency. The ancient
mind could understand how corn put into the ground would
by the agency of time alone produce twentyfold, thirtyfold,
or a hundredfold; they could understand how cattle left to
themselves would without human assistance increase from a
small to a large flock : but how could metal grow? how
could lifeless gold and silver increase and multiply like
animals and human beings? The Greek word for interest,
lokos, is the exact equivalent of the English word *breed*, and
the idea underlying the two was regularly connected with
that of interest in ancient discussions. The same idea is
present throughout the dispute between Antonio and Shylock.
Antonio indignantly asks :

> when did friendship take i iii. 134.
> A *breed* for *barren metal* of his friend?

Shylock illustrates usury by citing the patriarch Jacob and his i. iii. 72.
clever trick in cattle-breeding; showing how, at a time when
cattle were the currency, the natural rate of increase might
be diverted to private advantage. Antonio interrupts him :

> Is your gold and silver ewes and rams? i. iii. 96.

Shylock answers :

> I cannot tell; I make it *breed* as fast;

both parties thus showing that they considered the distinction
between the using of flesh and metal for the medium of
wealth to be the essential point in their dispute. With this
notion then of flesh *versus* money floating in the air between
them the interview goes on to the outbursts of mutual hatred
which reach a climax in Antonio's challenge to Shylock to do

Chap. II.

i. iii, from
138.
his worst; this challenge suddenly combines with the root
idea of the conversation to flash into Shylock's mind the suggestion of the bond. In an instant he smoothes his face and
proposes friendship. He will lend the money without interest,
in pure kindness, nay more, he will go to that extent of good
understanding implied in joking, and will have a merry bond;
while as to the particular joke (he says in effect), since you
Christians cannot understand interest in the case of money
while you acknowledge it in the case of flesh and blood,
suppose I take as my interest in this bond a pound of your
own flesh. In such a context the monstrous proposal sounds
almost natural. It has further been ushered in in a manner
which makes it almost impossible to decline it. When one
who is manifestly an injured man is the first to make ad-
vances, a generous adversary finds it almost impossible to
hold back. A sensitive man, again, will shrink from nothing
more than from the ridicule attaching to those who take serious
precautions against a jest. And the more incongruous Shylock's proposal is with commercial negotiations the better
evidence it is of his non-commercial intentions. In a word,
the essence of the difficulty was the incongruity between
human flesh and money transactions: it has been surmounted
by a discussion, flowing naturally from the position of the
two parties, of which the point is the relative position of
flesh and money as the medium of wealth in the past.

*Difficulty
of legally
recognising
the bond
evaded*

iv. i. 104.

iv. i. 17.
The bond thus proposed and accepted, there follows the
difficulty of representing it as entertained by a court of
justice. With reference to Shakespeare's handling of this
point it may be noted, first, that he leaves us in doubt
whether the court would have entertained it: the Duke is
intimating an intention of adjourning at the moment when
the entrance of Portia gives a new turn to the proceedings.
Again, at the opening of the trial, the Duke gives expression
to the universal opinion that Shylock's conduct was intelligible only on the supposition that he was keeping up to the

last moment the appearance of insisting on his strange terms, CHAP. II.
in order that before the eyes of the whole city he might
exhibit his enemy at his mercy, and then add to his ignominy
by publicly pardoning him : a fate which, it must be admitted,
was no more than Antonio justly deserved. This will explain
how Shylock comes to have a hearing at all : when once he
is admitted to speak it is exceedingly difficult to resist the
pleas Shakespeare puts into his mouth. He takes his stand iv. i. 38.
on the city's charter and the letter of the law, and declines
to be drawn into any discussion of natural justice ; yet even as
a question of natural justice what answer can be found when iv. i. 90.
he casually points to the institution of slavery, which we
must suppose to have existed in Venice at the period ? Shylock's only offence is his seeking to make Antonio's life a
matter of barter : what else is the accepted institution of
slavery but the establishment of power over human flesh and
blood and life, simply because these have been bought with
money, precisely as Shylock has given good ducats for his
rights over the flesh of Antonio ? No wonder the perplexed
Duke is for adjourning.

There remains one more difficulty, the mode in which, *Difficulty*
according to the traditional story, the bond is upset. It is *as to the*
traditional
manifest that the agreement as to the pound of flesh, if it is *mode of*
to be recognised by a court of justice at all, cannot without *upsetting*
the bond
the grossest perversion of justice be cancelled on the ground *met.*
of its omitting to mention blood. Legal evasion can go
to great lengths. It is well known that an Act requiring
cabs to carry lamps at night has been evaded through the
omission of a direction that the lamps were to be lighted ;
and that importers have escaped a duty on foreign gloves at
so much the pair by bringing the right-hand and left-hand
gloves over in different ships. But it is perfectly possible to
carry lamps without lighting them, while it is a clear impossibility to cut human flesh without shedding blood. Nothing
of course would be easier than to upset the bond on rational

CHAP. II. grounds—indeed the difficulty is rather to imagine it receiving rational consideration at all; but on the other hand no solution of the perplexity could be half so dramatic as the one tradition has preserved.   The dramatist has to choose between a course of procedure which shall be highly dramatic but leave a sense of injustice, and one that shall be sound and legal but comparatively tame.   Shakespeare contrives to secure both alternatives.   He retains the traditional plea as to the blood, but puts it into the mouth of one known to his audience to be a woman playing the lawyer for the nonce; iv. i. 314, and again, before we have time to recover from our surprise 347. and feel the injustice of the proceeding, he follows up the brilliant evasion by a sound legal plea, the suggestion of a real lawyer.   Portia has come to the court from a conference with her cousin Bellario, the most learned jurist of Venice. iii. iv. 47; Certainly it was not this doctor who hit upon the idea of the iv. i. 143. blood being omitted.   His contribution to the interesting consultation was clearly the old statute of Venice, which every one else seems to have forgotten, which made the mere attempt on the life of a citizen by an alien punishable with death and loss of property: according to this piece of statute law not only would Shylock's bond be illegal, but the demand of such security constituted a capital offence.   Thus Shakespeare surmounts the final difficulty in the story of the Jew in a mode which retains dramatic force to the full, yet does this without any violation of legal fairness.

The inter-weaving of the two stories.   The second purpose of the present study is to show how Shakespeare has improved his two stories by so weaving them together that they assist one another's effect.

First, it is easy to see how the whole movement of the play rises naturally out of the union of the two stories.   One of the main distinctions between the progress of events in real life or history and in Drama is that the movement of a drama runs into the form technically known as Complication

and Resolution. A dramatist fastens our attention upon some
train of events: then he sets himself to divert this train of
events from its natural course by some interruption; this
interruption is either removed, and the train of events returns
to its natural course, or the interruption is carried on to some
tragic culmination. In *The Merchant of Venice* our interest
is at the beginning fixed on Antonio as rich, high-placed, the
protector and benefactor of his friends. By the events following upon the incident of the bond we see what would seem
the natural life of Antonio diverted into a totally different
channel; in the end the old course is restored, and Antonio
becomes prosperous as before. Such interruption of a train
of incidents is its Complication, and the term Complication
suggests a happy Resolution to follow. Complication and
Resolution are essential to dramatic movement, as discords
and their 'resolution' into concords constitute the essence of
music. The Complication and Resolution in the story of the
Jew serve for the Complication and Resolution of the drama
as a whole; and my immediate point is that these elements of
movement in the one story spring directly out of its connection with the other. But for Bassanio's need of money and
his blunder in applying to Shylock the bond would never have
been entered into, and the change in Antonio's fortunes would
never have come about: thus the cause for all the Complication
of the play (technically, the Complicating Force) is the happy
lover of the Caskets Story. Similarly Portia is the means by
which Antonio's fortunes are restored to their natural flow:
in other words, the source of the Resolution (or Resolving
Force) is the maiden of the Caskets Story. The two leading
personages of the one tale are the sources respectively of the
Complication and Resolution in the other tale, which carry
the Complication and Resolution of the drama as a whole.
Thus simply does the movement of the whole play flow from
the union of the two stories. ●

One consequence flowing from this is worth noting; that

CHAP. II.

*play sym-
metrical
about its
central
scene.*

the scene in which Bassanio makes his successful choice of the casket is the Dramatic Centre of the whole play, as being the point in which the Complicating and Resolving Forces meet. This Dramatic Centre is, according to Shakespeare's favourite custom, placed in the exact mechanical centre of the drama, covering the middle of the middle Act. There is again an amount of poetic splendour lavished upon this scene which throws it up as a poetic centre to the whole. More than this, it is the real crisis of the play. Looking philosophically upon the whole drama as a piece of history, we must admit that the true turning-point is the success of Bassanio; the apparent crisis is the Trial Scene, but this is in reality governed by the scene of the successful choice, and if Portia and Bassanio had not been united in the earlier scene no lawyer would have interposed to turn the current of events in the trial. There is yet another sense in which the same scene may be called central. Hitherto I have dealt with only two tales; the full plot however of *The Merchant of Venice* involves two more, the Story of Jessica and the Episode of the Rings : it is to be observed that all four stories meet in the scene of the successful choice. This scene is

1

the climax of the Caskets Story. It is connected with the

iii. ii, from catastrophe in the Story of the Jew : Bassanio, at the moment
221.*?*.
of his happiness, learns that the friend through whom he has been able to contend for the prize has forfeited his life to his foe as the price of his liberality. The scene is

3

connected with the Jessica Story ! for Jessica and her husband are the messengers who bring the sad tidings, and thus link together the bright and gloomy elements of the play. Finally,

4 .

the Episode of the Rings, which is to occupy the end of the

iii. ii. 173– drama, has its foundation in this scene, in the exchange of the
187.
rings which are destined to be the source of such ironical perplexity. Such is the symmetry with which the plot of *The Merchant of Venice* has been constructed : the incident which is technically its Dramatic Centre is at once its 'mechanical

centre, its poetic centre, and, philosophically considered, its true turning-point; while, considering the play as a Romantic drama with its union of stories, we find in the same central incident all the four stories dovetailed together.

These points may appear small and merely technical. But *Shake-* it is a constant purpose with me in the present exposition of *speare as* Shakespeare as a Dramatic Artist to combat the notion, so *of Plot.* widely prevalent amongst ordinary readers, that Shakespeare, *a master* though endowed with the profoundest grasp of human nature, is yet careless in the construction of his plots: a notion in itself as improbable as it would be that a sculptor could be found to produce individual figures exquisitely moulded and chiselled, yet awkwardly and clumsily grouped. It is the minuter points that show the finish of an artist; and such symmetry of construction as appears in *The Merchant of Venice* is not likely to characterise a dramatist who sacrifices plot to character-painting.

There remains another point, which no one will consider *The union* small or technical, connected with the union of the two *of a light* stories: the fact that Shakespeare has thus united a light and *serious* a serious story, that he has woven together gloom and bright- *story.* ness. This carries us to one of the great battlefields of dramatic history; no feature is more characteristic of the Romantic Drama than this mingling of light and serious in the same play, and at no point has it been more stoutly assailed by critics trained in an opposite school. I say nothing of the wider scope this practice gives to the dramatist, nor the way in which it brings the world of art nearer to the world of reality; my present purpose is to review the dramatic effects which flow from the mingling of the two elements in the present play.

In general human interest the stories are a counterpoise *Dramatic* to one another, so different in kind, so equal in the degree *effects* of interest their progress continues to call forth. The inci- *of this* dents of the two tales gather around Antonio and Portia *union.* *arising out*

respectively; each of these is a full and rounded character,
Effects of Human Interest.
i. i. 1.
and they are both centres of their respective worlds. The
stories seem to start from a common point. The keynote to
the story of the Jew is the strange 'sadness'—the word implies no more than seriousness—which overpowers Antonio,
and which seems to be the shadow of his coming trouble.
Compare with this the first words we hear of Portia:

i. ii. 1.
> By my troth, Nerissa, my little body is aweary of this great
> world.

Such a humorous languor is a fitting precursor to the excitement and energy of the scenes which follow. But from
this common starting-point the stories move in opposite
directions; the spectator's sympathies are demanded alternately for two independent chains of circumstances, for the
fortunes of Antonio sinking lower and lower, and the fortunes of Portia rising higher and higher. He sees the
merchant and citizen become a bankrupt prisoner, the lordly
benefactor of his friends a wretch at the mercy of his foe.
He sees Portia, already endowed with beauty, wealth, and
character, attain what to her heart is yet higher, the power to
lay all she has at the feet of the man she loves. Then, when
they are at the climax of their happiness and misery, when
Portia has received all that this world can bestow, and Antonio has lost all that this world can take away, for the first
time these two central personages meet face to face in the
Effects of Plot.
Trial Scene. And if from general human interest we pass
on to the machinery of plot, we find this also governed by the
same combination: a half-serious frolic is the medium in
which a tragic crisis finds its solution.

Emotional effects: in-crease of tragic passion;
But it is of course passion and emotional interest which
are mainly affected by the union of light and serious: these
we shall appreciate chiefly in connection with the Trial Scene,
where the emotional threads of the play are gathered into
a knot, and the two personages who are the embodiments of
the light and serious elements face one another as judge and

prisoner. In this scene it is remarkable how Portia takes CHAP. II.
pains to prolong to the utmost extent the crisis she has come iv. i, from
to solve ; she holds in her fingers the threads of the tangled 225
situation, and she is strong enough to play with it before she
will consent to bring it to an end. She has intimated her 178.
opinion that the letter of the bond must be maintained, she 184-207.
has made her appeal to Shylock for mercy and been refused,
she has heard Bassanio's appeal to wrest the law for once to 214-222.
her authority and has rejected it; there remains nothing but
to pronounce the decree. But at the last moment she asks 225.
to see the bond, and every spectator in court holds his
breath and hears his heart beat as he follows the lawyer's eye
down line after line. It is of no avail; at the end she can 227–230.
only repeat the useless offer of thrice the loan, with the effect
of drawing from Shylock an oath that he will not give way.
Then Portia admits that the bond is forfeit, with a needless 230-244.
reiteration of its horrible details ; yet, as if it were some evenly
balanced question, in which after-thoughts were important,
she once more appeals to Shylock to be merciful and bid
her tear the bond, and evokes a still stronger asseveration
from the malignant victor, until even Antonio's stoicism begins to give way, and he begs for a speedy judgment. Portia 243.
then commences to pass her judgment in language of legal
prolixity, which sounds like a recollection of her hour with
Bellario :—

> For the intent and purpose of the law
> Hath full relation to the penalty,
> Which here appeareth due upon the bond, &c.

Next she fads about the details of the judicial barbarity, 255–261.
the balance to weigh the flesh, a surgeon as a forlorn hope ;
and when Shylock demurs to the last, stops to argue that he
might do this for charity. At last surely the intolerable
suspense will come to a termination. But our lawyer of 263.
half-an-hour's standing suddenly remembers she has forgotten to call on the defendant in the suit, and the pathos is

CHAP. II. intensified by the dying speech of Antonio, calmly welcoming death for himself, anxious only to soften Bassanio's remorse, his last human passion a rivalry with Portia for the love of his friend.

iv. i. 276.

> Bid her be judge
> Whether Bassanio had not once a love.

iv. i, from 299. When the final judgment can be delayed no longer its opening sentences are still lengthened out by the jingling repetitions of judicial formality,

> The law allows it, and the court awards it, &c.

Only when every evasion has been exhausted comes the thunderstroke which reverses the whole situation. Now it is clear that had this situation been intended to have a tragic termination this prolonging of its details would have been impossible ; thus to harrow our feelings with items of agony would be not art but barbarity. It is because Portia knows what termination she is going to give to the scene that she can indulge in such boldness; it is because the audience have recognised in Portia the signal of deliverance that the lengthening of the crisis becomes the dramatic beauty of suspense. It appears then that, if this scene be regarded only as a crisis of tragic passion, the dramatist has been able to extract more *tragic* effect out of it by the device of assisting the tragic with a light story.

reaction and comic effect; Again, it is a natural law of the human mind to pass from strain to reaction, and suspense relieved will find vent in vehement exhilaration. By giving Portia her position in the crisis scene the dramatist is clearly furnishing the means for a reaction to follow, and the reaction is found in the iv. i, from 425. Episode of the Rings, by which the disguised wives entangle their husbands in a perplexity affording the audience the bursts of merriment needed as relief from the tension of the Trial Scene. The play is thus brought into conformity with the laws of mental working, and the effect of the reaction

is to make the serious passion more keen because more
healthy.

Finally, there are the effects of mixed passion, neither *effects of*
wholly serious nor wholly light, but compounded of the two, *mixed*
which are impossible to a drama that can admit only a *passion.*
single tone.   The effect of Dramatic Irony, which Shakespeare inherited from the ancient Drama, but greatly
modified and extended, is powerfully illustrated at the most
pathetic point of the Trial Scene, when Antonio's chance iv. i. 273-
reference to Bassanio's new wife calls from Bassanio and ²⁹⁴·
his followers agonised vows to sacrifice even their wives
if this could save their patron—little thinking that these
wives are standing by to record the vow.   But there is an
effect higher than this.   Portia's outburst on the theme of iv. i. 184-
mercy, considered only as a speech, is one of the noblest in ²⁰²·
literature, a gem of purest truth in a setting of richest
music.   But the situation in which she speaks it is so framed
as to make Portia herself the embodiment of the mercy she
describes.   How can we imagine a higher type of mercy,
the feminine counterpart of justice, than in the bright
woman, at the moment of her supreme happiness, appearing
in the garb of the law to deliver a righteous unfortunate
from his one error, and the justice of Venice from the in-
soluble perplexity of having to commit a murder by legal
process ? And how is this situation brought about but by the
most intricate interweaving of a story of brightness with a
story of trouble ?

In all branches then of dramatic effect, in Character, in
Plot and in Passion, the union of a light with a serious story
is found to be a source of power and beauty.   The fault
charged against the Romantic Drama has upon a deeper view
proved a new point of departure in dramatic progress ; and
in this particular case the combination of tales so opposite
in character must be regarded as one of the leading points
in which Shakespeare has improved the tales in the telling.

III.

How Shakespeare makes his plot more Complex in order to make it more Simple.

A Study in Underplot.

CHAP. III.

Paradox of simplicity by means of increased complexity.

THE title of the present study is a paradox : that Shakespeare makes a plot more complex[1] in order to make it more simple. It is however a paradox that finds an illustration from the material world in every open roof. The architect's problem has been to support a heavy weight without the assistance of pillars, and it might have been expected that in solving the problem he would at least have tried every means in his power for diminishing the weight to be supported. On the contrary, he has increased this weight by the addition of massive cross-beams and heavy iron-girders. Yet, if these have been arranged according to the laws of construction, each of them will bring a supporting power considerably greater than its own weight ; and thus, while in a literal sense increasing the roof, for all practical purposes they may be said to have diminished it. Similarly a dramatist of the Romantic school, from his practice of uniting more than one story in the same plot, has to face the

[1] It is a difficulty of literary criticism that it has to use as technical terms words belonging to ordinary conversation, and therefore more or less indefinite in their significations. In the present work I am making a distinction between 'complex' and 'complicated': the latter is applied to the diverting a story out of its natural course with a view to its ultimate 'resolution'; 'complex' is reserved for the interweaving of stories with one another. Later on 'single' will be opposed to 'complex,' and 'simple' to 'complicated.'

difficulty of complexity. This difficulty he solves not by seeking how to reduce combinations as far as possible, but, on
the contrary, by the addition of more and inferior stories ;
yet if these new stories are so handled as to emphasise
and heighten the effect of the main stories, the additional
complexity will have resulted in increased simplicity. In the
play at present under consideration, Shakespeare has interwoven into a common pattern two famous and striking tales ;
his plot, already elaborate, he has made yet more elaborate
by the addition of two more tales less striking in their
character—the Story of Jessica and the Episode of the Rings.
If it can be shown that these inferior stories have the effect *The Jessica*
of assisting the main stories, smoothing away their difficulties *Story and*
the Rings
and making their prominent points yet more prominent, it *Episode*
will be clear that he has made his plot more complex only in *assist the*
main
reality to make it more simple. The present study is de- *stories.*
voted to noticing how the Stories of Jessica and of the Rings
minister to the effects of the Story of the Jew and the
Caskets Story.

   To begin with : it may be seen that in many ways the *The Jessica*
mechanical working out of the main stories is assisted by the *Story. It*
serves as
Jessica story. In the first place it relieves them of their *Underplot*
superfluous personages. Every drama, however simple, must *for me-*
chanical
contain 'mechanical' personages, who are introduced into *personages.*
the play, not for their own sake, but to assist in presenting
incidents or other personages. The tendency of Romantic
Drama to put a story as a whole upon the stage multiplies
the number of such mechanical personages : and when
several such stories come to be combined in one, there is a
danger of the stage being crowded with characters which
intrinsically have little interest. Here the Underplots become of service and find occupation for these inferior personages. In the present case only four personages are essential to the main plot—Antonio, Shylock, Bassanio, Portia.
But in bringing out the unusual tie that binds together

CHAP. III.

e.g. i. i;
iii. iii;
iv. i.

a representative of the city and a representative of the nobility, and upon which so much of the plot rests, it is an assistance to introduce the rank and file of gay society and depict these paying court to the commercial magnate. The high position of Antonio and Bassanio in their respective spheres will come out still clearer if these lesser social per-

i. i; compare iii. i,
esp. 14–18.

sonages are graduated. Salanio, Salerio, and Salarino are mere parasites; Gratiano has a certain amount of in-

i. i. 74–118. dividuality in his wit; while, seeing that Bassanio is a scholar
i. ii. 124.   as well as a nobleman and soldier, it is fitting to give pro-
v. i, &c.   minence amongst his followers to the intellectual and artistic
i. ii, &c.   Lorenzo. Similarly the introduction of Nerissa assists in
iii. i. 80,
&c.   presenting Portia fully; Shylock is seen in his relations with his race by the aid of Tubal, his family life is seen in connection with Jessica, and his behaviour to dependants in connection with Launcelot; Launcelot himself is set off by Gobbo. Now the Jessica story is mainly devoted to these inferior personages, and the majority of them take an animated part in the successful elopement. It is further to be noted that the Jessica Underplot has itself an inferior story attached

ii. ii, iii;
iii. v.

to it, that of Launcelot, who seeks scope for his good nature by transferring himself to a Christian master, just as his mistress seeks a freer social atmosphere in union with a Christian husband. And, similarly, side by side with the Caskets Story, which unites Portia and Bassanio, we have a

iii. ii. 188,
&c.

faintly-marked underplot which unites their followers, Nerissa and Gratiano. In one or other of these inferior stories the mechanical personages find attachment to plot; and the multiplication of individual figures, instead of leaving an impression of waste, is made to minister to the sense of Dramatic Economy.

*It assists
mechanical
development:
occupying
the three*

Again: as there are mechanical personages so there are mechanical difficulties—difficulties of realisation which do not belong to the essence of a story, but which appear when the story comes to be worked out upon the stage. The Story of

the Jew involves such a mechanical difficulty in the interval
of three months which elapses between the signing of the *months' in-*
bond and its forfeiture. In a classical setting this would be *terval,*
avoided by making the play begin on the day the bond falls
due; such treatment, however, would shut out the great
dramatic opportunity of the Bond Scene. The Romantic
Drama always inclines to exhibiting the whole of a story; it
must therefore in the present case *suppose* a considerable
interval between one part of the story and another, and such
suppositions tend to be weaknesses. The Jessica Story con-
veniently bridges over this interval. The first Act is given
up to bringing about the bond, which at the beginning of the
third Act appears to be broken. The intervening Act consists
of no less than nine scenes, and while three of them carry
on the progress of the Caskets Story, the other six are
devoted to the elopement of Jessica: the bustle and activity
implied in such rapid change of scene indicating how an
underplot can be used to keep the attention of the audience
just where the natural interest of the main story would flag.

The same use of the Jessica Story to bridge over the *and so*
three months' interval obviates another mechanical difficulty *breaking*
of the main plot. The loss of all Antonio's ships, the *the news of*
supposition that all the commercial ventures of so prudent a *Antonio's*
merchant should simultaneously miscarry, is so contrary to *losses.*
the chances of things as to put some strain upon our sense
of probability; and this is just one of the details which, too
unimportant to strike us in an anecdote, become realised
when a story is presented before our eyes. The artist, it
must be observed, is not bound to find actual solutions for
every possible difficulty; he has merely to see that they do
not interfere with dramatic effect. Sometimes he so arranges
his incidents that the difficulty is met and vanishes; sometimes it is kept out of sight, the portion of the story which
contains it going on behind the scenes; at other times he is
content with reducing the difficulty in amount. In the pre-

CHAP. III. sent instance the improbability of Antonio's losses is les-
sened by the gradual way in which the news is broken to us,
distributed amongst the numerous scenes of the three months'
ii. viii. 25. interval. We get the first hint of it in a chance conversation between Salanio and Salarino, in which they are
chuckling over the success of the elopement and the fury of
the robbed father. Salanio remarks that Antonio must look
that he keep his day; this reminds Salarino of a ship he has
just heard of as lost somewhere in the English Channel:

> I thought upon Antonio when he told me;
> And wish'd in silence that it were not his.

iii. i. In the next scene but one the same personages meet, and
one of them, enquiring for the latest news, is told that the
rumour yet lives of Antonio's loss, and now the exact place
of the wreck is specified as the Goodwin Sands; Salarino
adds: 'I would it might prove the end of his losses.'
Before the close of the scene Shylock and Tubal have been
added to it. Tubal has come from Genoa and gives Shylock
the welcome news that at Genoa it was *known* that Antonio
had lost an argosy coming from Tripolis; while on his
journey to Venice Tubal had travelled with creditors of
Antonio who were speculating upon his bankruptcy as a
iii. ii. certainty. Then comes the central scene in which the full
news reaches Bassanio at the moment of his happiness: all
Antonio's ventures failed—

> From Tripolis, from Mexico and England,
> From Lisbon, Barbary, and India,

iii. iii. not one escaped. In the following scene we see Antonio in
custody.

The Jessica These are minor points such as may be met with in any
Story play, and the treatment of them belongs to ordinary Dra-
assists matic Mechanism. But we have already had to notice that
Dramatic
Hedging in the Story of the Jew contains special difficulties which belong
regard to to the essence of the story, and must be met by special
Shylock.

devices. One of these was the monstrous character of the CHAP. III.
Jew himself; and we saw how the dramatist was obliged to
maintain in the spectators a double attitude to Shylock,
alternately letting them be repelled by his malignity and
again attracting their sympathy to him as a victim of wrong.
Nothing in the play assists this double attitude so much as
the Jessica Story. Not to speak of the fact that Shylock
shows no appreciation for the winsomeness of the girl who
attracts every one else in the drama, nor of the way in which
this one point of brightness in the Jewish quarter throws up
the sordidness of all her surroundings, we hear the Jew's
own daughter reflect that his house is a 'hell,' and we see ii. iii. 2.
enough of his domestic life to agree with her. A Shylock e.g. ii. v.
painted without a tender side at all would be repulsive; he
becomes much more repulsive when he shows a tenderness
for one human being, and yet it appears how this tenderness
has grown hard and rotten with the general debasement of
his soul by avarice, until, in his ravings over his loss, his iii. 1, from
ducats and his daughter are ranked as equally dear.   25.

> I would my daughter were dead at my foot, and the jewels in iii. 1. 92.
> her ear! Would she were hearsed at my foot, and the ducats in her
> coffin!

For all this we feel that he is hardly used in losing her.
Paternal feeling may take a gross form, but it is paternal
feeling none the less, and cannot be denied our sympathy;
bereavement is a common ground upon which not only high
and low, but even the pure and the outcast, are drawn
together. Thus Jessica at home makes us hate Shylock:
with Jessica lost we cannot help pitying him. The perfection of Dramatic Hedging lies in the equal balancing of
the conflicting feelings, and one of the most powerful
scenes in the whole play is devoted to this twofold display of
Shylock. Fresh from the incident of the elopement, he is
encountered by the parasites and by Tubal: these amuse
themselves with alternately 'chaffing' him upon his losses,

*Jessica
Shake-
speare's
compensa-
tion to
Shylock.*

iv. i. 348–
394.

ii. iv. 34.

*The Jessica
Story ex-
plains Shy-
lock's un-
yielding-
ness.*

iv. i. 17.

and 'drawing' him in the matter of the expected gratification of his vengeance, while his passions rock him between extremes of despair and fiendish anticipation. We may go further. Great creative power is accompanied by great attachment to the creations and keen sense of justice in disposing of them. Looked at as a whole, the Jessica Story is Shakespeare's compensation to Shylock. The sentence on Shylock, which the necessities of the story require, is legal rather than just; yet large part of it consists in a requirement that he shall make his daughter an heiress. And, to put it more generally, the repellent character and hard fate of the father have set against them the sweetness and beauty of the daughter, together with the full cup of good fortune which her wilful rebellion brings her in the love of Lorenzo and the protecting friendship of Portia. Perhaps the dramatist, according to his wont, is warning us of this compensating treatment when he makes one of the characters early in the play exclaim :

> If e'er the Jew her father come to heaven,
> It will be for his gentle daughter's sake.

The other main source of difficulty in the Story of the Jew is, as we have seen, the detail concerning the pound of flesh, which throws improbability over every stage of its progress. In one at least of these stages the difficulty is directly met by the aid of the Jessica Story: it is this which explains Shylock's resolution not to give way. When we try in imagination to realise the whole circumstances, common sense must take the view taken in the play itself by the Duke :

> Shylock, the world thinks, and I think so too,
> That thou but lead'st this fashion of thy malice
> To the last hour of act ; and then 'tis thought
> Thou'lt show thy mercy and remorse more strange
> Than is thy strange apparent cruelty.

A life-long training in avarice would not easily resist an offer of nine thousand ducats. But further, the alternatives between which Shylock has to choose are not so simple as

the alternatives of Antonio's money or his life.   On the one
hand, Shylock has to consider the small chance that either
the law or the mob would actually suffer the atrocity to be
judicially perpetrated, and how his own life would be likely
to be lost in the attempt.   Again, turning to the other alternative, Shylock is certainly deep in his schemes of vengeance, and the finesse of malignity must have suggested to
him how much more cruel to a man of Antonio's stamp it
would be to fling him a contemptuous pardon before the
eyes of Venice than to turn him into a martyr, even supposing this to be permitted.   But at the moment when the
choice becomes open to Shylock he has been maddened by
the loss of his daughter, who, with the wealth she has stolen,
has gone to swell the party of his deadly foe.   It is fury, not
calculating cruelty, that makes Shylock with a madman's
tenacity cling to the idea of blood, while this passion is
blinding him to a more keenly flavoured revenge, and risking
the chance of securing any vengeance at all[1].

From the mechanical development of the main plot and *The Jessica*
the reduction of its difficulties, we pass to the interweaving of *Story assists*
the inter-
the two principal stories, which is so leading a feature of the *weaving of*
play.   In the main this interweaving is sufficiently provided *the main*
stories.
for by the stories themselves, and we have already seen how
the leading personages in the one story are the source of the
whole movement in the other story.   But this interweaving
is drawn closer still by the affair of Jessica: technically *It is thus*
described the position in the plot of Jessica's clopement is *a Link*
Action,
that of a Link Action between the main stories.   This

---

[1] This seems to me a reasonable view notwithstanding what Jessica
says to the contrary (iii ii. 286), that she has often heard her father swear
he would rather have Antonio's flesh than twenty times the value of the
bond.   It is one thing to swear vengeance in private, another thing to
follow it up in the face of a world in opposition.   A man of over-
bearing temper surrounded by inferiors and dependants often utters
threats, and seems to find a pleasure in uttering them, which both he
and his hearers know he will never carry out.

G

CHAP. III. linking appears in the way in which Jessica and her suite are in the course of the drama transferred from the one tale to the other. At the opening of the play they are personages in the Story of the Jew, and represent its two antagonistic sides, Jessica being the daughter of the Jew and Lorenzo a friend and follower of Bassanio and Antonio. First the contrivance of the elopement assists in drawing together these opposite sides of the Jew Story, and aggravating the feud on which it turns. Then, as we have seen, Jessica and

iii. ii, from her husband in the central scene of the whole play come into
221.
contact with the Caskets Story at its climax. From this point they become adopted into the Caskets Story, and settle down

helping to in the house and under the protection of Portia. This
restore the
balance be- transference further assists the symmetry of interweaving by
tween the helping to adjust the balance between the two main stories.
main
stories, In its *mass*, if the expression may be allowed, the Caskets tale, with its steady progress to a goal of success, is over-weighted by the tale of Antonio's tragic peril and startling deliverance: the Jessica episode, withdrawn from the one and added to the other, helps to make the two more equal. Once more, the case, we have seen, is not merely that of a union between stories, but a union between stories opposite in kind, a combination of brightness with gloom.

and a bond The binding effect of the Jessica Story extends to the union
between
their bright between these opposite tones. We have already had occasion
and dark to notice how the two extremes meet in the central scene, how
climaxes.
from the height of Bassanio's bliss we pass in an instant to the total ruin of Antonio, which we then learn in its fulness for the first time : the link which connects the two is the arrival of Jessica and her friends as bearers of the news.

Character So far, the points considered have been points of Mechan-
effects. Cha- ism and Plot ; in the matter of Character-Interest the Jessica
racter of
Jessica. episode is to an even greater degree an addition to the whole effect of the play, Jessica and Lorenzo serving as a foil to Portia and Bassanio. The characters of Jessica and Lorenzo

are charmingly sketched, though liable to misreading unless Chap. III.
carefully studied.   To appreciate Jessica we must in the first
place assume the grossly unjust mediæval view of the Jews as
social outcasts.   The dramatist has vouchsafed us a glimpse
of Shylock at home, and brief as the scene is it is remark- ii. v.
able how much of evil is crowded into it.   The breath of
home life is trust, yet the one note which seems to pervade
the domestic bearing of Shylock is the lowest suspiciousness.
Three times as he is starting for Bassanio's supper he draws 12, 16, 36.
back to question the motives for which he has been invited.
He is moved to a shriek of suspicion by the mere fact of his
servant joining him in shouting for the absent Jessica, by the 7.
mention of masques, by the sight of the servant whispering 28, 44.
to his daughter.   Finally, he takes his leave with the words

> Perhaps I will return immediately,   52.

a device for keeping order in his absence which would be
a low one for a nurse to use to a child, but which he is not
ashamed of using to his grown-up daughter and the lady of
his house.   The short scene of fifty-seven lines is sufficient
to give us a further reminder of Shylock's sordid house-
keeping, which is glad to get rid of the good-natured
Launcelot as a 'huge feeder'; and his aversion to any form 3, 46.
of gaiety, which leads him to insist on his shutters being put 28.
up when he hears that there is a chance of a pageant in
the streets.   Amidst surroundings of this type Jessica has
grown up, a motherless girl, mingling only with harsh men
(for we nowhere see a trace of female companionship for
her): it can hardly be objected against her that she should
long for a Christian atmosphere in which her affections might ii. iii. 20.
have full play.   Yet even for this natural reaction she feels
compunction :

> Alack, what heinous sin is it in me   ii. iii. 16.
> To be ashamed to be my father's child!
> But though I am a daughter to his blood,
> I am not to his manners.

G 2

CHAP. III.   Formed amidst such influences it would be a triumph to a
character if it escaped repulsiveness; Jessica, on the contrary,
is full of attractions.   She has a simplicity which stands to
her in the place of principle.   More than this she has a high
degree of feminine delicacy.   Delicacy will be best brought
out in a person who is placed in an equivocal situation, and
we see Jessica engaged, not only in an elopement, but in an
ii. iv. 30.   elopement which, it appears, has throughout been planned by
herself and not by Lorenzo.   Of course a quality like feminine
delicacy is more conveyed by the bearing of the actress than
by positive words; we may however notice the impression
which Jessica's part in the elopement scenes makes upon
ii. iv. 30–   those who are present.   When Lorenzo is obliged to make a
40.   confidant of Gratiano, and tell him how it is Jessica who has
planned the whole affair, instead of feeling any necessity of
apologising for her the thought of her childlike innocence
moves him to enthusiasm, and it is here that he exclaims:

> If e'er the Jew her father come to heaven,
> It will be for his gentle daughter's sake.

ii. vi.   In the scene of the elopement itself, Jessica has steered clear
of both prudishness and freedom, and when after her pretty
confusion she has retired from the window, even Gratiano
breaks out:

ii. vi. 51.   Now, by my hood, a Gentile and no Jew;

while Lorenzo himself has warmed to see in her qualities
he had never expected:

ii. vi. 52.   Beshrew me but I love her heartily;
> For she is wise, if I can judge of her,
> And fair she is, if that mine eyes be true,
> And true she is, as she has proved herself,
> And therefore, like herself, wise, fair, and true,
> Shall she be placed in my constant soul.

So generally, all with whom she comes into contact feel
ii. iii. 10.   her spell: the rough Launcelot parts from her with tears he
iii. i. 41.   is ashamed of yet cannot keep down; Salarino—the last of

men to take high views of women—resents as a sort of blas-　CHAP. III.
phemy Shylock's claiming her as his flesh and blood ; while
between Jessica and Portia there seems to spring in an iii. iv, v;
instant an attraction as mysterious as is the tie between v. i.
Antonio and Bassanio.

Lorenzo is for the most part of a dreamy inactive nature, *Character*
as may be seen in his amused tolerance of Launcelot's *of Lorenzo.*
word-fencing—word-fencing being in general a challenge 75.
which none of Shakespeare's characters can resist; similarly,
Jessica's enthusiasm on the subject of Portia, which in reality iii v. 75-
he shares, he prefers to meet with banter : 89.

> Even such a husband
> Hast thou of me as she is for a wife.

But the strong side of his character also is shown us in the
play : he has an artist soul, and to the depth of his passion
for music and for the beauty of nature we are indebted for v. i. 1-24,
some of the noblest passages in Shakespeare. This is the 54-88.
attraction which has drawn him to Jessica, her outer beauty
is the index of artistic sensibility within : 'she is never merry v 1 69, 1-
when she hears sweet music,' and the soul of rhythm is 24.
awakened in her, just as much as in her husband, by the
moonlight scene. Simplicity again, is a quality they have
in common, as is seen by their ignorance in money- iii. i. 113,
matters, and the way a valuable turquoise ring goes for a 123.
monkey—if, at least, Tubal may be believed : a carelessness
of money which mitigates our dislike of the free hand Jessica
lays upon her father's ducats and jewels. On the whole,
however, Lorenzo's dreaminess makes a pretty contrast to
Jessica's vivacity. And Lorenzo's inactivity is capable of
being roused to great things. This is seen by the elopement
itself : for the suggestion of its incidents seems to be that esp. ii. iv.
Lorenzo meant at first no more than trifling with the 20, 30; ii.
pretty Jewess, and that he rose to the occasion as he found vi. 30, &c.
and appreciated Jessica's higher tone and attraction. Finally,
we must see the calibre of Lorenzo's character through the

CHAP. III.

iii. iv. 24,
32.

*Jessica and
Lorenzo a
foil to Por-
tia and
Bassanio.*

eyes of Portia, who selects him at first sight as the represen- tative to whom to commit her household in her absence, of which commission she will take no refusal.

So interpreted the characters of Jessica and Lorenzo make the whole episode of the elopement an antithesis to the main plot. To a wedded couple in the fresh happiness of their union there can hardly fall a greater luxury than to further the happiness of another couple; this luxury is granted to Portia and Bassanio, and in their reception of the fugitives what picturesque contrasts are brought together! The two pairs are a foil to one another in kind, and set one another off like gold and gems. Lorenzo and Jessica are negative characters with the one positive quality of intense capacity for enjoyment; Bassanio and Portia have every- thing to enjoy, yet their natures appear dormant till roused by an occasion for daring and energy. The Jewess and her husband are distinguished by the bird-like simplicity that so often goes with special art-susceptibility; Portia and Bassa- nio are full and rounded characters in which the whole of human nature seems concentrated. The contrast is of degree as well as kind: the weaker pair brought side by side with the stronger throw out the impression of their strength. Portia has a fulness of power which puts her in her most natural position when she is extending protection to those who are less able to stand by themselves. Still more with Bassanio: he has so little scope in the scenes of the play itself, which from the nature of the stories present him always in situations of dependence on others, that we see his strength almost entirely by the reflected light of the attitude which others hold to him; in the present instance we have no difficulty in catching the intellectual power of Lorenzo, and Lorenzo looks up to Bassanio as a superior. And the couples thus contrasted in character present an equal like- ness and unlikeness in their fortunes. Both are happy for ever, and both have become so through a bold stroke. Yet

in the one instance it is blind obedience, in face of all temptations, to the mere whims of a good parent, who is dead, that
has been guided to the one issue so passionately desired; in
the case of the other couple open rebellion, at every practical
risk, against the legitimate authority of an evil father, still
living, has brought them no worse fate than happiness in one
another, and for their defenceless position the best of
patrons.

It seems, then, that the introduction of the Jessica Story is
justified, not only by the purposes of construction which it
serves, but by the fact that its human interest is at once a
contrast and a supplement to the main story, with which
it blends to produce the ordered variety of a finished
picture.

A few words will be sufficient to point out how the effects *The Rings*
of the main plot are assisted by the Rings Episode, which, *Episode*
though rich in fun, is of a slighter character than the Jessica *assists the*
Story, and occupies a much smaller space in the field of view. *mechanism*
of the main
The dramatic points of the two minor stories are similar. *stories,*
Like the Jessica Story the Rings Episode assists the mechanical working out of the main plot. An explanation
must somehow be given to Bassanio that the lawyer is Portia
in disguise; mere mechanical explanations have always an
air of weakness, but the affair of the rings utilises the
explanation in the present case as a source of new dramatic
effects. This arrangement further assists, to a certain extent,
in reducing the improbability of Portia's project. The point
at which the improbability would be most felt would be, not
the first appearance of the lawyer's clerk, for then we are
engrossed in our anxiety for Antonio, but when the explanation of the disguise came to be made; there might be a
danger lest here the surprise of Bassanio should become
infectious, and the audience should awake to the improbability of the whole story: as it is, their attention is at the
critical moment diverted to the perplexity of the penitent

CHAP. III. husbands. The Story of the Rings, like that of Jessica, assists
and their the interweaving of the two main stories with one another,
interweav- its subtlety suggesting to what a degree of detail this inter-
ing; lacing extends. Bassanio is the main point which unites the
Story of the Jew and the Caskets Story; in the one he
occupies the position of friend, in the other of husband.
iv. i. 425- The affair of the rings, slight as it is, is so managed by
454. Portia that its point becomes a test as between his friendship
and his love; and so equal do these forces appear that,
though his friendship finally wins and he surrenders his
betrothal ring, yet it is not until after his wife has given him
a hint against herself:

> An if your wife be not a mad-woman,
> And know how well I have deserved the ring,
> She would not hold out enemy for ever
> For giving it to me.

The Rings Episode, even more than the Jessica Story, assists
in restoring the balance between the main tales. The chief
inequality between them lies in the fact that the Jew Story is
complicated and resolved, while the Caskets Story is a simple
progress to a goal; when, however, there springs from the
latter a sub-action which has a highly comic complication
and resolution the two halves of the play become dramatically on a par. And the interweaving of the dark and
bright elements in the play is assisted by the fact that the
Episode of the Rings not only provides a comic reaction
to relieve the tragic crisis, but its whole point is a Dramatic
Irony in which serious and comic are inextricably mixed.

and assists Finally, as the Jessica Story ministers to Character effect in
in the de- connection with the general ensemble of the personages, so
velopment the Episode of the Rings has a special function in bringing
of Portia's out the character of Portia. The secret of the charm which
character. has won for Portia the suffrages of all readers is the perfect
balance of qualities in her character: she is the meeting-
point of brightness, force, and tenderness. And, to crown the

union, Shakespeare has placed her at the supreme moment of Chap. III.
life, on the boundary line between girlhood and womanhood,
when the wider aims and deeper issues of maturity find
themselves in strange association with the abandon of youth.
The balance thus becomes so perfect that it quivers, and dips
to one side and the other. Portia is the saucy child as she
sprinkles her sarcasms over Nerissa's enumeration of the i. ii. 39.
suitors: in the trial she faces the world of Venice as a
heroine. She is the ideal maiden in the speech in which she iii. ii. 150.
surrenders herself to Bassanio: she is the ideal woman as
she proclaims from the judgment seat the divinity of mercy. iv. i. 184.
Now the fourth Act has kept before us too exclusively one
side of this character. Not that Portia in the lawyer's gown
is masculine: but the dramatist has had to dwell too long on
her side of strength. He will not dismiss us with this impression, but indulges us in one more daring feat surpassing
all the madcap frolics of the past. Thus the Episode of the
Rings is the last flicker of girlhood in Portia before it merges
in the wider life of womanhood. We have rejoiced in a great
deliverance wrought by a noble woman: our enjoyment rises
higher yet when the Rings Episode reminds us that this
woman has not ceased to be a sportive girl.

It has been shown, then, that the two inferior stories in
The Merchant of Venice assist the main stories in the most
varied manner, smoothing their mechanical working, meeting
their special difficulties, drawing their mutual interweaving
yet closer, and throwing their character effects into relief:
the additional complexity they have brought has resulted in
making emphatic points yet more prominent, and the total
effect has therefore been to increase clearness and simplicity.
Enough has now been said on the building up of Dramas out
of Stories, which is the distinguishing feature of the Romantic
Drama ; the studies that follow will be applied to the more
universal topics of dramatic interest, Character, Plot, and
Passion.

IV.

A picture of Ideal Villainy in Richard III.

A Study in Character-Interpretation.

I HOPE that the subject of the present study will not be considered by any reader forbidding. On the contrary, there is surely attractiveness in the thought that nothing is so repulsive or so uninteresting in the world of fact but in some way or other it may be brought under the dominion of art-beauty. The author of *L'Allegro* shows by the companion poem that he could find inspiration in a rainy morning; and the great master in English poetry is followed by a great master in English painting who wins his chief triumphs by his handling of fog and mist. Long ago the masterpiece of Virgil consecrated agricultural toil; Murillo's pictures have taught us that there is a beauty in rags and dirt; rustic commonplaces gave a life passion to Wordsworth, and were the cause of a revolution in poetry; while Dickens has penetrated into the still less promising region of low London life, and cast a halo around the colourless routine of poverty. Men's evil passions have given Tragedy to art, crime is beautified by being linked to Nemesis, meanness is the natural source for brilliant comic effects, ugliness has reserved for it a special form of art in the grotesque, and pain becomes attractive in the light of the heroism that suffers and the devotion that watches. In the infancy of modern English poetry Drayton found a poetic side to topography and maps, and Phineas Fletcher idealised anatomy; while of the two

greatest imaginations belonging to the modern world Milton CHAP. IV.
produced his masterpiece in the delineation of a fiend, and
Dante in a picture of hell. The final triumph of good over
evil seems to have been already anticipated by art.

The portrait of Richard satisfies a first condition of ide- *The*
ality in the scale of the whole picture. The sphere in which he *villainy of*
Richard
is placed is not private life, but the world of history, in which *ideal in its*
moral responsibility is the highest : if, therefore, the quality *scale,*
of other villainies be as fine, here the issues are deeper. As *and in its*
another element of the ideal, the villainy of Richard is pre- *fulness of*
develop-
sented to us fully developed and complete. Often an artist *ment.*
of crime will rely—as notably in the portraiture of Tito
Melema—mainly on the succession of steps by which a character, starting from full possession of the reader's sympathies,
arrives by the most natural gradations at a height of evil which
shocks. In the present case all idea of growth is kept outside the field of this particular play ; the opening soliloquy
announces a completed process :

> I am determined to prove a villain.   i. i. 30.

What does appear of Richard's past, seen through the
favourable medium of a mother's description, only seems to
extend the completeness to earlier stages :

> A grievous burthen was thy birth to me;   iv. iv. 167.
> Tetchy and wayward was thy infancy ;   .
> Thy school-days frightful, desperate, wild, and furious,
> Thy prime of manhood daring, bold, and venturous,
> Thy age confirm'd, proud, subtle, bloody, treacherous,
> More mild, but yet more harmful, kind in hatred.

So in the details of the play there is nowhere a note of the
hesitation that betrays tentative action. When even Buckingham is puzzled as to what can be done if Hastings should
resist, Richard answers :

> Chop off his head, man ; somewhat we will do.   iii. i. 193.

His choice is only between different modes of villainy, never
between villainy and honesty.

CHAP. IV.

It has no sufficient motive.

Othello: i. iii. 392, &c.

Lear · i. ii. 1-22.

Again, it is to be observed that there is no suggestion of impelling motive or other explanation for the villainy of Richard. He does not labour under any sense of personal injury, such as Iago felt in believing, however groundlessly, that his enemies had wronged him through his wife; or Edmund, whose soliloquies display him as conscious that his birth has made his whole life an injury. Nor have we in this case the morbid enjoyment of suffering which we associate with Mephistopheles, and which Dickens has worked up into one of his most powerful portraits in Quilp. Richard never turns aside to gloat over the agonies of his victims; it is not so much the details as the grand schemes of villainy, the handling of large combinations of crime, that have an interest for him : he is a strategist in villainy, not a tactician. Nor can we point to ambition as a sufficient motive. He is ambitious in a sense which belongs to all vigorous natures; he has the workman's impulse to rise by his work. But ambition as a determining force in character must imply more than this; it is a sort of moral dazzling, its symptom is a fascination by ends which blinds to the ruinous means leading up to these ends. Such an ambition was Macbeth's; but in Richard the symptoms are wanting, and in all his long soliloquies he is never found dwelling upon the prize in view. A nearer approach to an explanation would be Richard's sense of bodily deformity. Not only do all who come in contact with him shrink from the 'bottled spider,' but he

i. iii. 242, 228; iv. iv. 81, &c.

himself gives a conspicuous place in his meditations to the thought of his ugliness; from the outset he connects his criminal career with the reflection that he 'is not shaped for

i. i. 14.

sportive tricks :'

> Deform'd, unfinish'd, sent before my time
> Into this breathing world, scarce half made up,
> And that so lamely and unfashionable
> That dogs bark at me as I halt by them ;
> Why, I, in this weak piping time of peace,
> Have no delight to pass away the time,

> Unless to spy my shadow in the sun
> And descant on mine own deformity.

Still, it would be going too far to call this the motive of his crimes : the spirit of this and similar passages is more accurately expressed by saying that he has a morbid pleasure in contemplating physical ugliness analogous to his morbid pleasure in contemplating moral baseness. *esp. 1. ii. 252–264.*

There appears, then, no sufficient explanation and motive for the villainy of Richard : the general impression conveyed is that to Richard villainy has become an end in itself needing no special motive. This is one of the simplest principles of human development—that a means to an end tends to become in time an end in itself. The miser who began accumulating to provide comforts for his old age finds the process itself of accumulating gain firmer and firmer hold upon him, until, when old age has come, he sticks to accumulating and foregoes comfort. So in previous plays Gloster may have been impelled by ambition to his crimes : by the time the present play is reached crime itself becomes to him the dearer of the two, and the ambitious end drops out of sight. This leads directly to one of the two main features of Shakespeare's portrait : Richard is an *artist in villainy.* What form and colour are to the painter, what rhythm and imagery are to the poet, that crime is to Richard : it is the medium in which his soul frames its conceptions of the beautiful. The gulf that separates between Shakespeare's Richard and the rest of humanity is no gross perversion of sentiment, nor the development of abnormal passions, nor a notable surrender in the struggle between interest and right. It is that he approaches villainy as a thing of pure intellect, a region of moral indifference in which sentiment and passion have no place, attraction to which implies no more motive than the simplest impulse to exercise a native talent in its natural sphere. *Villainy has become to Richard an end in itself.*

compare 3 Henry VI: iii. ii. 165-181.

Richard an artist in villainy.

Of the various barriers that exist against crime, the most powerful are the checks that come from human emotions. It *Richard lacks the emotions*

is easier for a criminal to resist the objections his reason
naturally interposes to evildoing than to overcome these emotional
attending restraints : either his own emotions, woven by generations of
crime. hereditary transmission into the very framework of his
nature, which make his hand tremble in the act of sinning ;
or the emotions his crimes excite in others, such as will
cause hardened wretches, who can die calmly on the scaffold,
to cower before the menaces of a mob. Crime becomes
possible only because these emotions can be counteracted by
more powerful emotions on the other side, by greed, by thirst
for vengeance, by inflamed hatred. In Richard, however,
when he is surveying his works, we find no such evil emotions
raised, no gratified vengeance or triumphant hatred. The
reason is that there is in him no restraining emotion to be
overcome. Horror at the unnatural is not subdued, but
absent; his attitude to atrocity is the passionless attitude of
the artist who recognises that the tyrant's cruelty can be set
i. ii. to as good music as the martyr's heroism. Readers are
shocked at the scene in which Richard wooes Lady Anne
beside the bier of the parent he has murdered, and wonder
that so perfect an intriguer should not choose a more favourable time. But the repugnance of the reader has no place in
Richard's feelings : the circumstances of the scene are so
many *objections*, to be met by so much skill of treatment. A
single detail in the play illustrates perfectly this neutral attitude to horror. Tyrrel comes to bring the news of the
princes' murder; Richard answers :

iv. iii. 31.　　　Come to me, Tyrrel, soon at after supper,
　　　　　And thou shalt tell the process of their death.

Quilp could not have waited for his gloating till after supper ;
other villains would have put the deed out of sight when done ;
the epicure in villainy reserves his *bonbouche* till he has leisure
to do it justice. Callous to his own emotions, he is equally
callous to the emotions he rouses in others. When Queen
Margaret is pouring a flood of curses which make the inno-

cent courtiers' hair stand on end, and the heaviest curse of CHAP. IV.
all, which she has reserved for Richard himself, is rolling on i iii 216-
to its climax,   239.

> Thou slander of thy mother's heavy womb!
> Thou loathed issue of thy father's loins!
> Thou rag of honour! thou detested—

he adroitly slips in the word 'Margaret' in place of the
intended 'Richard,' and thus, with the coolness of a schoolboy's small joke, disconcerts her tragic passion in a way that
gives a moral wrench to the whole scene.   His own mother's iv. iv, from
curse moves him not even to anger; he caps its clauses with 136.
bantering repartees, until he seizes an opportunity for a pun,
and begins to move off: he treats her curse, as in a previous
scene he had treated her blessing, with a sort of gentle im- ii. ii 109.
patience as if tired of a fond yet somewhat troublesome
parent.   Finally, there is an instinct which serves as resultant
to all the complex forces, emotional or rational, which sway
us between right and wrong; this instinct of conscience is
formally disavowed by Richard:

> Conscience is but a word that cowards use,   v. iii. 309.
> Devised at first to keep the strong in awe.

But, if the natural heat of emotion is wanting, there is, on *But he re-*
the other hand, the full intellectual warmth of an artist's *gards*
villainy
enthusiasm, whenever Richard turns to survey the game he is *with the*
playing.   He reflects with a relish how he does the wrong *intellectual*
enthusiasm
and first begins the brawl, how he sets secret mischief *of the*   .
abroach and charges it on to others, beweeping his own *artist.*
i. iii, from
victims to simple gulls, and, when these begin to cry for 324.
vengeance, quoting Scripture against returning evil for evil,
and thus seeming a saint when most he plays the devil.   The
great master is known by his appreciation of details, in the
least of which he can see the play of great principles: so the
magnificence of Richard's villainy does not make him in-
sensible to commonplaces of crime.   When in the long

CHAP. IV. usurpation conspiracy there is a moment's breathing space
iii. v. 1–11. just before the Lord Mayor enters, Richard and Buckingham
utilise it for a burst of hilarity over the deep hypocrisy with
which they are playing their parts ; how they can counterfeit
the deep tragedian, murder their breath in the middle of a
word, tremble and start at wagging of a straw :—here we have
the musician's flourish upon his instrument from very wantonness of skill.   Again :

i. i. 118.   Simple, plain Clarence! I do love thee so
                        That I will shortly send thy soul to heaven—

is the composer's pleasure at hitting upon a readily workable
theme.   Richard appreciates his murderers as a workman
appreciates good tools :

i. iii. 354.   Your eyes drop millstones, when fools' eyes drop tears :
                        I like you, lads.

i. ii, from   And at the conclusion of the scene with Lady Anne we have
228.   the artist's enjoyment of his own masterpiece :

                        Was ever woman in this humour woo'd ?
                        Was ever woman in this humour won ? . . .
                        What! I, that kill'd her husband and his father,
                        To take her in her heart's extremest hate,
                        With curses in her mouth, tears in her eyes,
                        The bleeding witness of her hatred by ;
                        Having God, her conscience, and these bars against me,
                        And I nothing to back my suit at all,
                        But the plain devil and dissembling looks,
                        And yet to win her, all the world to nothing !

The tone in this passage is of the highest : it is the tone of a
musician fresh from a triumph of his art, the sweetest point
in which has been that he has condescended to no adven-
titious aids, no assistance of patronage or concessions to
popular tastes ; it has been won by pure music.   So the artist
in villainy celebrates a triumph of *plain devil !*

The   This view of Richard as an artist in crime is sufficient to
villainy   explain the hold which villainy has on Richard himself : but
ideal in

ideal villainy must be ideal also in its success; and on this CHAP. IV.
side of the analysis another conception in Shakespeare's *success. a*
portraiture becomes of first importance. It is obvious enough *fascination*
that Richard has all the elements of success which can be *bility in*
reduced to the form of skill: but he has something more. *Richard*
No theory of human action will be complete which does not
recognise a dominion of will over will operating by mere contact, without further explanation so far as conscious influence
is concerned. What is it that takes the bird into the jaws of
the serpent? No persuasion or other influence on the bird's
consciousness, for it struggles to keep back; we can only
recognise the attraction as a force, and give it a name,
fascination. In Richard there is a similar Fascination of
Irresistibility, which also operates by his mere presence, and
which fights for him in the same way in which the idea of
their invincibility fought for conquerors like Napoleon, and
was on occasions as good to them as an extra twenty or thirty
thousand men. A consideration like this will be appreciated
in the case of *tours de force* like the Wooing of Lady Anne,
which is a stumblingblock to many readers—a widow beside
the bier of her murdered husband's murdered father wooed
and won by the man who makes no secret that he is the
murderer of them both. The analysis of ordinary human
motives would make it appear that Anne would not yield at
points at which the scene represents her as yielding; some
other force is wanted to explain her surrender, and it is found
in this secret force of irresistible will which Richard bears about
with him. But, it will be asked, in what does this fascination
appear? The answer is that the idea of it is furnished to us
by the other scenes of the play. Such a consideration illustrates the distinction between real and ideal. An ideal incident is not an incident of real life simply clothed in beauty of
expression; nor, on the other hand, is an ideal incident
divorced from the laws of real possibility. Ideal implies that
the transcendental has been made possible by treatment: that

H

an incident (for example) which might be impossible in itself
becomes possible through other incidents with which it is associated, just as in actual life the action of a public personage
which may have appeared strange at the time becomes
intelligible when at his death we can review his life as a
whole. Such a scene as the Wooing Scene might be impossible as a fragment; it becomes possible enough in the
play, where it has to be taken in connection with the rest of
the plot, throughout which the irresistibility of the hero is
The fasci- prominent as one of the chief threads of connection. Nor is
nation is to it any objection that the Wooing Scene comes early in the
be conveyed action. The play is not the book, but the actor's interpreta-
in the tion on the stage, and the actor will have collected even from
acting. the latest scenes elements of the interpretation he throws
into the earliest: the actor is a lens for concentrating the
light of the whole play upon every single detail. The fascination of irresistibility, then, which is to act by instinct in
every scene, may be arrived at analytically when we survey
the play as a whole — when we see how by Richard's
innate genius, by the reversal in him of the ordinary relation
of human nature to crime, especially by his perfect mastery of the successive situations as they arise, the dramatist steadily builds up an irresistibility which becomes
a secret force clinging to Richard's presence, and through
the operation of which his feats are half accomplished by
the fact of his attempting them.

The irre- To begin with: the sense of irresistible power is brought
sistibility out by the way in which the unlikeliest things are con-
analysed. tinually drawn into his schemes and utilised as means. Not
Unlikely to speak of his regular affectation of blunt sincerity, he
means. makes use of the simple brotherly confidence of Clarence as
i. i, from an engine of fratricide, and founds on the frank famili-
42. arity existing between himself and Hastings a plot by
iii. iv; esp. which he brings him to the block. The Queen's com-
76 com- punction at the thought of leaving Clarence out of the
pared with
iii. i. 184.

general reconciliation around the dying king's bedside is the CHAP. IV.
fruit of a conscience tenderer than her neighbours' : Richard ii. i, from
adroitly seizes it as an opportunity for shifting on to the 73 ; cf. 134.
Queen and her friends the suspicion of the duke's murder.
The childish prattle of little York Richard manages to sug- iii. i. 154.
gest to the bystanders as dangerous treason; the solemnity
of the king's deathbed he turns to his own purposes by out- ii. i. 52–72.
doing all the rest in Christian forgiveness and humility; and
he selects devout meditation as the card to play with the iii. v. 99,
Lord Mayor and citizens. On the other hand, amongst &c.
other devices for the usurpation conspiracy, he starts a
slander upon his own mother's purity; and further—by one iii. v. 75–
of the greatest strokes in the whole play—makes capital 94.
in the Wooing Scene out of his own heartlessness, de- i. ii. 156–
scribing in a burst of startling eloquence the scenes of 167.
horror he has passed through, the only man unmoved to
tears, in order to add :

> And what these sorrows could not thence exhale,
> Thy beauty hath, and made them blind with weeping.

There are things which are too sacred for villainy to touch,
and there are things which are protected by their own foulness : both alike are made useful by Richard.

Similarly it is to be noticed how Richard can utilise the *The sensa-*
very sensation produced by one crime as a means to bring *tion pro-*
duced by
about more; as when he interrupts the King's dying moments *one crime*
to announce the death of Clarence in such a connection as *made to*
bring about
must give a shock to the most unconcerned spectator, and *others.*
then draws attention to the pale faces of the Queen's friends ii. i, from
as marks of guilt. He thus makes one crime beget another 77 ; cf. 134.
without further effort on his part, reversing the natural law
by which each criminal act, through its drawing more suspicion to the villain, tends to limit his power for further
mischief. It is to the same purpose that Richard chooses *Richard's*
own plans
sometimes instead of acting himself to foist his own schemes *foisted on to*
on to others; as when he inspires Buckingham with the *others.*

CHAP. IV.
ll. ii. 112–
154; esp.
149.

idea of the young king's arrest, and, when Buckingham seizes the idea as his own, meekly accepts it from him:

> I, like a child, will go by thy direction.

There is in all this a dreadful *economy* of crime: not the economy of prudence seeking to reduce its amount, but the artist's economy which delights in bringing the largest number of effects out of a single device. Such skill opens up a vista of evil which is boundless.

No signs of effort in Richard: imperturb- ability of mind;

The sense of irresistible power is again brought out by his perfect imperturbability of mind: villainy never ruffles his spirits. He never misses the irony that starts up in the circumstances around him, and says to Clarence:

1. i. 111.

> This deep disgrace in brotherhood
> *Touches* me deeply.

While taking his part in entertaining the precocious King he treats us to continual asides—

lll. i. 79, 94.

> So wise so young, they say, do never live long—

showing how he can stop to criticise the scenes in which he is an actor. He can delay the conspiracy on which his chance of the crown depends by coming late to the council, and then while waiting the moment for turning upon his victim is cool enough to recollect the Bishop of Ely's straw- berries. But more than all these examples is to be noted Richard's *humour*. This is *par excellence* the sign of a mind at ease with itself: scorn, contempt, bitter jest belong to the storm of passion, but humour is the sunshine of the soul. Yet Shakespeare has ventured to endow Richard with unquestionable humour. Thus, in one of his earliest meditations, he prays, 'God take King Edward to his mercy,' for then he will marry Warwick's youngest daughter:

lll. iv. 24.
llf. iv. 32.
humour;

1. l. 151–156.

> What though I kill'd her husband and her father!
> The readiest way to make the wench amends
> Is to become her husband and her father!

e.g. 1. l. 118; ll. ii.

And all through there perpetually occur little turns of lan-

guage into which the actor can throw a tone of humorous
enjoyment; notably, when he complains of being 'too
childish-foolish for this world,' and where he nearly ruins the
effect of his edifying penitence in the Reconciliation Scene,
by being unable to resist one final stroke :

CHAP. IV.
109; iv. iii.
38, 43; i.
iii. 142; ii.
i. 72; iii.
vii. 51-54,
&c.

> I thank my God for my humility!

Of a kindred nature is his perfect frankness and fairness to
his victims : villainy never clouds his judgment. Iago,
astutest of intriguers, was deceived, as has been already
noted, by his own morbid acuteness, and firmly believed—
what the simplest spectator can see to be a delusion—that
Othello has tampered with his wife. Richard, on the contrary, is a marvel of judicial impartiality; he speaks of King
Edward in such terms as these—

freedom from pre-judice.

> If King Edward be as true and just
> As I am subtle, false and treacherous ;

i. i. 36.

and weighs elaborately the superior merit of one of his
victims to his own :

> Hath she forgot already that brave prince,
> Edward, her lord, whom I, some three months since,
> Stabb'd in my angry mood at Tewksbury ?
> A sweeter and a lovelier gentleman,
> Framed in the prodigality of nature,
> Young, valiant, wise, and, no doubt, right royal,
> The spacious world cannot again afford :
> And will she yet debase her eyes on me,
> That cropped the golden prime of this sweet prince,
> And made her widow to a woful bed ?
> On me, whose all not equals Edward's moiety ?

i. ii, from
240.

Richard can rise to all his height of villainy without its
leaving on himself the slightest trace of struggle or even
effort.

Again, the idea of boundless resource is suggested by an
occasional recklessness, almost a slovenliness, in the details
of his intrigues. Thus, in the early part of the Wooing

A reckless-ness sug-gesting boundless resources.

Scene he makes two blunders of which a tyro in intrigue might be ashamed. He denies that he is the author of Edward's death, to be instantly confronted with the evidence of Margaret as an eye-witness. Then a few lines further on he goes to the opposite extreme :

> *Anne.* Didst thou not kill this king ?
> *Glouc.*   I grant ye.
> *Anne.* Dost grant me, hedgehog ?

The merest beginner would know better how to meet accusations than by such haphazard denials and acknowledgments. But the crack billiard-player will indulge at the beginning of the game in a little clumsiness, giving his adversaries a prospect of victory only to have the pleasure of making up the disadvantage with one or two brilliant strokes. And so Richard, essaying the most difficult problem ever attempted in human intercourse, lets half the interview pass before he feels it worth while to play with caution.

General character of Richard's intrigue: inspiration rather than calculation. The mysterious irresistibility of Richard, pointed to by the succession of incidents in the play, is assisted by the very improbability of some of the more difficult scenes in which he is an actor. Intrigue in general is a thing of reason, and its probabilities can be readily analysed ; but the genius of intrigue in Richard seems to make him avoid the caution of other intriguers, and to give him a preference for feats which seem impossible. The whole suggests how it is not by calculation that he works, but he brings the *touch* of an artist to his dealing with human weakness, and follows whither his artist's inspiration leads him. If, then, there is nothing so remote from evil but Richard can make it tributary; if he can endow crimes with power of self-multiplying ; if he can pass through a career of sin without the taint of distortion on his intellect and with the unruffled calmness of innocence ; if Richard accomplishes feats no other would attempt with a carelessness no other reputation would risk, even slow reason may well believe him irresistible. When,

further, such qualifications for villainy become, by unbroken CHAP. IV.
success in villainy, reflected in Richard's very bearing; when
the only law explaining his motions to onlookers is the law-
lessness of genius whose instinct is more unerring than the
most laborious calculation and planning, it becomes only
natural that the *opinion* of his irresistibility should become
converted. into a mystic *fascination*, making Richard's very
presence a signal to his adversaries of defeat, chilling with
hopelessness the energies with which they are to face his
consummate skill.

The two main ideas of Shakespeare's portrait, the idea of
an artist in crime and the fascination of invincibility which
Richard bears about with him, are strikingly illustrated in
the wooing of Lady Anne. For a long time Richard will not i. ii.
put forth effort, but meets the loathing and execration hurled
at him with repartee, saying in so many words that he regards
the scene as a 'keen encounter of our wits.' All this time 115
the mysterious power of his presence is operating, the more
strongly as Lady Anne sees the most unanswerable cause
that denunciation ever had to put produce no effect upon
her adversary, and feels her own confidence in her wrongs
recoiling upon herself. When the spell has had time to from 152.
work then he assumes a serious tone: suddenly, as we have
seen, turning the strong point of Anne's attack, his own
inhuman nature, into the basis of his plea—he who never
wept before has been softened by love to her. From this
point he urges his cause with breathless speed; he presses a 175.
sword into her hand with which to pierce his breast, knowing
that she lacks the nerve to wield it, and seeing how such
forbearance on her part will be a starting-point in giving
way. We can trace the sinking of her will before the un-
conquerable will of her adversary in her feebler and feebler from 193.
refusals, while as yet very shame keeps her to an outward
defiance. Then, when she is wishing to yield, he suddenly
finds her an excuse by declaring that all he desires at this

CHAP. IV. moment is that she should leave the care of the King's
funeral

> To him that hath more cause to be a mourner.

By yielding this much to penitence and religion we see she
has commenced a downward descent from which she will
never recover.   Such consummate art in the handling of
human nature, backed by the spell of an irresistible presence, the weak Anne has no power to combat.   To the last
iv. i. 66– she is as much lost in amazement as the reader at the way
87. it has all come about :

> Lo, ere I can repeat this curse again,
> Even in so short a space, my woman's heart
> Grossly grew captive to his honey words.

Ideal v. To gather up our results.   A dramatist is to paint a por-
real trait of ideal villainy as distinct from villainy in real life.   In
villainy real life it is a commonplace that a virtuous life is a life of
effort; but the converse is not true, that he who is prepared
to be a villain will therefore lead an easy life.   On the contrary, 'the *way* of transgressors is hard.'   The metaphor
suggests a path, laid down at first by the Architect of the
universe, beaten plain and flat by the generations of men
who have since trodden it : he who keeps within this path of
rectitude will walk, not without effort, yet at least with
safety ; but he who ' steps aside' to the right or left will
find his way beset with pitfalls and stumblingblocks. ` In
real life a man sets out to be a villain, but his mental power
is deficient, and he remains a villain only in intention.   Or
he has stores of power, but lacks the spark of purpose to set
them aflame.   Or, armed with both will to plan and mind to
execute, yet his efforts are hampered by unfit tools.   Or, if
his purpose needs reliance alone on his own clear head and
his own strong arm, yet in the critical moment the emotional nature he has inherited with his humanity starts into
rebellion and scares him, like Macbeth, from the half-

accomplished deed. Or, if he is as hardened in nature as CHAP. IV. corrupt in mind and will, yet he is closely pursued by a mocking fate, which crowns his well-laid plans with a mysterious succession of failures. Or, if there is no other limitation on him from within or from without, yet he may move in a world too narrow to give him scope : the man with a heart to be the scourge of his country proves in fact no more than the vagabond of a country side.—But in Shakespeare's portrait we have infinite capacity for mischief, needing no purpose, for evil has become to it an end in itself; we have one who for tools can use the baseness of his own nature or the shame of those who are his nearest kin, while at his touch all that is holiest becomes transformed into weapons of iniquity. We have one whose nature in the past has been a gleaning ground for evil in every stage of his development, and who in the present is framed to look on unnatural horror with the eyes of interested curiosity. We have one who seems to be seconded by fate with a series of successes, which builds up for him an irresistibility that is his strongest safeguard ; and who, instead of being cramped by circumstances, has for his stage the world of history itself, in which crowns are the prize and nations the victims. In such a portrait is any element wanting to arrive at the ideal of villainy?

The question would rather be whether Shakespeare has *Ideal* not gone too far, and, passing outside the limits of art, ex- *villainy* hibited a monstrosity. Nor is it an answer to point to the *strosity.* 'dramatic hedging' by which Richard is endowed with undaunted personal courage, unlimited intellectual power, and every good quality not inconsistent with his perfect villainy. The objection to such a portrait as the present study presents is that it offends against our sense of the principles upon which the universe has been constructed; we feel that before a violation of nature could attain such proportions nature must have exerted her recuperative force to crush it. If, however,

CHAP. IV. the dramatist can suggest that such reassertion of nature is actually made, that the crushing blow is delayed only while it is accumulating force: in a word, if the dramatist can draw out before us a *Nemesis* as ideal as the villainy was ideal, then the full demands of art will be satisfied. The Nemesis that dominates the whole play of *Richard III* will be the subject of the next study.

V.

RICHARD III : HOW SHAKESPEARE WEAVES NEMESIS INTO HISTORY.

A Study in Plot.

I HAVE alluded already to the dangerous tendency, which, as it appears to me, exists amongst ordinary readers of Shakespeare, to ignore plot as of secondary importance, and to look for Shakespeare's greatness mainly in his conceptions of character. But the full character effect of a dramatic portrait cannot be grasped if it be dissociated from the plot; and this is nowhere more powerfully illustrated than in the play of *Richard III*. The last study was devoted exclusively to the Character side of the play, and on this confined view the portrait of Richard seemed a huge offence against our sense of moral equilibrium, rendering artistic satisfaction impossible. Such an impression vanishes when, as in the present study, the drama is looked at from the side of Plot. The effect of this plot is, however, missed by those who limit their attention in reviewing it to Richard himself. These may feel that there is nothing in his fate to compensate for the spectacle of his crimes: man must die, and a death in fulness of energy amid the glorious stir of battle may seem a fate to be envied. But the Shakespearean Drama with its complexity of plot is not limited to the individual life and fate in its interpretation of history; and when we survey all the distinct trains of interest in the play of *Richard III*, with their blendings and mutual influence, we shall obtain a sense of dramatic satisfaction

CHAP. V. amply counterbalancing the monstrosity of Richard's villainy. Viewed as a study in character the play leaves in us only an intense craving for Nemesis: when we turn to consider the plot, this presents to us the world of history transformed into an intricate design of which the recurrent pattern is Nemesis.

The under-plot: a set of separate Nemesis Actions. This notion of tracing a pattern in human affairs is a convenient key to the exposition of plot. Laying aside for the present the main interest of Richard himself, we may observe that the bulk of the drama consists in a number of minor interests—single threads of the pattern—each of

Clarence. which is a separate example of Nemesis. The first of these trains of interest centres around the Duke of Clarence. He has betrayed the Lancastrians, to whom he had solemnly sworn

i. iv. 50, 66. fealty, for the sake of the house of York; this perjury is his bitterest recollection in his hour of awakened conscience, and is urged home by the taunts of his murderers; while his only defence is that he did it all for his brother's love. Yet his

ii. i. 86. lot is to fall by a treacherous death, the warrant for which is signed by this brother, the King and head of the Yorkist house,

i. iv. 250. while its execution is procured by the bulwark of the house,

The King. the intriguing Richard. The centre of the second nemesis is the King, who has thus allowed himself in a moment of suspicion to be made a tool for the murder of his brother,

ii. i. 77-133. seeking to stop it when too late. Shakespeare has contrived that this death of Clarence, announced as it is in so terrible a manner beside the King's sick bed, gives him a shock from which he never rallies, and he is carried out to die with the words on his lips:

> O God, I fear Thy justice will take hold
> On me, and you, and mine, and yours for this.

The Queen and her kindred. In this nemesis on the King are associated the Queen and her kindred. They have been assenting parties to the measures against Clarence (however little they may have contemplated the bloody issue to which those measures have

been brought by the intrigues of Gloster). This we must CHAP. V.
understand from the introduction of Clarence's children, ii. ii. 62–
who serve no purpose except to taunt the Queen in her 65.
bereavement :

> *Boy.* Good aunt, you wept not for our father's death ;
> How can we aid you with our kindred tears?
> *Girl.* Our fatherless distress was left unmoan'd ;
> Your widow-dolour likewise be unwept !

The death of the King, so unexpectedly linked to that of
Clarence, removes from the Queen and her kindred the sole ii. ii. 74,
bulwark to the hated Woodville family, and leaves them at &c.
the mercy of their enemies.   A third nemesis Action has *Hastings.*
Hastings for its subject. Hastings is the head of the court- i. i. 66; iii.
faction which is opposed to the Queen and her allies, and he ii. 58, &c.
passes all bounds of decency in his exultation at the fate
which overwhelms his adversaries :

> But I shall laugh at this a twelvemonth hence,
> That they who brought me in my master's hate,
> I live to look upon their tragedy.

He even forgets his dignity as a nobleman, and stops on his
way to the Tower to chat with a mere officer of the court, in iii. ii. 97.
order to tell him the news of which he is full, that his
enemies are to die that day at Pomfret.   Yet this very
journey of Hastings is his journey to the block ; the same
cruel fate which had descended upon his opponents, from
the same agent and by the same unscrupulous doom, is dealt
out to Hastings in his turn.   In this treacherous casting off *Bucking-*
of Hastings when he is no longer useful, Buckingham has *ham.*
been a prime agent. Buckingham amused himself with the iii. ii, from
false security of Hastings, adding to Hastings's innocent 114.
expression of his intention to stay dinner at the Tower the
aside

> And supper too, although thou know'st it not;

while in the details of the judicial murder he plays second to
Richard. By precisely similar treachery he is himself cast

CHAP. V. off when he hesitates to go further with Richard's villainous
schemes; and in precisely similar manner the treachery is
iv. ii, from flavoured with contempt.
86.

> *Buck.* I am thus bold to put your grace in mind
>   Of what you promised me.
> *K. Rich.*   Well, but what 's o'clock?
> *Buck.* Upon the stroke of ten.
> *K. Rich.*   Well, let it strike.
> *Buck.* Why let it strike?
> *K. Rich.* Because that, like a Jack, thou keep'st the stroke
>   Betwixt thy begging and my meditation.
>   I am not in the giving vein to-day.
> *Buck.* Why, then resolve me whether you will or no.
> *K. Rich.* Tut, tut,
>   Thou troublest me; I am not in the vein.
>   [*Exeunt all but Buckingham.*
> *Buck.* Is it even so? rewards he my true service
>   With such deep contempt? made I him king for this?
>   O, let me think on Hastings, and be gone
>   To Brecknock, while my fearful head is on!

The four nemeses formed into a system by nemesis as a link.

These four Nemesis Actions, it will be observed, are not
separate trains of incident going on side by side, they are
linked together into a system, the law of which is seen to be
that those who triumph in one nemesis become the victims
of the next; so that the whole suggests a 'chain of destruction,' like that binding together the orders of the brute
creation which live by preying upon one another. When
Clarence perished it was the King who dealt the doom and
the Queen's party who triumphed: the wheel of Nemesis goes
round and the King's death follows the death of his victim,
the Queen's kindred are naked to the vengeance of their
enemies, and Hastings is left to exult. Again the wheel of
Nemesis revolves, and Hastings at the moment of his highest
exultation is hurled to destruction, while Buckingham stands
by to point the moral with a gibe. Once more the wheel
goes round, and Buckingham hears similar gibes addressed
to himself and points the same moral in his own person.
Thus the portion of the drama we have so far considered

yields us a pattern within a pattern, a series of Nemesis CHAP. V.
Actions woven into a complete underplot by a connecting-link
which is also Nemesis.

Following out the same general idea we may proceed to *The 'En-*
notice how the dramatic pattern is surrounded by a fringe or *veloping*
border. The picture of life presented in a play will have the *Action' a*
more reality if it be connected with a life wider than its own.
There is no social sphere, however private, but is to some
extent affected by a wider life outside it, this by one wider
still, until the great world is reached the story of which is
History. The immediate interest may be in a single family,
but it will be a great war which, perhaps, takes away some
member of this family to die in battle, or some great commercial crisis which brings mutation of fortune to the
obscure home. The artists of fiction are solicitous thus to
suggest connections between lesser and greater; it is the
natural tendency of the mind to pass from the known to the
unknown, and if the artist can derive the movements in his
little world from the great world outside, he appears to have
given his fiction a basis of admitted truth to rest on. This
device of enclosing the incidents of the actual story in a framework of great events—technically, the 'Enveloping Action'
—is one which is common in Shakespeare; it is enough to
instance such a case as *A Midsummer Night's Dream*, in which
play a fairy story has a measure of historic reality given to it
by its connection with the marriage of personages so famous
as Theseus and Hippolyta. In the present case, the main
incidents and personages belong to public life; nevertheless
the effect in question is still secured, and the contest of
factions with which the play is occupied is represented as
making up only a few incidents in the great feud of Lancaster and York. This Enveloping Action of the whole play,
the War of the Roses, is marked with special clearness: two
personages are introduced for the sole purpose of giving it
prominence. The Duchess of York is by her years and ii. ii. 80.

CHAP. V.   position the representative of the whole house; the factions
who in the play successively triumph and fall are all descended from herself; she says:

> Alas, I am the mother of these moans!
> Their woes are parcell'd, mine are general.

i. iii, from   And probabilities are forced to bring in Queen Margaret,
111; and   the head and sole rallying-point of the ruined Lancastrians:
iv. iv. 1-   when the two aged women are confronted the whole civil
125.   war is epitomised.   It is hardly necessary to point out that
this Enveloping Action is itself a Nemesis Action.   All the
rising and falling, the suffering and retaliation that we
actually see going on between the different sections of the
Yorkist house, constitute a detail in a wider retribution: the
esp. ii. ii;   presence of the Duchess gives to the incidents a unity, Queen
iv.i;iv.iv.   Margaret's function is to point out that this unity of woe is
ii. iii; and   only the nemesis falling on the house of York for their
iv. iv.   wrongs to the house of Lancaster.   Thus the pattern made
up of so many reiterations of nemesis is enclosed in a
border which itself repeats the same figure.

The En-   The effect is carried further.   Generally the Enveloping
veloping   Action is a sort of curtain by which our view of a drama is
Nemesis
carried on   bounded; in the present case the curtain is at one point
into indefi-   lifted, and we get a glimpse into the world beyond.   Queen
niteness.   Margaret has surprised the Yorkist courtiers, and her prophetic denunciations are still ringing, in which she points to
the calamities her foes have begun to suffer as retribution for
the woes of which her fallen greatness is the representative
i. iii. 174-   —when Gloster suddenly turns the tables upon her.
194.

> The curse my noble father laid on thee,
> When thou didst crown his warlike brows with paper
> And with thy scorns drew'st rivers from his eyes,
> And then, to dry them, gavest the duke a clout
> Steep'd in the faultless blood of pretty Rutland,—
> His curses, then from bitterness of soul
> Denounced against thee, are all fall'n upon thee;
> And God, not we, hath plagu'd thy bloody deed.

And the new key-note struck by Gloster is taken up in CHAP. V.
chorus by the rest, who find relief from the crushing effect of
Margaret's curses by pressing the charge home upon her.
This is only a detail, but it is enough to carry the effect of
the Enveloping Action a degree further back in time : the
events of the play are nemesis on York for wrongs done to
Lancaster, but now, it seems, these old wrongs against
Lancaster were retribution for yet older crimes Lancaster had
committed against York.   As in architecture the vista is
contrived so as to carry the general design of the building
into indefiniteness, so here, while the grand nemesis, of
which Margaret's presence is the representative, shuts in the
play like a veil, the momentary lifting of the veil opens up a
vista of nemeses receding further and further back into
history.

Once more.   All that we have seen suggests it as a sort *The one*
of law to the feud of York and Lancaster that each is *attempt to reverse the*
destined to wreak vengeance on the other, and then itself *nemesis*
suffer in turn.   But at one notable point of the play an *confirms it.* i. ii.
attempt is made to evade the hereditary nemesis by the
marriage of Richard and Lady Anne.   Anne, daughter to
Warwick—the grand deserter to the Lancastrians and martyr
to their cause—widow to the murdered heir of the house
and chief mourner to its murdered head, is surely the
greatest sufferer of the Lancastrians at the hands of the
Yorkists.   Richard is certainly the chief avenger of York
upon Lancaster.   When the chief source of vengeance and
the chief sufferer are united in the closest of all bonds, the
attempt to evade Nemesis becomes ideal.   Yet what is the
consequence ?   This attempt of Lady Anne to evade the
hereditary curse proves the very channel by which the curse
descends upon herself.   We see her once more : she is then *iv. i.* 66–
on her way to the Tower, and we hear her tell the strange 87.
story of her wooing, and wish the crown were 'red hot steel
to sear her to the brain'; never, she says, since her union

CHAP. V.   with Richard has she enjoyed the golden dew of sleep; she is but waiting for the destruction, by which, no doubt, Richard will shortly rid himself of her.

To counter-act the effect of re-petition the nemeses are specially empha-sised: An objection may, however, here present itself, that continual repetition of an idea like Nemesis, tends to weaken its artistic effect, until it comes to be taken for granted. No doubt it is a law of taste that force may be dissipated by repetition if carried beyond a certain point. But it is to be noted, on the other hand, what pains Shakespeare has taken to counteract the tendency in the present instance. The force of a nemesis may depend upon a fitness that addresses itself to the spectator's reflection, or it may be measured by the degree to which the nemesis is brought into prominence in the incidents themselves. In the incidents of the present play special means are adopted to make the recognition of the successive nemeses as they arise emphatic. In the first place the nemesis is in each case pointed out at the moment of its fulfilment. In the case of Clarence his story of crime and retribution is reflected in his dream before it is brought to a conclusion in reality; and wherein the bitterness of this review consists, we see when he turns to his sympathising jailor and says:

by recog-nition,

i. iv, from 18.

i. iv. 66.

> O Brackenbury, I have done those things,
> Which now bear evidence against my soul,
> For Edward's sake: and see how he requites me!

The words have already been quoted in which the King recognises how God's justice has overtaken him for his part in Clarence's death, and those in which the children of Clarence taunt the Queen with her having herself to bear the bereavement she has made them suffer. As the Queen's kindred are being led to their death, one of them exclaims:

iii. iii. 15.

> Now Margaret's curse is fall'n upon our heads
> For standing by when Richard stabb'd her son.

Hastings, when his doom has wakened him from his infatuation, recollects a priest he had met on his way to the

Tower, with whom he had stopped to talk about the dis- CHAP. V.
comfiture of his enemies:

> O, now I want the priest that spake to me! iii. iv. 89.

Buckingham on his way to the scaffold apostrophises the
souls of his victims:

> If that your moody discontented souls v. 1 7.
> Do through the clouds behold this present hour,
> Even for revenge mock my destruction.

And such individual notes of recognition are collected into a
sort of chorus when Margaret appears the second time to iv. iv. 1, 35.
point out the fulfilment of her curses, and sits down beside
the old Duchess and her daughter-in-law to join in the
'society of sorrow' and 'cloy her' with beholding the revenge for which she has hungered.

Again, the nemeses have a further emphasis given to *by pro-*
them by prophecy. As Queen Margaret's second appear- *phecy,*
ance is to mark the fulfilment of a general retribution, so her i iii, from
first appearance denounced it beforehand in the form of 195.
curses. And the effect is carried on in individual prophecies: the Queen's friends as they suffer foresee that the
turn of the opposite party will come:

> You live that shall cry woe for this hereafter; iii. iii. 7.

and Hastings prophesies Buckingham's doom:

> They smile at me that shortly shall be dead. iii. iv. 109.

It is as if the atmosphere cleared for each sufferer with the
approach of death, and they then saw clearly the righteous
plan on which the universe is constructed, and which had
been hidden from them by the dust of life.

But there is a third means, more powerful than either re- *and especi-*
cognition or prophecy, which Shakespeare has employed to *ally by*
make his Nemesis Actions emphatic. The danger of an effect *irony.*
becoming tame by repetition he has met by giving to each
train of nemesis a flash of irony at some point of its course.
In the case of Lady Anne we have already seen how the
exact channel Nemesis chooses by which to descend upon

CHAP. V. her is the attempt she made to avert it. She had bitterly
cursed her husband's murderer :

iv. i. 75.
> And be ·thy wife—if any be so mad—
> As miserable by the life of thee
> As thou hast made me by my dear lord's death !

In spite of this she had yielded to Richard's mysterious
power, and so, as she feels, proved the *subject of her own
heart's curse*. Again, it was noticed in the preceding study
how the Queen, less hard than the rest in that wicked court,
or perhaps softened by the spectacle of her dying husband,
essayed to reverse, when too late, what had been done
against Clarence ; Gloster skilfully turned this compunction
ii. i. 134. of conscience into a ground of suspicion on which he traded
to bring all the Queen's friends to the block, and thus a
moment's relenting was made into a means of destruction.
In Clarence's struggle for life, as one after another the
i. iv. 187, threads of hope snap, as the appeal to law is met by the
199, 200, King's command, the appeal to heavenly law by the re-
206, minder of his own sin, he comes to rest for his last and surest
i. iv. 232. hope upon his powerful brother Gloster—and the very murderers catch the irony of the scene :

> *Clar.* If you be hired for meed, go back again,
> And I will send you to my brother Gloster,
> Who shall reward you better for my life
> Than Edward will for tidings of my death.
> *Sec. Murd.* You are deceived, your brother Gloster hates you.
> *Clar.* O, no, he loves me, and he holds me dear:
> Go you to him from me.
> *Both.*   Ay, so we will.
> *Clar.* Tell him, when that our princely father York
> Bless'd his three sons with his victorious arm,
> And charg'd us from his soul to love each other,
> He little thought of this divided friendship :
> Bid Gloster think of this, and he will weep.
> *First Murd.* Ay, millstones; as he lesson'd us to weep.
> *Clar.* O, do not slander him, for he is kind.
> *First Murd.*   Right,
> As snow in harvest. Thou deceivest thyself:
> 'Tis he that sent us hither now to slaughter thee.

Clar. It cannot be; for when I parted with him,
    He hugg'd me in his arms, and swore, with sobs,
    That he would labour my delivery.
Sec. Murd. Why, so he doth, now he delivers thee
    From this world's thraldom to the joys of heaven.

In the King's case a special incident is introduced into the ii. i. 95. scene to point the irony. Before Edward can well realise the terrible announcement of Clarence's death, the decorum of the royal chamber is interrupted by Derby, who bursts in, anxious not to lose the portion of the king's life that yet remains, in order to beg a pardon for his follower. The King feels the shock of contrast:

    Have I a tongue to doom my brother's death,
    And shall the same give pardon to a slave?

The prerogative of mercy that exists in so extreme a case as the murder of a 'righteous gentleman,' and is so passionately sought by Derby for a servant, is denied to the King himself for the deliverance of his innocent brother. The nemesis iii. ii, from on Hastings is saturated with irony; he has the simplest 41. reliance on Richard and on 'his servant Catesby,' who has come to him as the agent of Richard's treachery; and the very words of the scene have a double significance that all see but Hastings himself.

Hast. I tell thee, Catesby,—
Cate.   What, my lord?
Hast. Ere a fortnight make me elder
    I'll send some packing that yet think not on it.
Cate. 'Tis a vile thing to die, my gracious lord,
    When men are unprepared, and look not for it.
Hast. O monstrous, monstrous! and so falls it out
    With Rivers, Vaughan, Grey: and so 'twill do
    With some men else, who think themselves as safe
    As thou and I.

As the scenes with Margaret constituted a general summary of the individual prophecies and recognitions, so the Recon- ii. i. ciliation Scene around the King's dying bed may be said to gather into a sort of summary the irony distributed through the play; for the effect of the incident is that the different parties pray for their own destruction.   In this scene Buckingham has taken the lead and struck the most solemn notes in his pledge of amity ; when Buckingham comes to die, his bitterest thought seems to be that the day of his death is All

Souls' Day.

> *This is the day* that, in King Edward's time,
> I wish'd might fall on me, when I was found
> False to his children or his wife's allies ;
> This is the day wherein I wish'd to fall
> By the false faith of him I trusted most; . . . .
> That high All-Seer that I dallied with
> Hath turn'd my feigned prayer on my head
> And given in earnest what I begg'd in jest.

By devices, then, such as these ; by the sudden revelation of a remedy when it is just too late to use it ; by the sudden memory of clear warnings blindly missed ; by the spectacle of a leaning for hope upon that which is known to be ground for despair ; by attempts to retreat or turn aside proving short cuts to destruction ; above all by the sufferer's perception that he himself has had a chief share in bringing about his doom :—by such irony the monotony of Nemesis is relieved, and fatality becomes flavoured with mockery.

*This multi-
plication of
Nemesis
a dramatic
background
for the
villainy of
Richard.*   Dramatic design, like design which appeals more directly to the eye, has its perspective: to miss even by a little the point of view from which it is to be contemplated is enough to throw the whole into distortion.   So readers who are not careful to watch the harmony between Character and Plot have often found in the present play nothing but wearisome repetition.   Or, as there is only a step between the sublime and the ridiculous, this masterpiece of Shakespearean plot has suggested to them only the idea of Melodrama,—that curious product of dramatic feeling without dramatic inventiveness, with its world in which poetic justice has become prosaic, in which conspiracy is never so superhumanly secret but there comes a still more superhuman detection, and how-

ever successful villainy may be for a moment the spectator Chap. V.
confidently relies on its being eventually disposed of by a
summary ' off with his head.' The point of view thus missed
in the present play is that this network of Nemesis is all
needed to give dramatic reality to the colossal villainy of the
principal figure. When isolated, the character of Richard is
unrealisable from its offence against an innate sense of retribution. Accordingly Shakespeare projects it into a world
of which, in whatever direction we look, retribution is the sole
visible pattern; in which, as we are carried along by the
movement of the play, the unvarying reiteration of Nemesis
has the effect of *giving rhythm to fate.*

What the action of the play has yielded so far to our in- *The motive*
vestigation has been independent of the central personage : *force of the*
whole play
we have now to connect Richard himself with the plot. *is another*
Although the various Nemesis Actions have been carried on *nemesis:*
the Life
by their own motion and by the force of retribution as a *and Death*
principle of moral government, yet there is not one of them *of Richard.*
which reaches its goal without at some point of its course
receiving an impetus from contact with Richard. Richard
is thus the source of movement to the whole drama, commu-
nicating his own energy through all parts. It is only fitting
that the motive force to this system of nemeses should be
itself a grand Nemesis Action, the *Life and Death*, or crime
and retribution, *of Richard III.* The hero's rise has been
sufficiently treated in the preceding study; it remains to trace
his fall.

This fall of Richard is constructed on Shakespeare's *The fall of*
favourite plan; its force is measured, not by suddenness and *Richard:*
not a shock
violence, but by protraction and the perception of distinct *but a suc-*
stages—the crescendo in music as distinguished from the *cession of*
stages.
fortissimo. Such a fall is not a mere passage through the air
—one shock and then all is over—but a slipping down the
face of the precipice, with desperate clingings and consciously increasing impetus : its effect is the one inexhaust-

CHAP. V. ible emotion of suspense. If we examine the point at which
the fall begins we are reminded that the nemesis on Richard
Not a is different in its type from the others in the play. These
nemesis of
equality but are (like that on Shylock) of the *equality* type, of which the
of sureness. motto is measure for measure : and, with his usual exactness,
Shakespeare gives us a turning-point in the precise centre
iii. iii. 15. of the play, where, as the Queen's kindred are being borne
to their death, we get the first recognition that the general
retribution denounced by Margaret has begun to work. But
the turning-point of Richard's fate is reserved till long past
the centre of the play ; his is the nemesis of *sureness*, in
which the blow is delayed that it may accumulate force.
Not that this turning-point is reserved to the very end; the
The turn- change of fortune appears just when Richard has *com-*
ing-point:
irony of its *mitted himself* to his final crime in the usurpation—the
delay. murder of the children—the crime from which his most
iv. ii, from unscrupulous accomplice has drawn back. The effect of
46. this arrangement is to make the numerous crimes which
follow appear to come by necessity ; he is ' so far in blood
that sin will pluck on sin '; he is forced to go on heaping up
his villainies with Nemesis full in his view. This turning-
point appears in the simple announcement that ' Dorset has
fled to Richmond.' There is an instantaneous change in
Richard to an attitude of defence, which is maintained to the
end. His first instinct is action : but as soon as we have
heard the rapid scheme of measures—most of them crimes—
by which he prepares to meet his dangers, then he can give
from 98. himself up to meditation ; and we now begin to catch the
significance of what has been announced. The name of
Richmond has been just heard for the first time in this play.
But as Richard meditates we learn how Henry VI prophesied that Richmond should be a king while he was but a
peevish boy. Again, Richard recollects how lately, while
viewing a castle in the west, the mayor, who showed him
over it, mispronounced its name as 'Richmond'—and he had

started, for a bard of Ireland had told him he should not live long after he had seen Richmond.   Thus the irony that has given point to all the other retributions in the play is not wanting in the chief retribution of all : Shakespeare compensates for so long keeping the grand Nemesis out of sight by thus representing Richard as gradually realising that *the finger of Nemesis has been pointing at him all his life and he has never seen it !*

Tantalising mockery in Richard's fate. From this point fate never ceases to tantalise and mock Richard.   He engages in his measures of defence, and with their villainy his spirits begin to recover :

> The sons of Edward sleep in Abraham's bosom,   iv. iii. 38.
> And Anne my wife hath bid the world good night ;

young Elizabeth is to be his next victim, and

> To her I go, a jolly thriving wooer.

comp. 49. *iv. iii. 45.* Suddenly the Nemesis appears again with the news that Ely, the shrewd bishop he dreads most of all men, is with Richmond, and that Buckingham has raised an army. Again, his defence is completing, and the wooing of Elizabeth—his masterpiece, since it is the second of its kind—has been brought to an issue that deserves his surprised exultation :

> Relenting fool, and shallow, changing woman !   iv. iv. 431.

His equanimity affected. *iv. iv. 444-540.* Suddenly the Nemesis again interrupts him, and this time is nearer : a puissant navy has actually appeared on the west. And now his equanimity begins at last to be disturbed.   He storms at Catesby for not starting, forgetting that he has given him no message to take.   More than this, a little further on *Richard changes his mind !*   Through the rest of the long scene destiny is openly playing with him, giving him just enough hope to keep the sense of despair warm. Messenger follows messenger in hot haste : Richmond is on the seas—Courtenay has risen in Devonshire—the Guildfords are up in Kent.—But Buckingham's army is dis-

CHAP. V. persed.—But Yorkshire has risen.—But, a gleam of hope, the Breton navy is dispersed—a triumph, Buckingham is taken.—Then, finally, Richmond has landed!' The suspense is telling upon Richard. In this scene he strikes a messenger before he has time to learn that he brings good tidings.

v. iii. 2, 5, 8, &c. When we next see him he wears a forced gaiety and scolds his followers into cheerfulness; but with the gaiety go sudden fits of depression :

> Here will I lie to-night;
> But where to-morrow ?

v. iii, from 47. A little later he becomes nervous, and we have the minute attention to details of the man who feels that his all depends upon one cast; he will not sup, but calls for ink and paper to plan the morrow's fight, he examines carefully as to his beaver and his armour, selects White Surrey to ride, and at last calls for wine and *confesses* a change in himself :

> I have not that alacrity of spirit,
> Nor cheer of mind, that 1 was wont to have.

Climax of Richard's fate: significance of the apparitions.
v. iii, from 118.
Then comes night, and with it the full tide of Nemesis. By the device of the apparitions the long accumulation of crimes in Richard's rise are made to have each its due re-presentation in his fall. It matters not that they are only apparitions. Nemesis itself is the ghost of sin : its sting lies not in the physical force of the blow, but in the close *connection* between a sin and its retribution. So Richard's victims rise from the dead only to secure that the weight of each several crime shall lie heavy on his soul in the morrow's doom. This point moreover must not be missed—that the

Significance of Richard's sleep.
climax of his fate comes to Richard in his *sleep*. The supreme conception of resistance to Deity is reached when God is opposed by God's greatest gift, the freedom of the will. God, so it is reasoned, is omnipotent, but God has made man omnipotent in setting no bounds to his will; and God's omnipotence to punish may be met by man's omni-potence to endure. Such is the ancient conception of Pro-

metheus, and such are the reasonings Milton has imagined CHAP. V.
for his Satan : to whom, though heaven be lost,

> All is not lost, the unconquerable will . . .
> And courage never to submit or yield.

But when that strange bundle of greatness and littleness
which makes up man attempts to oppose with such weapons
the Almighty, how is he to provide for those states in which
the will is no longer the governing force in his nature ; for
the sickness, in which the mind may have to share the
feebleness of the body, or for the daily suspension of will in
sleep ? Richard can to the last preserve his will from faltering. But, like all the rest of mankind, he must some time
sleep : that which is the refuge of the honest man, when he
may relax the tension of daily care, sleep, is to Richard his
point of weakness, when the safeguard of invincible will can
protect him no longer. It is, then, this weak moment which
a mocking fate chooses for hurling upon Richard the whole
avalanche of his doom ; as he starts into the frenzy of his
half-waking soliloquy we see him, as it were, tearing off
layer after layer of artificial reasonings with which the will-
struggles of a lifetime have covered his soul against the touch
of natural remorse. With full waking his will is as strong
as ever : but meanwhile his physical nature has been shattered to its depths, and it is only the wreck of Richard that
goes to meet his death on Bosworth Field.

There is no need to dwell on the further stages of the *Remaining*
fall : to the last the tantalising mockery continues. Richard's *stages of the fall.*
spirits rise with the ordering of the battle, and there comes v. iii. 303.
the mysterious scroll to tell him he is bought and sold. His
spirits rise again as the fight commences, and news comes of v. iii. 342.
Stanley's long feared desertion. Five times in the battle he
has slain his foe, and five times it proves a false Richmond. v. iv. 11.
Thus slowly the cup is drained to its last dregs and Richard
dies. The play opened with the picture of peace, the peace 1. i, from 1.
which led Richard's turbid soul, no longer finding scope in

CHAP. V. physical warfare, to turn to the moral war of villainy; from that point through all the crowded incidents has raged the tumultuous battle between Will and Nemesis; with Richard's death it ceases, and the play may return to its keynote:

V. v. 40.   Now civil wounds are stopp'd, peace lives again.

VI.

How Nemesis and Destiny are inter-woven in Macbeth.

A further Study in Plot.

THE present study, like the last, is a study in Plot. The last illustrated Shakespeare's grandeur of conception, how a single principle is held firm amidst the intricacies of history, and reiterated in every detail. The present purpose is to give an example of Shakespeare's *subtlety*, and to exhibit the incidents of a play bound together not by one, but by three, distinct threads of connection – or, if a technical term may be permitted, three Forms of Dramatic Action—all working harmoniously together into a design equally involved and symmetrical. One of these forms is Nemesis; the other two are borrowed from the ancient Drama: it thus becomes necessary to digress for a moment, in order to notice certain differences between the ancient and modern Drama, and between the ancient and modern thought of which the Drama is the expression.

In the ancient Classical Drama the main moral idea under-lying its action is the idea of Destiny. The ancient world recognised Deity, but their deities were not supreme in the universe; Zeus had gained his position by a revolution, and in his turn was to be overthrown by revolution; there was thus, in ancient conception, behind Deity a yet higher force to which Deity itself was subject. The supreme force of the universe has by a school of modern thought been de-fined as a stream of tendency in things not ourselves making for righteousness : if we attempt to adapt this formula to the ideas of antiquity the difficulty will be in finding anything to substitute for the word ' righteousness.' Sometimes the sum of forces in the universe did seem, in the conception of the ancients, to make for righteousness, and Justice became the highest law. At other times the world seemed to them governed by a supernatural Jealousy, and human prosperity was struck down for no reason except that it was prosperity. In such philosophy as that of Lucretius, again, the tendency of all things was towards Destruction ; while in the handling of legends such as that of Hippolytus there is a suggestion of a dark interest to ancient thought in conceiving Evil itself as an irresistible force. It appears, then, that the ancient mind had caught the idea of *force* in the universe, without adding to it the further idea of a motive by which that force was guided : *blind* fate was the governing power over all other powers. With this simple conception of force as ruling the world, modern thought has united as a motive righteousness or law : the transition from ancient to modern thought may be fairly described by saying that Destiny has become changed into Providence as the supreme force of the uni-

The change reflected in ancient and modern Nemesis. verse. The change may be well illustrated by comparing the ancient and modern conception of Nemesis. To ancient thought Nemesis was simply one phase of Destiny; the story of Polycrates has been quoted in a former study to illustrate how Nemesis appeared to the Greek mind as capricious a deity as Fortune, a force that might at any time, heedless of desert, check whatever happiness was high enough to attract its attention. But in modern ideas Nemesis and justice are strictly associated : Nemesis may be defined as the artistic side of justice.

So far as Nemesis then is concerned, it has, in modern thought, passed altogether out of.the domain of Destiny and been absorbed into the domain of law : it is thus fitted to be one of the regular forms into which human history may be

represented as falling, in harmony with our modern moral CHAP. VI.
conceptions. But even as regards Destiny itself, while the
notion as a whole is out of harmony with the modern notion
of law and Providence as ruling forces of the world, yet
certain minor phases of Destiny as conceived by antiquity
have survived into modern times and been found not irre- *Nemesis*
concilable with moral law. Two of these minor phases of *and Destiny in-*
Destiny are, it will be shown, illustrated in *Macbeth*: and *terwoven*
we may thus take as a general description of its plot, the *in the plot of Macbeth.*
interweaving of Destiny with Nemesis.

That the career of Macbeth is an example of Nemesis *The whole*
needs only to be stated. As in the case of *Richard III*, we *plot a Nemesis*
have the rise and fall of a leading personage; the rise is a *Action,*
crime of which the fall is the retribution. Nemesis has just
been defined as the artistic aspect of justice; we have in
previous studies seen different artistic elements in different
types of Nemesis. Sometimes, as with Richard III, the
retribution becomes artistic through its sureness; its long
delay renders the effect of the blow more striking when it
does come. More commonly the artistic element in Nemesis *of the type*
consists in the perfect equality between the sin and its retribu- *of equality.*
tion; and of the latter type the Nemesis in the play of
Macbeth is perhaps the most conspicuous illustration. The
rise and fall of Macbeth, to borrow the illustration of
Gervinus, constitute a perfect arch, with a turning-point in
the centre. Macbeth's series of successes is unbroken till it
ends in the murder of Banquo; his series of failures is unbroken from its commencement in the escape of Fleance.
Success thus constituting the first half and failure the second
half of the play, the transition from the one to the other is
the expedition against Banquo and Fleance, in which success
and failure are mingled : and this expedition, the keystone to
the arch, is found to occupy the exact middle of the middle iii. iii.
Act.

But this is not all: not only the play as a whole is an

CHAP. VI.

The rise of Macbeth a separate Nemesis action.

example of nemesis, but if its two halves be taken separately they will be found to constitute each a nemesis complete in itself. To begin with the first half, that which is occupied with the rise of Macbeth. If the plan of the play extended no further than to make the hero's fall the retribution upon his rise, it might be expected that the turning-point of the action would be reached upon Macbeth's elevation to the throne. As a fact, however, Macbeth's rise does not stop here; he still goes on to win one more success in his attempt upon the life of Banquo. What the purpose of this prolonged flow of fortune is will be seen when it is considered that this final success of the hero is in reality the source of his ruin. In Macbeth's progress to the attainment of the crown, while of course it was impossible that crimes so violent as his should not incur suspicion, yet circumstances had strangely combined to soothe these suspicions to sleep. But—so Shakespeare manipulates the story—when Macbeth, seated on the throne, goes on to the attempt against Banquo, this additional crime not only brings its own punishment, but has the further effect of unmasking the crimes that have gone before. This important point in the plot is brought out to us in a scene, specially introduced for the purpose, in which Lennox and another lord represent the opinion of the court.

iii. vi. 1.

> *Lennox.* My former speeches have but hit your thoughts,
> Which can interpret further: only, I say,
> Things have been strangely borne. The gracious Duncan
> Was pitied of Macbeth: marry, he was dead:
> And the right-valiant Banquo walk'd too late;
> Whom, you may say, if't please you, Fleance kill'd,
> For Fleance fled: men must not walk too late.
> Who cannot want the thought how monstrous
> It was for Malcolm and for Donalbain
> To kill their gracious father? damned fact!
> How it did grieve Macbeth! did he not straight
> In pious rage the two delinquents tear,
> That were the slaves of drink and thralls of sleep?

Was not that nobly done? Ay, and wisely too;
For 'twould have anger'd any heart alive
To hear the men deny't. So that, I say,
He has borne all things well: and I do think
That had he Duncan's sons under his key—
As, an 't please heaven, he shall not—they should find
What 'twere to kill a father; so should Fleance.

Under the bitter irony of this speech we can see clearly enough that Macbeth has been exposed by his *series* of suspicious acts; he has 'done all things well;' and in particular by peculiar resemblances between this last incident of Banquo and Fleance and the previous incident of Duncan and his son. It appears then that Macbeth's last successful crime proves the means by which retribution overtakes all his other crimes; the latter half of the play is needed to develop the steps of the retribution, but, in substance, Macbeth's fall is latent in the final step of his rise. Thus the first half of the play, that which traces the rise of Macbeth, is a complete Nemesis Action—a career of sins in which the last sin secures the punishment of all.

The same reasoning applies to the latter half of the play: the fall of Macbeth not only serves as the retribution for his rise, but further contains in itself a crime and its nemesis complete. What Banquo is to the first half of the play Macduff is to the latter half; the two balance one another as, in the play of *Julius Cæsar*, Cæsar himself is balanced by Antony; and Macduff comes into prominence upon Banquo's death as Antony upon the fall of Cæsar. Now Macduff, when he finally slays Macbeth, is avenging not only Scotland, but also his own wrongs; and the tyrant's crime against Macduff, with its retribution, just gives unity to the second half of the play, in the way in which the first half was made complete by the association between Macbeth and Banquo, from their joint encounter with the Witches on to the murder of Banquo as a consequence of the Witches' prediction. Accordingly we find that no sooner has Macbeth, by the appearance of the

The fall of Macbeth a separate Nemesis Action.

iii. i. 57–72.

K

CHAP. VI. Ghost at the banquet, realised the turn of fate, than his first
———   thoughts are of Macduff:

iii. iv. 128.   *Macbeth.*   How say'st thou, that Macduff denies his person
                  At our great bidding?
                Lady M.   Did you send to him, sir?
                Macbeth.   I hear it by the way; but I will send.

When the Apparitions bid Macbeth 'beware Macduff,' he
answers,
iv. i. 74.   Thou hast harp'd my fear aright!

iv. i, from On the vanishing of the Apparition Scene, the first thing that
139.   happens is the arrival of news that Macduff has fled to
             England, and is out of his enemy's power; then Macbeth's
             bloody thoughts devise a still more cruel purpose of vengeance
             to be taken on the fugitive's family.

> Time, thou anticipatest my dread exploits:
> The flighty purpose never is o'ertook
> Unless the deed go with it . . . .
> The castle of Macduff I will surprise;
> Seize upon Fife; give to the edge o' the sword
> His wife, his babes, and all unfortunate souls
> That trace him in his line.

iv. ii, iii. In succeeding scenes we have this diabolical massacre carried
             out, and see the effect which the news of it has in rousing
v. vii. 15.   Macduff to his revenge; until in the final scene of all he feels
             that if Macbeth is slain and by no stroke of his, his wife and
             children's ghosts will for ever haunt him.   Thus Macduff's
             function in the play is to be the agent not only of the grand
             nemesis which constitutes the whole plot, but also of a
             nemesis upon a private wrong which occupies the latter half
             of the play.   And, putting our results together, we find that
             a Nemesis Action is the description alike of the whole plot
             and of the rise and fall which are its two halves.

The Oracu-   With Nemesis is associated in the play of *Macbeth* Destiny
lar as one   in two distinct phases.   The first of these is *the Oracular.*   In
phase of
Destiny: ancient thought, as Destiny was the supreme governor of the
its partial universe, so oracles were the revelation of Destiny; and thus
revelation.

the term 'the Oracles of God' is appropriately applied to the CHAP. VI.
Bible as the Christian revelation. With the advent of
Christianity the oracles became dumb. But the triumph of
Christianity was for centuries incomplete; heathen deities
were not extirpated, but subordinated to the supernatural
personages of the new religion ; and the old oracles declined *A minor*
into oracular beings such as witches and wizards, and *form of the*
Oracular
oracular superstitions, such as magic mirrors, dreams, appa- *in modern*
ritions—all means of dimly revealing hidden destiny Shake- *oracular*
beings.
speare is never wiser than the age he is pourtraying; and
accordingly he has freely introduced witches and apparitions
into the machinery of *Macbeth*, though in the principles that
govern the action of this, as of all his other plays, he is true
to the modern notions of Providence and moral law. An *The Oracu-*
oracle and its fulfilment make up a series of events eminently *lar Action :*
Destiny
fitted to constitute a dramatic interest; and no form of *working*
ancient Drama and Story is more common than this of the *from*
mystery to
'Oracular Action.' Its interest may be formulated as Destiny *clearness ;*
working from mystery to clearness. At the commencement
of an oracular story the fated future is revealed indeed, but
in a dress of mystery, as when the Athenians are bidden to
defend themselves with only wooden walls ; but as the story
of Themistocles develops itself, the drift of events is throwing
more and more light on to the hidden meaning of the oracle,
until by the naval victory over the Persians the oracle is at
once clear and fulfilled.

The Oracular Action is so important an element in plot,
that it may be worth while to prolong the consideration of it
by noting the three principal varieties into which it falls, all
of which are illustrated in the play of *Macbeth*. In each case
the interest consists in tracing the working of Destiny out of
mystery into clearness : the distinction between the varieties
depends upon the agency by which Destiny works, and the (1) *by the*
agency of
relation of this agency to the original oracle. In the first *blind obedi-*
variety Destiny is fulfilled by the agency of blind obedience. *ence ;* .

CHAP. VI. The Spartans, unfortunate in their war with the Messenians, enquire of an oracle, and receive the strange response that they must apply for a general to the Athenians, their hereditary enemies. But they resolve to obey the voice of Destiny, though to all appearance they obey at their peril; and the Athenians mock them by selecting the most unfit subject they can find—a man whose bodily infirmities had excluded him from the military exercises altogether. Yet in the end the faith of the Spartans is rewarded. It had been no lack of generalship that had caused their former defeats, but discord and faction in their ranks; now Tyrtæus turned out to be a lyric poet, whose songs roused the spirit of the Spartans and united them as one man, and when united, their native military talent led them to victory. Thus in its fulfilment the hidden meaning of the oracle breaks out into clearness: and blind obedience to the oracle is the agency by which it has been fulfilled.

(2) by the agency of free will :   In the second variety the oracle is fulfilled by the agency of indifference and free will: it is neither obeyed nor disobeyed, but ignored. One of the best illustrations is to be found in the plot of Sir Walter Scott's novel, *The Betrothed.* Its heroine, more rational than her age, resists the family tradition that would condemn her to sleep in the haunted chamber; overborne, however, by age and authority, she consents, and the lady of the bloody finger appears to pronounce her doom:

> Widow'd wife, and wedded maid ;
> Betrothed, Betrayer, and Betrayed.

This seems a mysterious destiny for a simple and virtuous girl. The faithful attendant Rose declares in a burst of devotion that betrayed her mistress may be, but betrayer never ; the heroine herself braces her will to dismiss the foreboding from her thoughts, and resolves that she will not be influenced by it on the one side or on the other. Yet it all comes about. Gratitude compels her to give her hand to the elderly

Constable, who on the very day of betrothal is summoned Chap. VI.
away to the Crusade, from which, as it appears, he is never to
return, leaving his spouse at once a widowed wife and a
wedded maid. In the troubles of that long absence, by a
perfectly natural series of events, gratitude again leads the
heroine to admit to her castle her real deliverer and lover in
order to save his life, and in protecting him amidst strange
circumstances of suspicion to bid defiance to all comers.
Finally the castle is besieged by the royal armies, and the
heroine has to hear herself proclaimed a traitor by the herald
of England ; from this perplexity a deliverance is found only
when her best friend saves her by betraying the castle to the
king. So every detail in the unnatural doom has been in the
most natural manner fulfilled : and the woman by whose
action it has been fulfilled has been all the while maintaining
the freedom of her will and persistently ignoring the oracle.

But the supreme interest of the Oracular Action is reached (3) *by the*
when the oracle is fulfilled by an agency that has all the *agency of*
while set itself to oppose and frustrate it. A simple illustra- *opposing*
tion of this is seen in the Eastern potentate who, in opposition *will.*
to a prophecy that his son should be killed by a lion, forbad
the son to hunt, but heaped upon him every other indulgence.
In particular he built him a pleasure-house, hung with
pictures of hunting and of wild beasts, on which all that art
could do was lavished to compensate for the loss of the for-
bidden sport. One day the son, chafing at his absence from
the manly exercise in which his comrades were at that
moment engaged, wandered through his pleasure-house, until,
stopping at a magnificent picture of a lion at bay, he began
to apostrophise it as the source of his disgrace, and waxing
still more angry, drove his fist through the picture. A nail,
hidden behind the canvas entered his hand ; the wound
festered, and he died. So the measures taken to frustrate the
destiny proved the means of fulfilling it. But in this third
variety of the Oracular Action the classical illustration is the

CHAP. VI. story of Œdipus : told fully, it presents three examples woven together. Laius of Thebes learns from an oracle that the son about to be born to him is destined to be his murderer; accordingly he refuses to rear the child, and it is cast out to perish. A herdsman, Polybus, takes pity on the infant, carries it away to Corinth, and brings it up in secret. In due time this Œdipus becomes weary of the humble life of his supposed father; quitting Corinth, he seeks advice of the oracle as to his future career, and receives the startling response that he is destined to slay his own father. Resolved to frustrate so terrible a fate, he will not return to Corinth, but, as it happens, *takes the road to Thebes*, where he falls in accidentally with Laius, and, in ignorance of his person, quarrels with him and slays him. Now if Laius had not resisted the oracle by casting out the infant, it would have grown up like other sons, and every probability would have been against his committing so terrible a crime as parricide. Again, if Polybus had not by his removal to Corinth sought to keep the child in ignorance of his fate, he would have known the person of Laius and spared him. Once more, if Œdipus had not, in opposition to the oracle, avoided his supposed home, Corinth, he would never have gone to Thebes and fallen in with his real father. Three different persons acting separately seek to frustrate a declared destiny, and their action unites in fulfilling it.

The plot of *Macbeth*, both as a whole and in its separate parts, is constructed upon this form of the Oracular Action, in combination with the form of Nemesis. The play deals with the rise and fall of Macbeth: the rise, and the fall, and again the two taken together, present each of them an *The rise of* example of an Oracular Action. Firstly, the former half of *Macbeth an* the play, the rise of Macbeth, taken by itself, consists in an *Oracular* *Action,* oracle and its fulfilment—the Witches' promise of the crown and the gradual steps by which the crown is attained. Amongst the three varieties of the Oracular Action we have just distinguished, the present example wavers between the Chap. VI. first and the second. After his first excitement has passed *varying be-* away, Macbeth resolves that he will have nothing to do with *tween the* the temptation that lurked in the Witches' words; in his *second and* disjointed meditation we hear him saying:

> If chance will have me king, why chance may crown me i. iii. 143.
> Without my stir;

and again:

> Come what come may, i. iii. 146.
> Time and the hour runs through the roughest day;

in which last speech the very rhyming may, according to Shakespeare's subtle usage, be pointed to as marking a mind made up. So far then we appear to be following an Oracular Action of the second type, that of indifference and ignoring. But in the very next scene the proclamation of a Prince of Cumberland—that is, of an heir-apparent like our Prince of Wales—takes away Macbeth's 'chance':

> *Macb.* [*Aside*]. The prince of Cumberland! that is a step i. iv. 48.
> On which I must fall down, or else o'erleap,
> For in my way it lies.

He instantly commits himself to the evil suggestion, and thus changes the type of action to the first variety, that in which the oracle is fulfilled by the agency of obedience.

Similarly Macbeth's fall, taken by itself, constitutes an *The fall an* Oracular Action, consisting as it does of the ironical promises *Oracular* given by the Apparitions which the Witches raise for Macbeth *the first* on his visit to them, and the course of events by which these *type.* promises are fulfilled. Its type is a highly interesting example of the first variety, that of blind obedience. The *iv. i. 71-* responses of the Apparitions lay down impossible conditions, *100.* and as long as these conditions are unfulfilled Macbeth is to be secure; he will fall only when one not born of woman shall be his adversary, only when Birnam Wood shall come to Dunsinane. Macbeth trusts blindly to these promises; further he obeys them, so far as a man can be said to obey an oracle which enjoins no command: he obeys in the sense of relying on them, and making that reliance his ground of action.   But this reliance of Macbeth on the ironical promises is an agency in fulfilling them in their real mean- iv. i. 144–
156. ing.   In his reckless confidence he strikes out right and left, and amongst others injures one to whom the description 'not born of woman' applies.   In his reliance on the Apparitions he proceeds, when threatened by the English, to *shut himself up in Dunsinane Castle*; but for this fact the English army would not have approached Dunsinane Castle by the route of Birnam Wood, and the incident of the boughs would never have taken place.   Thus Macbeth's fate was made to depend upon impossibilities: by his action in reliance on these impossibilities he is all the while giving them occasion to become possible.   In this way an ironical oracle comes to be fulfilled by the agency of blind obedience.

The whole plot an Oracular Action of the third type.
i. iii. 48–50, 62–66.   Thirdly, the rise and fall of Macbeth are so linked together as to constitute the whole plot another example of the Oracular Action.   The original oracle given by the Witches on the blasted heath was a double oracle: besides the promise of the thaneships and the crown there was another revelation of destiny, that Banquo was to be lesser than Macbeth and yet greater, that he was to get kings though to be none.   In this latter half of the oracle is found the link which binds together the rise and fall of Macbeth.   When the first half of the Witches' promise has been fulfilled in his elevation to the throne, Macbeth sets himself to prevent the fulfilment of the second half by his attempt upon Banquo and Fleance. Now we have already seen how this attempt has the effect of drawing attention, not only to itself, but also to Macbeth's other crimes, and proves indeed the foundation of his ruin. Had Macbeth been content with the attainment of the crown, all might yet have been well: the addition of just one more precaution renders all the rest vain.   It appears, then, that that which binds together the rise and the fall, that which makes the fall the retribution upon the rise, is the expedition against the Banquo family; and the object of this crime is to frustrate the second part of the Witches' oracle. So the original oracle becomes the motive force to the whole play, setting in motion alike the rise and fall of the action. The figure of the whole plot we have taken as a regular arch; its movement might be compared to that terrible incident of mining life known as 'overwinding,' in which the steam engine pulls the heavy cage from the bottom to the top of the shaft, but, instead of stopping then, winds on till the cage is carried over the pulley and dashed down again to the bottom. So the force of the Witches' prediction is not exhausted when it has tempted Macbeth on to the throne, but carries him on to resist its further clauses, and in resisting to bring about the fall by which they are fulfilled. *¹* Not only then are the rise and the fall of Macbeth taken separately oracular, but the whole plot, compounded of the two taken together, constitutes another Oracular Action; and the last is of that type in which Destiny is fulfilled by the agency of a will that has been opposing it.

A second phase of Destiny enters into the plot of *Macbeth* : *Irony a* this is Irony. Etymologically the word means no more than *phase of* *malignant* *saying.* Pressing the idea of saying as distinguished from *Destiny.* meaning we get at the ordinary signification, ambiguous speech; from which the word widens in its usage to include double-dealing in general, such as the 'irony of Socrates,' his habit of assuming the part of a simple enquirer in order to entangle the pretentious sophists in their own wisdom. The particular extension of meaning with which we are immediately concerned is that by which irony comes to be applied to a double-dealing in Destiny itself; the link between this and the original sense being no doubt the ambiguous wording of oracular responses which has become proverbial. In ancient conception Destiny wavered between justice and

CHAP. VI. malignity; a leading phase of malignant destiny was this Irony or double-dealing; Irony was the laughter or mockery of Fate. It is illustrated in the angry measures of Œdipus for penetrating the mystery that surrounds the murder of Laius in order to punish the crime, impunity for which has brought the plague upon his city : when at last it is made clear that Œdipus himself has been unknowingly the culprit, there arises an irresistible sensation that Destiny has been all the while playing with the king, and using his zeal as a means for working his destruction. In modern thought the supreme force of the universe cannot possibly be represented

A modified as malignant. But mockery, though it may not be enthroned
Irony: Jus- in opposition to justice, may yet, without violating modern
tice in a ideas, be made to appear in the *mode of operation* by which
mocking justice is brought about; here mockery is no longer malig-
humour. nant, but simply an index of overpowering force, just as we smile at the helpless stubbornness of a little child, whereas a man's opposition makes us angry. For such a reconciliation of mockery with righteousness we have authority in the imagery of Scripture.

> Why do the heathen rage?
>   And the people imagine a vain thing?
> The kings of the earth set themselves
>   And the rulers take counsel together
> Against the Lord
>   And against His Anointed :
> Saying, Let us break their bonds,
>   And cast away their cords from us.
>
> He that sitteth in the heavens shall laugh :
> The Lord shall have them in derision.
>
> Then shall he speak unto them in his wrath ;
>   And vex them in his sore displeasure.

There could not be a more perfect type of Irony, in that form of it which harmonises with justice, than this pic-ture in three touches, of the busy security of the wicked, of justice pausing to mock their idle efforts, and then with a

burst of wrath and displeasure annihilating their projects at CHAP. VI.
a stroke.

In modern thought, then, Irony is Justice in a mocking
humour. The mockery that suddenly becomes apparent in
the mysterious operations of Providence, and is a measure of
their overpowering force, is clearly capable of giving a highly
dramatic interest to a train of events, and so is fitted to be a
form of dramatic action. The operation of Destiny as *Irony in*
exhibited in the plot of *Macbeth* is throughout tinctured with *the plot of*
irony: the element of mockery appearing always in this, that *obstacles*
apparent checks to Destiny turn out the very means Destiny *converted*
chooses by which to fulfil itself. Irony of this kind is *ping-stones.*
regularly attached to what I have called the third variety of
the Oracular Action, that in which the oracle is fulfilled by the
agency of attempts to oppose it ; but in the play under
consideration the destiny, whether manifesting itself in that
type of the Oracular Action or not, is never dissociated from
the attitude of mockery to resistance which converts
obstacles into stepping-stones. It remains to show how
the rise of Macbeth, the fall of Macbeth, and again the
rise and the fall taken together, are all of them Irony
Actions.

The basis of Macbeth's rise is the Witches' promise of the *The rise of*
crown. Scarcely has it been given when an obstacle starts *Macbeth an*
up to its fulfilment in the proclamation of Malcolm as heir- *Action.*
apparent. I have already pointed out that it is this very
proclamation which puts an end to Macbeth's wavering, and
leads him to undertake the treasonable enterprise which only
in the previous scene he had resolved he would have nothing
to do with. Later in the history a second obstacle appears : ii. iii. 141.
the king is slain, but his two sons, this heir-apparent and
his brother, escape from Macbeth's clutches and place two
lives between him and the fulfilment of his destiny. But, as
events turn out, it is this very flight of the princes that, by
diverting suspicion to them for a moment, causes Macbeth to

CHAP. VI.   be named as Duncan's successor. A conversation in the play
itself is devoted to making this point clear.

ii. iv. 22.   *Ross.* Is 't known who did this more than bloody deed?
Macduff. Those that Macbeth hath slain.
Ross.   Alas, the day!
What good could they pretend?
Macduff.   They were suborn'd:
Malcolm and Donalbain, the king's two sons,
Are stol'n away and fled; which puts upon them
Suspicion of the deed.
Ross.   'Gainst nature still!
Thriftless ambition, that will ravin up
Thine own life's means! Then 'tis most like
The soveieignty will fall upon Macbeth.
Macduff. He is already named, and gone to Scone
To be invested.

The fall an   Twice, then, in the course of the rise Destiny allows
Irony   obstacles to appear only for the sake of using them as an
Action.   unexpected means of fulfilment. The same mockery marks
the fall of the action. The security against a fall promised
by the Apparitions to Macbeth had just one drawback—
iv. i. 71.   'beware Macduff'; and we have already had occasion to
notice Macbeth's attempt to secure himself against this
iv. ii, &c.   drawback in the completest manner by extirpating the
dangerous thane and his family to the last scion of his stock,
· and also how this cruel purpose succeeded against all but
Macduff himself. Now it is to be noted that this attempt
against the fulfilment of the destined retribution proves the
very source of the fulfilment, without which it would never
have come about. For at one point of the story Macduff,
the only man who, according to the decrees of Fate, can
harm Macbeth, resolves to abandon his vengeance against
him. In his over-cautious policy Macduff was unwilling to
move without the concurrence of Malcolm the rightful heir.
iv. iii.   In one of the most singular scenes in all Shakespeare
Macduff is represented as urging Malcolm to assert his
rights, while Malcolm (in reality driven by the general panic

to suspect even Macduff) discourages his attempts, and CHAP. VI.
affects to be a monster of iniquity, surpassing the tyrant of
Scotland himself. At last he succeeds in convincing Macduff iv.iii, from
of his villainies, and in a burst of despair the fate-appointed 100.
avenger renounces vengeance.

> *Macduff.*   Fit to govern?
>   No, not to live . . . . Fare thee well !
> These evils thou repeat'st upon thyself
> Have banish'd me from Scotland. O my breast
> Thy hope ends here !

Malcolm, it is true, then drops the pretence of villainy, but
he does not succeed in reassuring his companion.

> *Macduff.* Such welcome and unwelcome things at once   iv. iii. 138.
>   'Tis hard to reconcile.

At this moment enters Ross with the news of Macbeth's
expedition against Fife, and tells how all Macduff's household, ' wife, children, servants, all,' have been cut off ' at
one swoop': before the agony of a bereavement like this
hesitation flies away for ever.

>   Gentle heavens,   iv. iii. 231.
>   Cut short all intermission ; front to front
> Bring thou this fiend of Scotland and myself ;
> Within my sword's length set him : if he 'scape,
> Heaven forgive him too !

The action taken by Macbeth with a view to prevent Macduff's being the instrument of retribution, is brought by a
mocking Fate to impel Macduff to his task at the precise
moment he had resolved to abandon it.

Finally, if the rise and the fall be contemplated together *The plot as*
as constituting one action, this also will be found animated *a whole an*
Irony
by the same spirit of irony. The original promise of the *Action.*
Witches, as well as the later promise of the Apparition, had
its drawback in the destiny that Banquo was to be lesser i. iii. 62–
than Macbeth and yet greater, to get kings though to be 66.
none ; and to secure against this drawback is Macbeth's

CHAP. VI. purpose in his plot against Banquo and Fleance, by which the rival family would be extirpated. The plot only *half succeeds*, and by its half-success contributes to the exactness with which the destiny is fulfilled. Had Macbeth's attempt fully succeeded, Banquo would neither have got kings nor been one; had no such attempt at all been made, then, for anything we see to the contrary in the play, Banquo would have preceded his sons on the throne, and so again the oracle would not have been fulfilled which made Banquo lesser than Macbeth. But by the mixture of success and failure in Macbeth's plot Banquo is slain before he can attain the crown, and Fleance lives to give a royal house to Scotland. Once more, then, mockery appears a characteristic of the Destiny that finds in human resistance just the one peculiar device needed for effecting the peculiar distribution of fortune it has promised.

Summary. Such is the subtlety with which Shakespeare has constructed this plot of *Macbeth*, and interwoven in it Nemesis and Destiny. To outward appearance it is connected with the rise and fall of a sinner: the analysis that searches for inner principles of construction traces through its incidents three forms of action working harmoniously together, by which the rise and fall of Macbeth are so linked as to exhibit at once a crime with its Nemesis, an Oracle with its fulfilment, and the Irony which works by the agency of that which resists it. Again the separate halves of the play, the rise and the fall of the hero, are found to present each the same triple pattern as the whole. Once more, with the career of Macbeth are associated the careers of Banquo and Macduff, and these also reflect the threefold spirit. Macbeth's rise involves Banquo's fall: this fall is the subject of oracular prediction, it is the starting-point of nemesis on Macbeth, and it has an element of irony in the fact that Banquo *all but* escaped. With Macbeth's fall is bound up Macduff's rise: this also had been predicted in oracles, it is an agency

in the main nemesis, and Macduff's fate has the irony that
he *all but* perished at the outset of his mission. Through all
the separate interests of this elaborate plot, the three forms
of action—Nemesis, the Oracular, Irony—are seen perfectly
harmonised and perfectly complete. And over all this is
thrown the supernatural interest of the Witches, who are
agents of nemesis working by the means of ironical oracles.

VII.

MACBETH, LORD AND LADY.

A Study in Character-Contrast.

CHAP. VII.

CONTRASTS of character form one of the simplest elements of dramatic interest. Such contrasts are often obvious; at other times they take definitiveness only when looked at from a particular point of view. The contrast of character which it is the object of the present study to sketch rests upon a certain distinction which is one of the fundamental *The anti-* ideas in the analysis of human nature—the distinction *thesis of the* between the outer life of action and the inner life of our *outer and* *inner life.* own experience. The recognition of the two is as old as the *Book of Proverbs*, which contrasts the man that ruleth his spirit with the man that taketh a city. The heathen oracle, again, opened out to an age which seemed to have exhausted knowledge a new world for investigation in the simple command, Know thyself. The Stoics, who so despised the busy vanity of state cares, yet delighted to call their ideal man a king; and their particular tenet is universalised by Milton when he says:

> Therein stands the office of a king,
> His honour, virtue, merit, and chief praise,
> That for the public all this weight he bears:
> Yet he who reigns within himself, and rules
> Passions, desires, and fears, is more a king.

And the modern humourist finds the idea indispensable for his pourtrayal of character and experience. 'Sir,' says one of Thackeray's personages, 'a distinct universe walks about under your hat and under mine . . . You and I are but a pair CHAP. VII. of infinite isolations with some fellow-islands more or less near to us.' And elsewhere the same writer says that 'each creature born has a little kingdom of thought of his own, which it is a sin in us to invade.'

This antithesis of the practical and inner life is so accepted a commonplace of the pulpit and of the essayist on morals and culture that it may seem tedious to expound it. But for the very reason that it belongs to all these spheres, and that these spheres overlap, the two sides of the antithesis are not kept clearly distinct, nor are the terms uniformly used in the same sense. For the present purpose the exact distinction is between the outer world, the world of practical action, the sphere of making and doing, in which we mingle with our fellow men, join in their enterprises, and influence them to our ideas, in which we investigate nature and society, or seek to build up a fabric of power : and, on the other hand, the inner intellectual life, in which our powers as by a mirror are turned inwards upon ourselves, finding a field for enterprise in self-discipline and the contest with inherited notions and passions, exploring the depths of our consciousness and our mysterious relations with the unseen, until the thinker becomes familiar with strange situations of the mind and at ease in the presence of its problems. The antithesis is thus not at all the same as that between worldly and religious, for the inner life may be cultivated for evil : self-anatomy, as Shelley says,

> Shall teach the will
> Dangerous secrets : for it tempts our powers,
> Knowing what must be thought and may be done,·
> Into the depth of darkest purposes.

Still less is it the antithesis between intellectual and commonplace ; the highest intellectual powers find employment in practical life. The various mental and moral qualities belong to both spheres, but have a different meaning for each.

L

CHAP. VII. Practical experience is a totally different thing from what the religious thinker means by his 'experience.' The discipline given by the world often consists in the dulling of those powers which self-discipline seeks to develope. Knowledge of affairs, with its rapid and instinctive grasp, is often possessed in the highest degree by the man who is least of all men versed in the other knowledge, which could explain and analyse the processes by which it operated. And every observer is struck by the different forms which courage takes in the two spheres, courage in action, and courage where nothing can be done and men have only to endure and wait. Macaulay in a well-known passage contrasts the active and passive courage as one of the distinctions between the West and the East.

> An European warrior, who rushes on a battery of cannon with a loud hurrah, will sometimes shriek under the surgeon's knife, and fall into an agony of despair at the sentence of death. But the Bengalee, who would see his country overrun, his house laid in ashes, his children murdered or dishonoured, without having the spirit to strike one blow, has yet been known to endure torture with the firmness of Mucius, and to mount the scaffold with the steady step and even pulse of Algernon Sidney.

The two lives are complete, each with its own field, its own qualities, culture, and fruit.

The antithesis an element in Character-Interpretation. It is obvious that relation to these two lives will have a very great effect in determining individual character. In the same man the two sides of experience may be most unequally developed; an intellectual giant is often a child in the affairs of the world, and a moral hero may be found in the person of some bedridden cripple. On the other hand, to some the inner life is hardly known: familiar perhaps with every other branch of knowledge they go down to their graves strangers to themselves.

> All things without, which round about we see,
> We seek to know and how therewith to do;
> But that whereby we reason, live, and be
> Within ourselves, we strangers are thereto.

> We seek to know the moving of each sphere,
>   And the strange cause of the ebbs and flows of Nile:
> But of that clock within our breasts we bear,
>   The subtle motions we forget the while.
>
> We, that acquaint ourselves with every zone,
>   And pass both tropics, and behold each pole,
> When we come home, are to ourselves unknown,
>   And unacquainted still with our own soul

The antithesis then between the outer and inner life will be among the ideas which lie at the root of Character-Interpretation.

When the idea is applied to an age like that of Macbeth, the antithesis between the two lives almost coincides with the distinction of the sexes: amid the simple conditions of life belonging to such an age the natural tendency would be for genius in men to find scope in the outer and practical world, while genius in women would be restricted to the inner life. And this is the idea I am endeavouring to work out in the present study:—that the key to Shakespeare's portraiture of Macbeth and Lady Macbeth will be found in regarding the two as illustrations of the outer and inner life. Both possess force in the highest degree, but the two have been moulded by the exercise of this force in different spheres; their characters are in the play brought into sharp contrast by their common enterprise, and the contrast of practical and intellectual mind. is seen maintained through the successive stages of their descent to ruin. *In a simple age it coincides with the distinction of the sexes.*

The antithesis the key to the characters of Macbeth and Lady Macbeth.

Thus Macbeth is essentially the practical man, the man of action, of the highest experience, power, and energy in military and political command, accustomed to the closest connection between willing and doing. He is one who in another age would have worked out the problem of free trade, or unified Germany, or engineered the Suez Canal. On the other hand, he has concerned himself little with things transcendental; he is poorly disciplined in thought and goodness; prepared for any emergency in which there is anything *Macbeth as the practical man.*

CHAP. VII. to be done, yet a mental crisis or a moral problem afflicts him with the shock of an unfamiliar situation. This is by no means a generally accepted view: amongst a large number of readers the traditional conception of Macbeth lingers as a noble disposition dragged down by his connection with the coarser nature of his wife. According to the view here suggested the nobility of Macbeth is of the flimsiest and most tawdry kind. The lofty tone he is found at times assuming means no more than virtuous education and surroundings. When the purely practical nature is examined in reference to the qualities which belong to the intellectual life, the result is not a blank but ordinariness: the practical nature will reflect current thought and goodness as they appear from the outside. So Macbeth's is the morality of inherited notions, retained just because he has no disposition to examine them; he has all the practical man's distrust of wandering from the beaten track of opinion, which gives the working politician his prejudice against doctrinaires, and has raised up stout defenders of the Church amongst men whose lives were little influenced by her teaching. And the traditionary morality is more than merely retained. When the seed fell into stony ground forthwith it sprang up *because* it had no deepness of earth: the very shallowness of a man's character may lend emphasis to his high professions, just as, on the other hand, earnestness in its first stage often takes the form of hesitation. So Macbeth's practical genius takes in strongly what it takes in at all, and gives it out vigorously. But that the nobility has gone beyond the stage of passive recognition, that it has become absorbed into his inner nature, there is not a trace; on the contrary, it is impossible to follow Macbeth's history far without abundant evidence that real love of goodness for its own sake, founded on intelligent choice or deep affection, has failed to root a single fibre in his nature.

First, we have the opportunity of studying Macbeth's

His nobility conventional.

character in the analysis given of it in the play itself by the
one person who not only saw Macbeth in his public life, but
knew also the side of him hidden from the world.

> *Lady Macbeth.*   I fear thy nature ;
>   It is too full o' the milk of human kindness
>   To catch the nearest way.

Lady Macbeth's analysis of her husband's character.
i. v. 16-31.

I believe that this phrase, the 'milk of human kindness,'
divorced from its context and become the most familiar of
all commonplaces, has done more than anything else towards giving a false twist to the general conception of
Macbeth's character. The words *kind, kindness* are amongst
the most difficult words in Shakespeare. The wide original
signification of the root, *natural, nature,* still retained in the
noun *kind,* has been lost in the adjective, which has been
narrowed by modern usage to one sort of naturalness, tender-heartedness; though in a derivative form the original
sense is still familiar to modern ears in the expression 'the
kindly fruits of the earth.' In Elizabethan English, however,
the root signification still remained in all usages of *kind* and
its derivatives. In Schmidt's analysis of the adjective, two
of its four significations agree with the modern use, the
other two are 'keeping to nature, natural,' and 'not dege-
nerate and corrupt, but such as a thing or person ought to
be.' Shakespeare delights to play upon the two senses of
this family of words: tears of joy are described as a 'kind
overflow of kindness'; the Fool says of Regan that she will
use Lear 'kindly,' i.e. according to her nature ; 'the worm
will do his kind,' i.e. bite. How far the word can wander
from its modern sense is seen in a phrase of the present
play, 'at your kind'st leisure,' where it is simply equivalent
to 'convenient.' Still more will the wider signification of
the word obtain, when it is associated with the word *human*;
'humankind' is still an expression for human nature, and
the sense of the passage we are considering would be more
obvious if the whole phrase were printed as one word, not

Much Ado, i. i. 26.

Lr. i. v. 15.

Ant. and Cleop. v. ii. 264.

ii. i. 24.

Chap. VII 'human kindness,' but 'humankind-ness': — that shrinking from what is not natural, which is a marked feature of the practical nature. The other part of the clause, *milk* of humankind-ness, no doubt suggests absence of hardness: but it equally connotes natural, inherited, traditional feelings, imbibed at the mother's breast. The whole expression of Lady Macbeth, then, I take to attribute to her husband an instinctive tendency to shrink from whatever is in any way unnatural. That this is the true sense further appears, not only from the facts—for nothing in the play suggests that I. ii 54. Macbeth, 'Bellona's bridegroom,' was distinguished by kindness in the modern sense—but from the context. The form of Lady Macbeth's speech makes the phrase under discussion a summing up of the rest of her analysis, or rather a general text which she proceeds to expand into details. Not one of these details has any connection with tender-heartedness: on the other hand, if put together the details do amount to the sense for which I am contending, that Macbeth's character is a type of commonplace morality, the shallow unthinking and unfeeling man's lifelong hesitation between God and Mammon.

> Thou would'st be great;
> Art not without ambition, but without
> The illness should attend it: what thou would'st highly
> That would'st thou holily; would'st not play false,
> And yet would'st wrongly win: thou'ldst have, great Glamis,
> That which cries 'Thus thou must do, if thou have it,
> And that which *rather thou dost fear to do*
> *Than wishest should be undone.'*

If the delicate balancing of previous clauses had left any doubt as to the meaning, the last two lines remove it, and assert distinctly that Macbeth has no objection to the evil itself, but only a fear of evil measures which must be associated to a practical mind with failure and disgrace. It is striking that at the very moment Lady Macbeth is so medi- I. iv. 48-53 tating, her husband is giving a practical confirmation of her

description in its details as well as its general purport. He CHAP. VII.
had resolved to take no steps himself towards the fulfilment i. iii. 143,
of the Witches' prophecy, but to leave all to chance; then 146.
the proclamation of Malcolm, removing all apparent chance
of succession, led him to change his mind and entertain the
scheme of treason and murder: the words with which he
surrenders himself seem like an echo of his wife's analysis.

> Stars, hide your fires;
> Let not light see my black and deep desires:
> The eye wink at the hand; *yet let that be*
> *Which the eye fears, when it is done, to see.*

But we are not left to descriptions of Macbeth by others. *Macbeth's*
We have him self-displayed; and that in a situation so *soliloquy:*
framed that if there were in him the faintest sympathy with *of an em-*
inently
goodness it must here be brought into prominence. Mac- *practical*
character.
beth has torn himself away from the banquet, and, his mind i. vii. 1–28.
full of the desperate danger of the treason he is meditating,
he ponders over the various motives that forbid its execution.
A strong nobility would even amid incentives *to* crime feel
the attraction of virtue and have to struggle against it; but
surely the weakest nobility, when facing motives *against* sin,
would be roused to some degree of virtuous passion. Yet,
if Macbeth's famous soliloquy be searched through and
through, not a single thought will be found to suggest that
he is regarding the deep considerations of sin and retribution in any other light than that of immediate practical
consequences. First, there is the thought of the sureness of
retribution even in this world. It may be true that hope of
heaven and fear of hell are not the highest of moral incentives, but at least they are a degree higher than the thought
of worldly prosperity and failure ; Macbeth however is willing
to take his chance of the next world if only he can be
guaranteed against penalties in this life.

> If it were done when 'tis done, then 'twere well
> It were done quickly : if the assassination

> Could trammel up the consequence, and catch
> With his surcease success; that but this blow
> Might be the be-all and the end-all here,
> But here, upon this bank and shoal of time,
> We'ld jump the life to come. But in these cases
> We still have judgement here; that we but teach
> Bloody instructions, which, being taught, return
> To plague the inventor: this even-handed justice
> Commends the ingredients of our poisoned chalice
> To our own lips.

So far he has reached no higher consideration, in reference to treason and murder, than the fear that he may be suggesting to others to use against himself the weapon he is intending for Duncan. Then his thoughts turn to the motives against crime which belong to the softer side of our nature.

> He's here in double trust,
> First, as I am his kinsman and his subject,
> Strong both against the deed; then, as his host,
> Who should against his murderer shut the door,
> Not bear the knife myself. Besides, this Duncan,
> Hath borne his faculties so meek, hath been
> So clear in his great office, that his virtues
> Will plead like angels, trumpet-tongued, against
> The deep damnation of his taking-off;
> And pity—

At all events it is clear this is no case of a man blinded for the moment to the emotions which resist crime; and as we hear him passing in review kinship, loyalty, hospitality, pity, we listen for the burst of remorse with which he will hurl from him the treachery he had been fostering. But, on the contrary, his thoughts are still practical, and the climax to which this survey of motives is to lead up is no more than the effect they will have on others: pity

> Shall blow the horrid deed in every eye,
> That tears shall drown the wind.

And then he seems to regret that he cannot find more incentives to his villainy.

> I have no spur
> To prick the sides of my intent, but only
> Vaulting ambition, which o'erleaps itself
> And falls on the other.

So Macbeth's searching self-examination on topics of sin and retribution, amid circumstances specially calculated to rouse compunction, results in thoughts not more noble than these— that murder is a game which two parties can play at, that heartlessness has the effect of drawing general attention, that ambition is apt to defeat its own object.

Again: that Macbeth's union of superficial nobility with real moral worthlessness is connected with the purely practical bent of his mind will be the more evident the wider the survey which is taken of his character and actions. It may be observed that Macbeth's spirits always rise with evil deeds: however he may have wavered in the contemplation of crime, its execution strings him up to the loftiest tone. This is especially clear in the Dagger Scene, and in the scene in which he darkly hints to his wife the murder of Banquo, which is in a brief space to be in actual perpetration. As he feels the moment of crime draw near, his whole figure seems to dilate, the language rises, and the imagery begins to flow. Like a poet invoking his muse, Macbeth calls on seeling night to scarf up the tender eye of pitiful day. He has an eye to dramatic surroundings for his dark deeds.

Macbeth rises with external deeds and sinks with internal conflicts.

ii. i, from 31; and iii. ii, from 39.

> Now, o'er the one half-world
> Nature seems dead, and wicked dreams abuse
> The curtain'd sleep; witchcraft celebrates
> Pale Hecate's offerings, and wither'd murder,
> Alarum'd by his sentinel, the wolf,
> Whose howl's his watch, thus with his stealthy pace,
> With Tarquin's ravishing strides, towards his design
> Moves like a ghost. Thou sure and firm-set earth,
> Hear not my steps, which way they walk, for fear
> The very stones prate of my whereabout,
> *And take the present horror from the time,*
> *Which now suits with it.*

The man who had an hour or two before been driven from

CHAP. VII. the table of his guests by the mere thought of a crime moves to the deed itself with the exalted language of a Hebrew prophet. On the other hand, in his spiritual struggles there is a simpleness that sometimes suggests childishness. His ii. ii. 31. trouble is that he could not say 'Amen' when the sleepers cried 'God bless us'; his conscience seems a voice outside ii. ii. 35–46. him; finally, the hardened warrior dare not return to the darkness and face the victim he had so exultingly done to death.

Macbeth, then, is the embodiment of one side of the antithesis with which we started; his is pre-eminently the practical nature, moulded in a world of action, but uninfluenced by the cultivation of the inner life. Yet he is not perfect as a man of action: for the practical cannot reach its per-
Two flaws in Macbeth as an em-bodiment of the practical: his su-perstition; fection without the assistance of the inner life. There are two flaws in Macbeth's completeness. For one, his lack of training in thought has left him without protection against the superstition of his age. He is a passive prey to super-natural imaginings. He himself tells us he is a man whose
v. v. 10. senses would cool to hear a night-shriek, and his fell of hair rouse at a dismal treatise. And we see throughout the play how he never for an instant doubts the reality of the super-natural appearances: a feature the more striking from its
e. g. iii. iv. 60; i. iii. 107, 122. iii. i. 6. contrast with the scepticism of Lady Macbeth, and the hesitating doubt of Banquo. Again: no active career can be without its periods when action is impossible, and it is in
and his helplessness under sus-pense. such periods that the training given by the intellectual life makes itself felt, with its self-control and passive courage. All this Macbeth lacks: in suspense he has no power of
compare i. iii. 137, and iii. ii. 16. self-restraint. When we come to trace him through the stages of the action we shall find that one of these two flaws springing out of Macbeth's lack of the inner life, his superstition and his helplessness in suspense, is at every turn the source of his betrayal.

In the case of Lady Macbeth, the old-fashioned view of

her as a second Clytæmnestra has long been steadily giving CHAP. VII.
way before a conception higher at least on the intellectual
side.   The exact key to her character is given by regarding
her as the antithesis of her husband, and an embodiment of
the inner life and its intellectual culture so markedly wanting
in him.   She has had the feminine lot of being shut out
from active life, and her genius and energy have been turned
inwards; her soul—like her ' little hand'—is not hardened
for the working-day world, but is quick, delicate, sensitive.
She has the keenest insight into the characters of those
around her.   She is accustomed to moral loneliness and
at home in mental struggles.   She has even solved for
herself some of their problems   In the very crisis of Duncan's murder she gives utterance to the sentiment:

Lady Mac-
beth as an
embodi-
ment of the
inner life.

v. i. 58.

the sleeping and the dead
Are but as pictures.

ii. ii. 53.

When we remember that she must have started with the
superstitions of her age such an expression, simple enough
in modern lips, opens up to us a whole drama of personal
history: we can picture the trembling curiosity, the struggle
between will and quivering nerves, the triumph chequered
with awe, the resurrection of doubts, the swayings between
natural repulsion and intellectual thirst, the growing courage
and the reiterated victories settling down into calm principle.   Accordingly, Lady Macbeth has won the grand
prize of the inner life: in the kingdom of her personal
experience her WILL is unquestioned king.   It may seem
strange to some readers that Lady Macbeth should be held
up as the type of the inner life, so associated is that phrase
to modern ears with the life fostered by religion.   But the
two things must not be confused—religion and the sphere in
which religion is exercised.   'The kingdom of God is within
you,' was the proclamation of Christ, but the world within
may be subjugated to other kings than God.   Mental discipline and perfect self-control, like that of Lady Macbeth,

CHAP. VII. would hold their sway over evil passions, but they would also be true to her when she chose to contend against goodness, and even against the deepest instincts of her feminine nature. This was ignored in the old conception of the character, and a struggle *against* the softer side of her nature was mistaken for its total absence. But her intellectual culture must have quickened her finer sensibilities at the same time that it built up a will strong enough to hold them down; nor is the subjugation so perfect but that a sympathetic insight can throughout trace a keen delicacy of nature striving to assert itself. In particular, when she calls upon the spirits that tend on mortal thoughts to unsex and fill her from crown to toe with direst cruelty, she is thrilling all over with feminine repugnance to the bloody enterprise, which nevertheless her royal will insists upon her undertaking. Lady Macbeth's career in the play is one long mental civil war: and the strain ends, as such a strain could only end, in madness.

A struggle against not absence of the softer qualities.

i. v. 41.

The Character-Contrast traced through the action.

Such is the general conception of Lord and Lady Macbeth from the point of view of the antithesis between the outer and inner life. We have now to turn from character to action, and trace the contrasted pair through the stages of their common career.

Situation at the opening of the play.

The two opposing natures have been united in a happy marriage, the happier because a link between characters so forceful and so antithetic, if it held at all, must be a source of interest: the dark tragedy of this unhappy pair is softened by the tenderness of demeanour which appears on both sides. Another source of marriage happiness is added: there is not a trace of self-seeking in Lady Macbeth. Throughout the play she is never found meditating upon what she is to gain by the crown; wife-like, she has no sphere but the career of her husband. In a picture of human characters, great in their scale, overwhelmed in moral ruin, the question of absorbing interest is the commencement of the descent, and

compare i. v. 55-60; i. vii. 38; iii. ii. 27, 29, 36, 45; iii. iv. 141.

The original impulse to evil came from Macbeth.

the source from which the impulse to evil has come.   This, CHAP. VII.
in the present case, Shakespeare has carefully hidden from
us : before the play opens the essential surrender of spirit
has taken place, and all that we are allowed to see is its
realisation in life and fact.   If, however, we use the slight
material afforded us for speculation on this point, it would
appear that the original choice for evil has for both been
made by Macbeth.   In the partnership of man and wife it is
generally safe to assume that the initiative of action has
come from the husband, if nothing appears to the contrary.
In the present case we are not left to assumptions, Lady
Macbeth distinctly speaks of her husband as first breaking i. vii. 48.
to her the enterprise of treacherous ambition.

> What beast was 't, then,
> Which made you break this enterprise to me?
> . . . . Nor time nor place
> Did then adhere, and yet you would make both.

The reference can only be to a period before the commencement of the play; and the general drift of the passage suggests that it was no mere choice, made by Macbeth with
deliberation during which he would be open to conviction,
but an impulse of uncontrollable passion that it would have
been vain for his wife to resist, supposing that she had had
the desire to resist it — so uncontrollable, indeed, that it
appears to Lady Macbeth stronger than the strongest of i. vii. 54.
feminine passions, a mother's love.

> I have given suck, and know
> How tender 'tis to love the babe that milks me.
> I would, while it was smiling in my face,
> Have pluck'd my nipple from his boneless gums,
> And dash'd the brains out, had I so sworn as you
> Have done to this.

The only sense in which Lady Macbeth can be pronounced
the ruin of her husband is that her firm nature holds him in
the path to which he has committed them both, and will not

CHAP. VII. allow his fatal faltering to lose both the virtue he has re-
nounced and the price for which he has bartered it. Denied
by her feminine position, the possibility—even if she had
had the desire—of directing the common lot for good, she
has recognised before we make her acquaintance that this
lot has been cast for evil, and she is too well-trained in self-
knowledge to attempt the self-deception her husband tries to
keep up. And to this evil lot she applies her full force. Her

i. vii. 54. children have died, and this natural outlet for passion is
wanting; the whole of her energy is brought to bear upon
her husband's ambition, and she is waiting only an occasion for concentrating her powers upon some definite
project.

Four
stages in
the action.
With such mutual relations between the hero and the
heroine the play opens: we are to watch the contrasted
characters through the successive stages of the Temptation,
the Deed, the Concealment, the Nemesis.

The Tempt-
ation.
The Temptation accosts the two personages when separated from one another, and we thus have the better
opportunity of watching the different forms it assumes in
adapting itself to the different characters. The expedition,
which has separated Macbeth from his wife, is one which
must have led him to brood over his schemes of ambition.
Certainly it exhibits to him an example of treason and shows
him the weakness of his sovereign. Probably he sees events
shaping in a direction that suggests opportunity; he may
have known that the king must pass in the direction of his
castle, or in some other way may have anticipated a royal
visit; at all events the king's intimation of this visit in the
play itself—

i. iv. 42.
From hence to Inverness,
And bind us further to you,—

does not look like a first mention of it. To a mind so pre-

i. iii. 38–
78.
pared the supernatural solicitation brings a shock of temptation; and as the Witches in their greeting reach the promise,

'Thou shalt be KING hereafter,' Macbeth gives a start that CHAP. VII.
astonishes Banquo :

> Good sir, why do you start ; and seem to fear
> Things that do sound so fair?

To Banquo this prediction of the Witches seems no more
than curious ; for it must be remembered that Macbeth's
position in the kingdom was not such as to exclude hope of
succession to the crown, though the hope was a remote one.
But Macbeth's start tells a tale of his inner thoughts at the
time. This alone should be sufficient to vindicate Shakespeare from the charge sometimes brought against him of
turning a great character from virtue to vice by demoniac
agency ; his is the higher conception that a soul which has
commenced the surrender to evil will find in the powers of
darkness agencies ready to expedite its descent, it matters
not what form these agencies assume. Macbeth has been
for years playing with the idea of treason, while never
bracing himself up to the point of acting it : suddenly the
thought he fancied so safe within his bosom appears outside
him in tangible form, gleaming at him in the malignant
glances of recognition the Witches are casting at him. To a
mind utterly undefended by culture against superstitious
terror this objective presentation of his own thought proves
a Rubicon of temptation which he never attempts to recross.
On Lady Macbeth the supernatural incident makes not the i. v. 1-55.
slightest impression of any kind ; we see her reading her
husband's excited account of the interview with the most
deliberate calmness, weighing its suggestions only with reference to the question how it can be used upon her husband.
To her temptation comes with the suggestion of *opportunity*.
The messenger enters during her quiet meditation ;

> *Mess.* The king comes here to-night.
> *Laay M.* 〉 Thou 'rt mad to say it.

The shock that passes over her is like the shock of chemical
change. In an instant her whole nature is strung up to

a single end; the long-expected occasion for the concentration of a whole life's energy upon a decisive stroke is come. So rapidly does her imagination move that she sees the deed before her as already done, and, as she casts her eyes upwards, the very ravens over her head seem to be croaking the fatal entrance of Duncan under her battlements.

The meeting afterwards. The stage of Temptation cannot be considered complete
i. v, from without taking in that important section of the play which
55; i. vii. intervenes between the meeting of the two personages after their separate temptations and the accomplishment of the treason. This is essentially a period of suspense, and accordingly exhibits Macbeth at his weakest. As he enters his castle his tell-tale face is as a book where men may read strange matters; and his utter powerlessness of self-control throws upon his wife's firm will the strongest of all strains, that of infusing her own tenacity into a vacillating ally. I have already dealt with the point at which Macbeth's suspense becomes intolerable, and he leaves the supper-table; and I have drawn attention to the eminently practical nature of his thoughts even at this crisis. The scene which follows, when his wife labours to hold him to the enterprise he has undertaken, illustrates perhaps better than any other incident in the play how truly this practical bent is the key to Macbeth's whole character. At first he takes high ground, and rests his hesitation on considerations of gratitude. Lady Macbeth appeals to consistency, to their mutual love, and, her anger beginning to rise at this wavering of will in a critical moment, she taunts her husband with cowardice. Then it is that Macbeth, irritated in his turn, speaks the noble words that have done so much to gain him a place in the army of martyrs to wifely temptations.

> Prithee, peace:
> I dare do all that may become a man;
> Who dares do more is none.

But it is difficult to share Macbeth's self-deception long.   At C<small>HAP.</small> VII.
his wife's reminder how he had been the one to first moot the
undertaking, and swear to it in spite of overwhelming obstacles, already the noble attitude looks more like the sour
grapes morality of the man who begins to feel indignation
against sin at the precise moment when the sin becomes
dangerous.   And the whole truth comes sneaking out at
Macbeth's next rejoinder : 'If we should fail?'   Here is
the critical point of the scene.   At its beginning Macbeth i. vii, from
is for abandoning the treason, at its end he prepares for 61.
his task of murder with animation : where does the change
come ?   *The practical man is nerved by having the practical.*
details supplied to him.   Lady Macbeth sketches a feasible
scheme : how that the King will be wearied, his chamberlains
can by means of the banquet be easily drugged, their confusion on waking can be interpreted as guilt—before she has
half done her husband interrupts her with a burst of enthusiasm, and completes her scheme for her.   The man who
had thought it was manliness that made him shrink from
murder henceforward never hesitates till he has plunged his
dagger in his sovereign's bosom.

In the perpetration of the Deed itself we have the woman *The Deed*
passing from weakness to strength, the man from strength to ii. i. 31 to
weakness.   To Lady Macbeth this actual contact with a deed ii. ii.
of blood is the severest point of the strain, the part most
abhorrent to her more delicate nature.   For a single moment
she feels herself on the verge of the madness which eventually
comes upon her :

> These deeds must not be thought   ii. ii. 33.
> After these ways; so, it will make us mad!

And at the beginning of the scene she has been obliged to
have recourse to stimulants in order to brace her failing
nerves :

> That which hath made them drunk hath made me bold.   ii. ii 1.

M

CHAP. VII. And in part the attempt to bring her delicate nature to the repugnant deed does fail. It is clear that, knowing how little her husband could be depended upon, she had intended to have a hand in the murder itself:

I. vii. 69;
compare
I. v. 68.

> What cannot *you and I* perform upon
> The unguarded Duncan?

But the will which was strong enough to hold down conscience gave way for a moment before an instinct of feminine tenderness:

ii. ii. 13.

> Had he not resembled
> My father as he slept, I had done 't.

The superiority, however, of the intellectual mind is seen in this, that it can nerve itself from its own agitation, it can draw strength out of the weakness surrounding it, or out of the necessities of the situation : *must* is the most powerful of spells to a trained will. And so it is that Lady Macbeth rises to the occasion when her husband fails. At first Macbeth in the perpetration of the murder appears in his proper sphere of action, and we have already noticed how the Dagger Soliloquy shows no shrinking, but rather excitement on the side of exultation. The change in him comes with a moment of suspense, caused by the momentary waking of the grooms :

ii. ii. 24.

'I stood and heard them.' With this, no longer sustained by action, he utterly breaks down under the unfamiliar terrors of a fight with his conscience. His prayer sticks in his throat; his thoughts seem so vivid that his wife can hardly tell whether he did not take them for a real voice outside him.

> Who was it that thus cried? Why, worthy thane,
> You do unbend your noble strength, to think
> So brainsickly of things.

In his agitation he forgets the plan of action, brings away the daggers instead of leaving them with the grooms, and finally dares not return to finish what he has left uncompleted. And accordingly his wife has to make another demand upon her overwrought nature : with one hysterical jest,

> If he do bleed,
> I'll *gild* the faces of the grooms withal,
> For it must seem their *guilt,*

her nature rallies, and the strength derived from the inner life fills up a gap in action where the mere strength of action had failed.

The Concealment of the murder forms a stage of the action which falls into two different parts: the single effort which faces the first shock of discovery, and the very different strain required to meet the slowly gathering evidence of guilt. In the Scene of the Discovery Macbeth is perfectly at home: energetic action is needed, and he is dealing with men. His acted innocence appears to me better than his wife's; Lady Macbeth goes near to suggesting a personal interest in the crime by her over-anxiety to disclaim it.

The first Shock of Conceal-ment. ii. iii, from 68.

> *Macduff.*   O Banquo, Banquo,
>   Our royal master's murder'd !
> *Lady M.*   Woe, alas !
>   What, in our house ?
> *Banquo.*   Too cruel anywhere.

Yet in this scene, as everywhere else, the weak points in Macbeth's character betray him: for one moment he is left to himself, and that moment's suspense ruins the whole episode. In the most natural manner in the world Macbeth had, on hearing the announcement, rushed with Lennox to the scene of the murder. Lennox quitted the chamber of blood first, and for an instant Macbeth was alone, facing the grooms still heavy with their drugged sleep, and knowing that in another moment they would be aroused and telling their tale: the sense of crisis proves too much for him, and under an ungovernable impulse he stabs them. He thus wrecks the whole scheme. How perfectly Lady Macbeth's plan would have served if it had been left to itself is seen by Lennox's account of what he had seen, and how the grooms

> stared, and were distracted; no man's life
> Was to be trusted with them.

M 2

CHAP. VII. Nothing, it is true, can be finer than the way in which Macbeth seeks to cover his mistake and announces what he has done. But in spite of his brilliant outburst,

> Who can be wise, amazed, temperate and furious,
> Loyal and neutral, in a moment?

and his vivid word-picture of his supposed sensations, his efforts are in vain, and at the end of his speech we feel that there has arisen in the company of nobles the indescribable effect known as 'a sensation,' and we listen for some one to speak some word that shall be irrevocable. The crisis is

ii. iii. 124. acute, but Lady Macbeth comes to the rescue *and faints!* It matters little whether we suppose the fainting assumed, or that she yields to the agitation she has been fighting against so long. The important point is that she chooses this exact moment for giving way: she holds out to the end of her husband's speech, then falls with a cry for help; there is at once a diversion, and she is carried out. But the crisis

ii. iii. 132. has passed, and a moment's consideration has suggested to the nobles the wisdom of adjourning for a fitter occasion the enquiry into the murder they all suspect: before that occasion

ii. iv. 24–32. arrives the flight of the king's sons has diverted suspicion into an entirely new channel. Lady Macbeth's fainting saved her husband.

The long Strain of Conceal-ment. iii. i, ii. To convey dramatically the continuous strain of keeping up appearances in face of steadily accumulating suspicion is more difficult than to depict a single crisis. Shakespeare manages it in the present case chiefly by presenting Macbeth to us on the eve of an important council, at which the whole truth is likely to come out.

iii. i. 30.
> We hear, our bloody cousins are bestowed
> In England and in Ireland, not confessing
> Their cruel parricide, filling their hearers
> With strange invention: but of that to-morrow.

It is enough to note here that Macbeth takes the step—the fatal step, as was pointed out in the last study—of contriving

Banquo's murder simply because he cannot face the suspense
of waiting for the morrow, and hearing the defence of the
innocent princes made in presence of Banquo, who knows
the inducement he had to such a deed. That he feels the
danger of the crime, which nevertheless he cannot hold himself back from committing, is clear from the fact that he will
not submit it to the calmer judgment of his wife. The con- iii. ii. 45.
trast of the two characters appears here as everywhere. Lady
Macbeth can *wait* for an opportunity of freeing themselves
from Banquo :

> *Macb.* Thou know'st that Banquo, and his Fleance, lives.   iii. ii. 37.
> *Lady M.* But in them nature's copy's not eterne.

To Macbeth the one thing impossible is to wait; and once
more his powerlessness to control suspense is his ruin.

We have reviewed the contrasted characters under Tempta- *The first*
tion, in the Deed of sin itself, and in the struggle for Conceal- *Shock of*
ment : it remains to watch them face to face with their *Nemesis.*
Nemesis. In the present play Shakespeare has combined the iii. iv.
nemesis which takes the form of a sudden shock with the yet
severer nemesis of a hopeless resistance through the stages of
a protracted fall. The first Shock of Nemesis comes in the
Banquet Scene. Macbeth has surrendered himself to the
supernatural, and from the supernatural his retribution comes.
This is not the place to draw out the terrible force of this
famous scene; for its bearing on the contrast of character
under delineation it is to be remarked that Macbeth faces his
ghostly visitation with unflinching courage, yet without a
shadow of doubt as to the reality of what nevertheless no one
sees but himself. Lady Macbeth is equally true to her
character, and fights on to the last in the now hopeless
contest—her double task of keeping up appearances for herself and for her husband. Her keen tact in dealing with
Macbeth is to be noted. At first she rallies him angrily, and
seeks to shame him into self-command; a moment shows

that he is too far gone to be reached by such motives. Instantly she changes her tactics, and, employing a device so
often effective with patients of disordered brain, she en-
deavours to recall him to his senses by assuming an ordinary
tone of voice ; hitherto she has whispered, now, in the hearing of all, she makes the practical remark :

iii. iv. 83.   My worthy lord,
      Your noble friends do lack you.

The device proves successful, his nerves respond to the tone
of everyday life, and recovering himself he uses all his skill
of deportment to efface the strangeness of the episode, until
the reappearance of his victim plunges the scene in confusion
past recovery. In the moment of crisis Lady Macbeth had
used roughness to rouse her husband ; when the courtiers

iii. iv, from are gone she is all tenderness. She utters not a word of re-
122. proach : perhaps she is herself exhausted by the strain she has
gone through ; more probably the womanly solicitude for the
physical sufferer thinks only how to procure for her husband
'the season of all natures, sleep.'

The full   At last the end comes. The final stage, like the first, is
Nemesis. brought to the two personages separately. Lady Macbeth
has faced every crisis by sheer force of nerve ; the nemesis
comes upon her fitly in madness, the brain giving way under
the strain of contest which her will has forced upon it. In
the delirium of her last appearance before us we can trace
three distinct tones of thought working into one another as if
in some weird harmony. There is first the mere reproduction
of the horrible scenes she has passed through.

One : two : why then 'tis time to do't. . . . Yet who would have
thought the old man to have had so much blood in him. . . . The thane
of Fife had a wife : where is she now ?

Again there is an inner thought contending with the first, the
struggle to keep her husband from betraying himself by his
irresolution.

No more o' that, my lord, no more o' that : you mar all with this

starting . . . Wash your hands, put on your night-gown ; look not so CHAP. VII.
pale . . . Fie ! a soldier and afear'd ?

And there is an inmost thought of all: the uprising of her
feminine nature against the foulness of the violent deed.

> Out, damned spot ! . . . Here's the smell of blood still : all the per-
> fumes of Arabia will not sweeten this little hand—

and the 'sorely charged heart' vents itself in a sigh which
the attendants shudder to hear. On Macbeth Nemesis heaps
itself in double form. The purely practical man, without
resources in himself, finds nemesis in an old age that receives
no honour from others.

> My way of life   v. iii. 22.
> Is fall'n into the sear, the yellow leaf;
> And that which should accompany old age,
> As honour, love, obedience, troops of friends,
> I must not look to have, but, in their stead,
> Curses, not loud, but deep.

Again, as the drunkard finds his refuge in drink, so the
victim of superstition longs for deeper draughts of the supernatural. Macbeth seeks the Witches, forces himself to hear iv. i.
the worst, and suffers nemesis in anticipation in viewing
future generations which are to see his foes on his throne. iv. i. 110-
Finally from the supernatural comes the climax of retribution 135.
when Macbeth is seen resting in unquestioning reliance on an from iv. i.
ironical oracle : till the shock of revelation comes, the pledge 80.
of his safety is converted into the sign of his doom, and the v. v, from
brave Macbeth, hero of a hundred battles, throws down his 33; v. viii,
sword and refuses to fight. from 13.
                                                  v. viii. 22.

VIII.

Ch. VIII.

Character-Grouping.

Every lover of art feels that the different fine arts form not a crowd but a family; the more familiar the mind becomes with them the more it delights to trace in them the application of common ideas to different media of expression. We are reminded of this essential unity by the way in which the arts borrow their terms from one another. 'Colour' is applied to music, 'tone' to painting; we speak of costume as 'loud,' of melody as 'bright,' of orchestration as 'massive.' Two classes of oratorical style have been distinguished as 'statuesque' and 'picturesque'; while the application of a musical term, 'harmony,' and a term of sculpture, 'relief,' to all the arts alike is so common that the transference is scarcely felt. Such usages are not the devices of a straitened vocabulary, but are significant of a single *Art* which is felt to underlie the special *arts*. So the more Drama is brought by criticism into the family of the fine arts the more it will be seen to present the common features. We have already had to notice repeatedly how the idea of pattern or design is the key to dramatic plot. We are in the present study to see how contrast of character, such as was traced in the last study between Lord and Lady Macbeth, when applied to a larger number of personages, produces an effect on the mind analogous to that of *grouping* in pictures and statuary: the different personages not only present points of contrast with one another, but their varieties suddenly fall into a unity of effect if looked at from some one point of view. An example of such Character-Grouping is seen in the play of *Julius Cæsar*, where the four leading figures, all on the grandest scale, have the elements of their characters thrown into relief by comparison with one another, and the contrast stands out boldly when the four are reviewed in relation to one single idea.

CH. VIII.

The grouping in Julius Cæsar rests on the antithesis of the practical and inner life.

This idea is the same as that which lay at the root of the Character-Contrast in *Macbeth*—the antithesis of the practical and inner life. It is, however, applied in a totally different sphere. Instead of a simple age in which the lives coincide with the sexes we are carried to the other extreme of civilisation, the final age of Roman liberty, and all four personages are merged in the busy world of political life. Naturally, then, the contrast of the two lives takes in this play a different form. In the play of *Macbeth* the inner life was seen in the force of will which could hold down alike bad and good impulses; while the outer life was made interesting by its confinement to the training given by action, and an exhibition of it devoid of the thoughtfulness and self-control for which the life of activity has to draw upon the inner life. But there is another aspect in which the two may be regarded. The idea of the inner life is reflected in the word 'individuality,' or that which a man has not in common with others. The cultivation of the inner life implies not merely cultivation of our own individuality, but to it also belongs sympathy with the individuality of others; whereas in the sphere of practical life men fall into classes, and each person has his place as a member of these classes. Thus benevolence may take the form of enquiring into individual wants and troubles and meeting these by personal assistance; but a man has an equal claim to be called benevolent who applies himself to such sciences as political economy, studies the springs which regulate human society,

This takes the form of individual sympathies v. public policy.

Ch. VIII. and by influencing these in the right direction confers
benefits upon whole classes at a time. Charity and political
science are the two forms benevolence assumes correspon-
dent to the inner life of individual sympathies and the outer
life of public action. Or, if we consider the contrast from
the side of rights as distinguished from duties, the supreme
form in which the rights of individuals may be summed
up is justice; the corresponding claim which public life
makes upon us is (in the highest sense of the term) policy:
wherever these two, justice and policy, seem to clash, the outer
and inner life are brought into conflict. It is in this form
that the conflict is raised in the play of *Julius Cæsar*. To
get it in its full force, the dramatist goes to the world of
antiquity, for one of the leading distinctions between ancient
and modern society is that the modern world gives the fullest
play to the individual, while in ancient systems the individual
was treated as existing solely for the state. 'Liberty' has
been a watchword in both ages ; but while we mean by liberty
the least amount of interference with personal activity, the
liberty for which ancient patriots contended was freedom of
the government from external or internal control, and the
ideal republic of Plato was so contrived as to reduce individual liberty to a minimum. And this subordination of
private to public was most fully carried out in Rome. 'The
common weal,' says Merivale, 'was after all the grand object
of the heroes of Roman story. Few of the renowned heroes
of old had attained their eminence as public benefactors
without steeling their hearts against the purest instincts of
nature. The deeds of a Brutus or a Manlius, of a Sulla
or a Cæsar, would have been branded as crimes in private
citizens; it was the public character of the actors that
stamped them with immortal glory in the eyes of their
countrymen.' Accordingly, the opposition of outer and
inner life is brought before us most keenly when, in Roman
life, a public policy, the cause of republican freedom, seems

to be bound up with the supreme crime against justice and the rights of the individual, assassination. Ch. VIII.

Brutus is the central figure of the group: in his character the two sides are so balanced that the antithesis disappears. This evenness of development in his nature is the thought of those who in the play gather around his corpse; giving prominence to the quality in Brutus hidden from the casual observer they say: *Brutus's character so evenly developed that the antithesis disappears.*

> His life was gentle; and the elements
> So mix'd in him that Nature might stand up
> And say to all the world 'This was a man!'

v. v. 73.

Of another it would be said that he was a poet, a philosopher; of Brutus the only true description was that he was a man! It is in very few characters that force and softness are each carried to such perfection. The strong side of Brutus's character is that which has given to the whole play its characteristic tone. It is seen in the way in which he appreciates the issue at stake. Weak men sin by hiding from themselves what it is they do; Brutus is fully alive to the foulness of conspiracy at the moment in which he is conspiring. *Force of his character.*

> O conspiracy,
> Shamest thou to show thy dangerous brow by night,
> When evils are most free? O, then by day
> Where wilt thou find a cavern dark enough
> To mask thy monstrous visage?

ii. i. 77.

His high tone he carries into the darkest scenes of the play. The use of criminal means has usually an intoxicating effect upon the moral sense, and suggests to those once committed to it that it is useless to haggle over the amount of the crime until the end be obtained. Brutus resists this intoxication, setting his face against the proposal to include Antony in Cæsar's fate, and resolving that not one life shall be unnecessarily sacrificed. He scorns the refuge of suicide; and with warmth adjures his comrades not to stain— ii. i. 162.

CH. VIII.

ii. i. 114.

The even virtue of our enterprise,
Nor the insuppressive mettle of our spirits,
To think that or our cause or our performance
Did need an oath; when every drop of blood
That every Roman bears, and nobly bears,
Is guilty of a several bastardy,
If he do break the smallest particle
Of any promise that hath pass'd fiom him.

The scale of Brutus's character is again brought out by his relations with other personages of the play. Casca, with all his cynical depreciation of others, has to bear unqualified testimony to Brutus's greatness:

i. iii. 157.

O, he sits high in all the people's hearts;
And that which would appear offence in us,
His countenance, like richest alchemy,
Will change to virtue and to worthiness.

ii. i, fin.
We see Ligarius coming from a sick-bed to join in he knows not what: 'it sufficeth that Brutus leads me on.' And the hero's own thought, when at the point of death he pauses to take a moment's survey of his whole life, is of the unfailing v. v. 34. power with which he has swayed the hearts of all around him:

My heart doth joy that yet in all my life
I found no man but he was true to me.

i. ii.
Above all, contact with Cassius throws into relief the greatness of Brutus. At the opening of the play it is Cassius that we associate with the idea of force; but his is the ruling mind only while Brutus is hesitating; as soon as Brutus has thrown in his lot with the conspirators, Cassius himself is swept along with the current of Brutus's irresistible influence. Cf. ii. i. 162–190; iii. i. 140–146, 231–243; iv. iii. 196–225, &c. In the councils every point is decided—and, so far as success is concerned, wrongly decided—against Cassius's better judgment. In the sensational moment when Popilius Lena enters the Senate-house and is seen to whisper Cæsar, Cassius's presence of mind fails him, and he prepares in despair for iii. i. 19. suicide; Brutus retains calmness enough to *watch faces*:

Cassius, be constant :
Popilius Lena speaks not of our purposes ;
For, look, he smiles, and Cæsar doth not change.

CH. VIII.

In the Quarrel Scene Cassius has lost all pretensions to iv. iii.
dignity of action in the impatience sprung from a ruined
cause; Brutus maintains principle in despair. Finally, at the
close of the scene, when it is discovered that under all the
hardness of this contest for principle Brutus has been hiding iv. iii, from
a heart broken by the loss of Portia, Cassius is forced to give 145.
way and acknowledge Brutus's superiority to himself even in
his own ideal of impassiveness :

I have as much of this in art as you, iv. iii. 194.
But yet my nature could not bear it so.

The force in Brutus's character is obvious : it is rather its *Its soft-
softer side that some readers find difficulty in seeing. But this *ness.*
difficulty is in reality a testimony to Shakespeare's skill, for
Brutus is a Stoic, and what gentleness we see in him appears
in spite of himself. It may be seen in his culture of art,
music, and philosophy, which have such an effect in softening
the manners. Nor is this in the case of the Roman Brutus
a mere conventional culture : these tastes are among his
strongest passions. When all is confusion around him on the
eve of the fatal battle he cannot restrain his longing for the iv. iii. 256.
refreshing tones of his page's lyre ; and, the music over, he
takes up his philosophical treatise at the page he had turned
down. Again Brutus's considerateness for his dependants is iv. iii. 242.
in strong contrast with the harshness of Roman masters.
On the same eve of the battle he insists that the men who
watch in his tent shall lie down instead of standing as discipline would require. An exquisite little episode brings out iv. iii, from
Brutus's sweetness of demeanour in dealing with his youthful 252.
page; this rises to womanly tenderness at the end when,
noticing how the boy, wearied out and fallen asleep, is lying
in a position to injure his instrument, he rises and disengages
it without waking him.

CH. VIII.

Bru. Look, Lucius, here's the book I sought for so;
        I put it in the pocket of my gown.
Luc. I was sure your loidship did not give it me.
Bru. Bear with me, good boy; I am much forgetful.
        Can'st thou hold up thy heavy eyes awhile,
        And touch thy instrument a strain or two?
Luc. Ay, my lord, an't please you.
Bru.   It does, my boy:
        I trouble thee too much, but thou ait willing.
Luc. It is my duty, sir.
Bru. I should not urge thy duty past thy might;
        I know young bloods look for a time of rest.
Luc. I have slept my lord, already.
Bru. It was well done; and thou shalt sleep again;
        I will not hold thee long: if I do live
        I will be good to thee.   [*Music and a song.*
        This is a sleepy tune. O murderous slumber,
        Lay'st thou thy leaden mace upon my boy,
        That plays thee music? Gentle knave, good night,
        I will not do thee so much wrong to wake thee.—
        If thou dost nod, thou break'st thy instrument;
        I'll take it from thee; and, good boy, good night.

ii. i, from   Brutus's relations with Portia bear the same testimony.
233.   Portia is a woman with as high a spirit as Lady Macbeth,
                and she can inflict a wound on herself to prove her courage
                and her right to share her husband's secrets.   But she lacks
                the physical nerve of Lady Macbeth; her agitation on the
ii. iv.   morning of the assassination threatens to betray the con-
                spirators, and when these have to flee from Rome the
                suspense is too much for her and she commits suicide.
                Brutus knew his wife better than she knew herself, and was
                right in seeking to withhold the fatal confidence; yet he
                allowed himself to be persuaded: no man would be so
                swayed by a tender woman unless he had a tender spirit of
                his own.   In all these ways we may trace an extreme of
This is   gentleness in Brutus. But it is of the essence of his character
concealed   that this softer side is concealed behind an imperturbability
under stoic   of outward demeanour that belongs to his stoic religion:
imper-
turbability. this struggle between inward and outward is the main feature

for the actor to bring out.   It is a master stroke of Shake- CH. VIII.
speare that he utilises the euphuistic prose of his age to iii. ii, from
express impassiveness in Brutus's oration.   The greatest 14.
man of the world has just been assassinated; the mob are
swaying with fluctuating passions; the subtlest orator of his
day is at hand to turn those passions into the channel of
vengeance for his friend: Brutus called on amid such surroundings to speak for the conspirators still maintains the
artificial style of carefully balanced sentences, such as
emotionless rhetoric builds up in the quiet of a study.

> As Cæsar loved me, I weep for him ; as he was fortunate, I rejoice
> at it ; as he was valiant, I honour him : but, as he was ambitious, I slew
> him. There is tears for his love; joy for his fortune; honour for his
> valour ; and death for his ambition.

Brutus's nature then is developed on all its sides; in his *The anti-*
character the antithesis of the outer and inner life disappears. *thesis re-*
It reappears, however, in the action; for Brutus is compelled *Brutus in*
to balance a weighty issue, with public policy on the one *the action.*
side, and on the other, not only justice to individual claims, ii. i. 10-85.
but further the claims of friendship, which is one of the
fairest flowers of the inner life.   And the balance dips to
the wrong side.   If the question were of using the
weapon of assassination against a criminal too high for
the ordinary law to reach, this would be a moral problem
which, however doubtful to modern thought, would have
been readily decided by a Stoic.   But the question which
presented itself to Brutus was distinctly not this.   Shake- ii. i. 18-34.
speare has been careful to represent Brutus as admitting to
himself that Cæsar has done no wrong: he slays him *for*
what he might do.

> The abuse of greatness is, when it disjoins
> Remorse from power: and, *to speak truth of Cæsar,*
> *I have not known when his affections sway'd*
> *More than his reason.* But 'tis a common proof,
> That lowliness is young ambition's ladder,
> Whereto the climber-upward turns his face;

But when he once attains the upmost round,
He then unto the ladder turns his back,
Looks in the clouds, scorning the base degrees
By which he did ascend. So Cæsar may.
Then, lest he may, prevent. And *since the quarrel
Will bear no colour for the thing he is,*
Fashion it thus ; that what he is, augmented,
Would run to these and these extremities :
And therefore think him as a serpent's egg
Which hatch'd, would, as his kind, grow mischievous,
And kill him in the shell.

It is true that Shakespeare, with his usual ' dramatic hedging,' softens down this immoral bias in a great hero by representing him as both a Roman, of the nation which beyond all other nations exalted the state over the individual, and a *compare 1. ii. 159.* Brutus, representative of the house which had risen to greatness by leading violence against tyranny. But, Brutus's own conscience being judge, the man against whom he moves is guiltless ; and so the conscious sacrifice of justice and friendship to policy is a fatal error which is source sufficient for the whole tragedy of which Brutus is the hero.

Cæsar: discrepancies in his character to be reconciled. The character of Cæsar is one of the most difficult in Shakespeare. Under the influence of some of his speeches we find ourselves in the presence of one of the master spirits of mankind ; other scenes in which he plays a leading part breathe nothing but the feeblest vacillation and weakness. It is the business of Character-Interpretation to harmonise this contradiction ; it is not interpretation at all to ignore one side of it and be content with describing Cæsar as vacillating. The force and strength of his character is seen in the impression he makes upon forceful and strong men. The attitude of Brutus to Cæsar seems throughout to be that of looking up ; and notably at one point the thought of Cæsar's greatness seems to cast a lurid gleam over the assassination plot itself, and Brutus feels that the grandeur of the victim gives a dignity to the crime :

ii. i. 173.   Let 's carve him as a dish fit for the gods.

The strength and force of Antony again no one will question ; and Antony, at the moment when he is alone with the corpse of Cæsar and can have no motive for hypocrisy, apostrophises it in the words—

> Thou art the ruins of the noblest man
> That ever lived in the tide of times.

iii. i. 256.

And we see enough of Cæsar in the play to bear out the opinions of Brutus and Antony.   Those who accept vacillation as sufficient description of Cæsar's character must explain his strong speeches as vaunting and self-assertion.   But surely it must be possible for dramatic language to distinguish between the true and the assumed force ; and equally surely there is a genuine ring in the speeches in which Cæsar's heroic spirit, shut out from the natural sphere of action in which it has been so often proved, leaps restlessly at every opportunity into pregnant words.   We may thus feel certain of his lofty physical courage.

> Cowards die many times before their deaths ;
> The valiant never taste of death but once.
> Of all the wonders that I yet have heard,
> It seems to me most strange that men should fear . . .
>
> .   .   .   .
>
> Danger knows full well
> That Cæsar is more dangerous than he :
> We are two lions litter'd in one day,
> And I the elder and more terrible.

ii. ii. 32.

ii. ii. 44.

A man must have felt the thrill of courage in search of its food, danger, before his self-assertion finds language of this kind in which to express itself.   In another scene we have the perfect *fortiter in re* and *suaviter in modo* of the trained statesman exhibited in the courtesy with which Cæsar receives the conspirators, combined with his perfect readiness to ' tell graybeards the truth.'   Nor could imperial firmness be more ideally painted than in the way in which Cæsar ' prevents ' Cimber's intercession.

ii. ii, from 57.

iii. i. 35.

> Be not fond,
> To think that Cæsar bears such rebel blood

N

That will be thaw'd from the true quality
With that which melteth fools; I mean, sweet words,
Low-crooked court'sies, and base spaniel-fawning.
Thy brother by decree is banished:
If thou dost bend and pray and fawn for him,
I spurn thee like a cur out of my way.
Know, Cæsar doth not wrong, nor without cause
Will he be satisfied.

Commonplace authority loudly proclaims that it will never relent: the true imperial spirit feels it a preliminary condition to see first that it never does wrong.

Reconcili-
ation:
Cæsar the
highest
type of the
practical;

It is the antithesis of the outer and inner life that explains this contradiction in Cæsar's character. Like Macbeth, he is the embodiment of one side and one side only of the antithesis; he is the complete type of the practical—though in special qualities he is as unlike Macbeth as his age is unlike Macbeth's age. Accordingly Cæsar appears before us perfect up to the point where his own personality comes in. The military and political spheres, in which he has been such a colossal figure, call forth practical powers, and do not involve introspection and meditation on foundation principles of thought.

Theirs not to reason why:
Theirs but to do.

The tasks of the soldier and the statesman are imposed upon them by external authority and necessities, and the faculties exercised are those which shape means to ends. But at last Cæsar comes to a crisis that does involve his personality; he attempts a task imposed on him by his own ambition. He plays in a game of which the prize is the world and the stake himself, and to estimate chances in such a game tests *but lacking* self-knowledge and self-command to its depths. How want-*in the inner* ing Cæsar is in the cultivation of the inner life is brought out *life.* by his contrast with Cassius. The incidents of the flood and *I. ii. 100–* the fever, retained by the memory of Cassius, illustrate this. *128.* The first of these was no mere swimming-match; the flood in the Tiber was such as to reduce to nothing the difference

between one swimmer and another. It was a trial of nerve: CH. VIII.
and as long as action was possible Cæsar was not only as
brave as Cassius, but was the one attracted by the danger. i. ii. 102.
Then some chance wave or cross current renders his chance
of life hopeless, and no buffeting with lusty sinews is of any
avail ; that is the point at which the *passive* courage born of
the inner life comes in, and gives strength to submit to the
inevitable in calmness. This Cæsar lacks, and he calls for
rescue : Cassius would have felt the water close over him and
have sunk to the bottom and died rather than accept aid from
his rival. In like manner the sick bed is a region in which
the highest physical and intellectual activity is helpless ; the
trained self-control of a Stoic may have a sphere for exercise
even here ; but the god Cæsar shakes, and cries for drink
like a sick girl. It is interesting to note how the two types *The con-*
of mind, when brought into personal contact, jar upon one *ception brought out*
another's self-consciousness. The intellectual man, judging *by personal*
the man of action by the test of mutual intercourse, sees *contact with*
nothing to explain the other's greatness, and wonders what *Cassius.*
people find in him that they so admire him and submit to his
influence. On the other hand, the man of achievement is
uneasily conscious of a sort of superiority in one whose intellectual aims and habits he finds it so difficult to follow—yet
superiority it is not, for what has he *done?* Shakespeare has
illustrated this in the play by contriving to bring Cæsar and
his suite across the ' public place ' in which Cassius is dis- i. ii. 182–
coursing to Brutus. Cassius feels the usual irritation at 214.
being utterly unable to find in his old acquaintance any
special qualities to explain his elevation.

> Now, in the names of all the gods at once, i. ii. 148.
> Upon what meat doth this our Cæsar feed,
> That he is grown so great ?

Similarly Cæsar, as he casts a passing glance at Cassius, becomes at once uneasy. ' He thinks too much,' is the ex-
clamation of the man of action :

> He loves no plays,
> As thou dost, Antony; he hears no music.

The practical man, accustomed to divide mankind into a few simple types, is always uncomfortable at finding a man he cannot classify. Finally there is a climax to the jealousy that exists between the two lives : Cæsar complains that Cassius *'looks quite through the deeds of men.'*

A change in Cæsar and a change in Rome itself.

comp. i. i, and iii. iii; i. ii. 151, 164; i. iii. 82, 105; iii. i 66–70; v. v. 69–72, &c.

There is another circumstance to be taken into account in explaining the weakness of Cæsar. A change has come over the spirit of Roman political life itself—such seems to be Shakespeare's conception : Cæsar on his return has found Rome no longer the Rome he had known. Before he left for Gaul, Rome had been the ideal sphere for public life, the arena in which principles alone were allowed to combat, and from which the banishment of personal aims and passions was the first condition of virtue. In his absence Rome has gradually degenerated ; the mob has become the ruling force, and introduced an element of uncertainty into political life ; politics has passed from science into gambling. A new order of public men has arisen, of which Cassius and Antony are the types ; personal aims, personal temptations, and personal risks are now inextricably interwoven with public action. This is a changed order of things to which the mind of Cæsar, cast in a higher mould, lacks the power to adapt itself. His vacillation is the vacillation of unfamiliarity with the new political conditions. He refuses the crown 'each time

i. ii. 230.

gentler than the other,' showing want of decisive reading in dealing with the fickle mob ; and on his return from the

i. ii. 183.

Capitol he is too untrained in hypocrisy to conceal the angry spot upon his face ; he has tried to use the new weapons which he does not understand, and has failed. It is a subtle touch of Shakespeare's to the same effect that Cæsar is repre-

ii. i. 195

sented as having himself undergone a change *of late* :

> For he is superstitious grown of late,
> Quite from the main opinion he held once
> Of fantasy, of dreams and ceremonies.

To come back to a world of which you have mastered the machinery, and to find that it is no longer governed by machinery at all, that causes no longer produce their effects— this, if anything, might well drive a strong intellect to super- stition. And herein consists the pathos of Cæsar's situation. The deepest tragedy of the play is not the assassination of Cæsar, it is rather seen in such a speech as this of Decius :

> If he be so resolved,
> I can o'ersway him ; for he loves to hear
> That unicorns may be betray'd with trees,
> And beais with glasses, elephants with holes,
> Lions with toils and men with flatterers ;
> But when I tell him, he hates flatterers,
> He says he does, being then most flattered.

ii. 1. 202.

Assassination is a less piteous thing than to see the giant intellect by its very strength unable to contend against the low cunning of a fifth-rate intriguer.

Such, then, appears to be Shakespeare's conception of Julius Cæsar. He is the consummate type of the practical : emphatically the public man, complete in all the greatness that belongs to action. On the other hand, the knowledge of self produced by self-contemplation is wanting, and so when he comes to consider the relation of his individual self to the state he vacillates with the vacillation of a strong man moving amongst men of whose greater intellectual subtlety he is dimly conscious : no unnatural conception for a Cæsar who has been founding empires abroad while his fellows have been sharpening their wits in the party contests of a decaying state.

The remaining members of the group are Cassius and *Cassius :* Antony. In Cassius thought and action have been equally *his whole character* developed, and he has the qualities belonging to both *developed* the outer and the inner life. But the side which in Brutus *and sub-jected to a* barely preponderated, absolutely tyrannises in Cassius ; his *master-* public life has given him a grand passion to which the whole *passion that is dis-* of his nature becomes subservient. Inheriting a 'rash *interested.*

CH. VIII.
—————
iv. iii. 120.

humour' from his mother, he was specially prepared for impatience of political anomalies; republican independence has become to him an ideal dearer than life.

i. ii. 95.

> I had as lief not be as live to be
> In awe of such a thing as I myself.

i. ii, iii; ii.
i; iii. i
177, &c.
i. ii. 312-
319.

He has thus become a professional politician. Politics is to him a game, and men are counters to be used; Cassius finds satisfaction in discovering that even Brutus's 'honourable metal may be wrought from that it is disposed.' He has the politician's low view of human nature; while Brutus talks of principles Cassius interposes appeals to interest: he says to Antony,

iii. i. 177.

> Your voice shall be as strong as any man's
> In the disposing of new dignities.

His party spirit is, as usual, unscrupulous; he seeks to work upon his friend's unsuspecting nobility by concocted

i. ii. 319.

letters thrown in at his windows; and in the Quarrel Scene loses patience at Brutus's scruples.

iv. iii. 7,
29, &c.

> I'll not endure it: you forget yourself,
> To hedge me in; I am a soldier, I,
> Older in practice, abler than yourself
> To make conditions

iii. i. 145.

*Antony:
his whole
character
developed
and sub-
jected to
selfish
passion.*

At the same time he has a party politician's tact; his advice throughout the play is proved by the event to have been right, and he does himself no more than justice when he says his misgiving 'still falls shrewdly to the purpose.' Antony also has all the powers that belong both to the intellectual and practical life; so far as these powers are concerned, he has them developed to a higher degree than even Brutus and Cassius. His distinguishing mark lies in the use to which these powers are put; like Cassius, he has concentrated his whole nature in one aim, but this aim is not a disinterested object of public good, it is unmitigated self-seeking. Antony has greatness enough to appreciate the greatness of Cæsar; hence in the first half of the play he has effaced himself,

choosing to rise to power as the useful tool of Cæsar. Here, CH. VIII.
indeed, he is famed as a devotee of the softer studies, but esp. i. ii,
it is not till his patron has fallen that his irresistible strength from 19ɔ:
is put forth. There seems to be but one element in Antony 16ɔ̠ comp. ii. i.
that is not selfish : his attachment to Cæsar is genuine, and
its force is measured in the violent imagery of the vow with iii 1, from
which, when alone for a moment with the corpse, he promises 254. comp.
vengeance till all pity is 'choked with custom of fell deeds.' 194-213.
And yet this perhaps is after all the best illustration of his
callousness to higher feelings ; for the one tender emotion of
his heart is used by him as the convenient weapon with which
to fight his enemies and raise himself to power.

Such, then, is the Grouping of Characters in the play of *The Group-*
Julius Cæsar. To catch it they must be contemplated in the *ing as a*
light of the antithesis between the outer and inner life. In *veyed.*
Brutus the antithesis disappears amid the perfect balancing
of his character, to reappear in the action, when Brutus has
to choose between his cause and his friend. In Cæsar the
practical life only is developed, and he fails as soon as action
involves the inner life. Cassius has the powers of both outer
and inner life perfect, and they are fused into one master-
passion, morbid but unselfish. Antony has carried to an even
greater perfection the culture of both lives, and all his powers
are concentrated in one purpose, which is purely selfish. In
the action in which this group of personages is involved the
determining fact is the change that has come over the spirit
of Roman life, and introduced into its public policy the
element of personal aggrandisement and personal risk. The
new spirit works upon Brutus: the chance of winning
political liberty by the assassination of one individual just
overbalances his moral judgment, and he falls. Yet in his fall
he is glorious : the one false judgment of his life brings him,
what is more to him than victory, the chance of maintaining
the calmness of principle amid the ruins of a falling cause,
and showing how a Stoic can fail and die. The new spirit

CH. VIII. affects Cæsar and tempts him into a personal enterprise in which success demands a meanness that he lacks, and he is betrayed to his fall. Yet in his fall he is glorious : the assassins' daggers purge him from the stain of his momentary personal ambition, and the sequel shows that the Roman world was not worthy of a ruler such as Cæsar. The spirit of the age effects Cassius, and fans his passion to work itself out to his own destruction, and he falls. Yet in his fall he is glorious : we forgive him the lowered tone of his political action when we see by the spirit of the new rulers how desperate was the chance for which he played, and how Cassius and his loved cause of republican freedom expire together. The spirit of the age which has wrought upon the rest is controlled and used by Antony, and he rises on their ruins. Yet in his rise he is less glorious than they in their fall : he does all for self ; he may claim therefore the prize of success, but in goodness he has no share beyond that he is permitted to be the passive instrument of punishing evil.

IX.

How the Play of Julius Cæsar works to a Climax at the Centre.

A Study in Passion and Movement.

THE preceding chapters have been confined to two of the main elements in dramatic effect, Character and Plot: the third remains to be illustrated. Amongst other devices of public amusement the experiment has been tried of arranging a game of chess to be played by living pieces on a monster board; if we suppose that in the midst of such a game the real combative instincts of the living pieces should be suddenly aroused, that the knight should in grim earnest plunge his spear into his nearest opponent, and that missiles should actually be discharged from the castles, then the shock produced in the feelings of the bystanders by such a change would serve to bring out with emphasis the distinction between Plot and the third element of dramatic effect, Passion. Plot is an interest of a purely intellectual kind, it traces laws, principles, order, and design in the incidents of life. Passion, on the other hand, depends on the human character of the personages involved; it consists in the effects produced on the spectator's emotional nature as his sympathy follows the characters through the incidents of the plot; it is War as distinguished from *Kriegspiel*. Effects of such Passion are numerous and various: the present study is concerned with its *Movement*. This Movement comprehends a class of dramatic effects differing in one obvious

Passion connected with the movement of a drama.

The regular arch-form applicable to Passion-Movement.

particular from the effects considered so far. Character-Interpretation and Plot are both analytical in their nature; the play has to be taken to pieces and details selected from various parts have to be put together to give the idea of a complete character, or to make up some single thread of design. Movement, on the contrary, follows the actual order of the events as they take place in the play itself. The emotional effects produced by such events as they succeed one another will not be uniform and monotonous; the skill of the dramatist will lie in concentrating effect at some points and relieving it at others; and to watch such play of passion through the progress of the action will be a leading dramatic interest. Now we have already had occasion to notice the prominence which Shakespeare in his dramatic construction gives to the central point of a play; symmetry more than sensation is the effect which has an attraction for his genius, and the finale to which the action is to lead is not more important to him than the balancing of the whole drama about a turning-point in the middle. Accordingly it is not surprising to find that in the Passion-Movement of his dramas a similar plan of construction is often followed; that all other variations are subordinated to one great Climax of Passion at the centre. To repeat an illustration already applied to Plot: the movement of the passion seems to follow the form of a regular arch, commencing in calmness, rising through emotional strain to a summit of agitation at the centre, then through the rest of the play declining into a calmness of a different kind. It is the purpose of the two remaining studies to illustrate this kind of movement in two very different plays. *Julius Cæsar* has the simplest of plots; our attention is engaged with a train of emotion which is made to rise gradually to a climax at the centre, and then equally gradually to decline. *Lear*, on the contrary, is amongst the most intricate of Shakespeare's plays; nevertheless the dramatist contrives to keep the same simple form of emotional

effect, and its complex passions unite in producing a concen- CHAP. IX.
tration of emotional agitation in a few central scenes.

The passion in the play of *Julius Cæsar* gathers around *In Julius*
the conspirators, and follows them through the mutations of *Cæsar the*
movement
their fortunes. If however we are to catch the different parts *follows the*
justifica-
of the action in their proper proportions we must remember *tion of the*
the character of these conspirators,' and especially of their *conspira-*
tors to the
leaders Brutus and Cassius. These are actuated in what *audience*
they do not by personal motives but by devotion to the
public good and the idea of republican liberty; accordingly
in following their career we must not look too exclusively at
their personal success and failure. The exact key to the
movement of the drama will be given by fixing attention
upon the *justification of the conspirators' cause* in the minds of
the audience; and it is this which is found to rise gradually *this rises to*
the centre
to its height in the centre of the play, and from that point to *and de-*
decline to the end. I have pointed out in the preceding *clines from*
study how the issue at stake in *Julius Cæsar* amounts to a *the centre.*
conflict between the outer and inner life, between devotion
to a public enterprise and such sympathy with the claims of
individual humanity as is specially fostered by the cultivation
of the inner nature. The issue is reflected in words of
Brutus already quoted:

> The abuse of greatness is, when it disjoins   ii i. 18
> Remorse from power.

Brutus applies this as a test to Cæsar's action, and is forced
to acquit him: but is not Brutus here laying down the very
principle of which his own error in the play is the violation?
The assassin's dagger puts Brutus and the conspirators in
the position of power; while 'remorse'—the word in Shakespearean English means human sympathy—is the due of
their victim Cæsar, whose rights to justice as a man, and to
more than justice as the friend of Brutus, the conspirators
have the responsibility of balancing against the claims of a
political cause. These claims of justice and humanity are

deliberately ignored by the stoicism of Brutus, while the rest of the conspirators are blinded to them by the mists of political enthusiasm ; this outraged human sympathy asserts itself after Cæsar's death in a monstrous form in the passions of the mob, which are guided by the skill of Antony to the destruction of the assassins. Of course both the original violation of the balance between the two lives and the subsequent reaction are equally corrupt. The stoicism of Brutus, with its suppression of the inner sympathies, arrives practically at the principle—destined in the future history of the world to be the basis of a yet greater crime—that it is expedient that one man should die rather than that a whole people should perish. On the other hand, Antony trades upon the fickle violence of the populace, and uses it as much for personal ends as for vengeance. This demoralisation of both the sides of character is the result of their divorce. Such is the essence of this play if its action be looked at as a whole ; but it belongs to the movement of dramatic passion that we see the action only in its separate parts at different times. Through the first half of the play, while the justification of the conspirators' cause is rising, the other side of the question is carefully hidden from us ; from the point of the assassination the suppressed element starts into prominence, and sweeps our sympathies along with it to its triumph at the conclusion of the play.

First stage: the con- spiracy forming. Passion indistin- guishable from mere interest. 1. i, ii.

In following the movement of the drama the action seems to divide itself into stages. In the first of these stages, which comprehends the first two scenes, the conspiracy is only forming ; the sympathy with which the spectator follows the details is entirely free from emotional agitation; passion so far is indistinguishable from mere interest. The opening scene strikes appropriately the key-note of the whole action.

Starting- point: signs of reaction in the

In it we see the tribunes of the people—officers whose whole *raison d'être* is to be the mouthpiece of the commonalty—re- straining their own clients from the noisy honours they are dis-

posed to pay to Cæsar. To the justification in our eyes of a CHAP. IX.
conspiracy against Cæsar, there could not be a better starting- *popular*
point than this hint that the popular worship of Cæsar, *worship of*
which has made him what he is, is itself reaching its *Cæsar.*
reaction-point. Such a suggestion moreover makes the *i. i.*
whole play one complete *wave* of popular fickleness from
crest to crest.

The second is the scene upon which the dramatist mainly *The Rise*
relies for the *crescendo* in the justification of the con- *begins. The*
spirators. It is a long scene, elaborately contrived so as to *cause seen*
keep the conspirators and their cause before us at their very *at its best,*
best, and the victim at his very worst. Cassius is the life *the victim*
and spirit of this scene, as he is of the whole republican *at his*
movement. Cassius is excellent soil for republican prin- *worst.*
ciples. The 'rash humour' his mother gave him would pre- *i. ii.*
dispose him to impatience of those social inequalities and conventional distinctions against which republicanism sets itself.
Again he is a hard-thinking man, to whom the perfect
realisation of an ideal theory would be as palpable an aim as
the more practical purposes of other men. He is a Roman
moreover, at once proud of his nation as the greatest in the
world, and aware that this national greatness had been
through all history bound up with the maintenance of a
republican constitution. His republicanism gives to Cassius
the dignity that is always given to a character by a grand
passion, whether for a cause, a woman, or an idea—the
unification of a whole life in a single aim, by which the
separate strings of a man's nature are, as it were, tuned into
harmony. In the present scene Cassius is expounding the
cause which is his life-object. Nor is this all. Cassius was
politician enough to adapt himself to his hearers, and could
hold up the lower motives to those who would be influenced
by them; but in the present case it is the 'honourable metal'
of a Brutus that he has to work upon, and his exposition
of republicanism must be adapted to the highest possible

CHAP. IX. standard. Accordingly, in the language of the scene we find
the idea of human equality expressed in its most ideal form.
Without it Cassius thinks life not worth living.

1. ii. 95.

> I had as lief not be as live to be
> In awe of such a thing as I myself.
> I was born free as Cæsar; so were you;
> We both have fed as well, and we can both
> Endure the winter's cold as well as he.

The examples follow of the flood and fever incidents, which
show how the majesty of Cæsar vanished before the violence
of natural forces and the prostration of disease.

115.

> And this man
> Is now become a god, and Cassius is
> A wretched creature and must bend his body,
> If Cæsar carelessly but nod on him.

In the eye of the state, individuals are so many members of a
class, in precisely the way that their names are so many
examples of the proper noun.

142.

> Brutus and Cæsar: what should be in that 'Cæsar'?
> Why should that name be sounded more than yours?
> Write them together, yours is as fair a name;
> Sound them, it doth become the mouth as well;
> Weigh them, it is as heavy; conjure with them,
> Brutus will start a spirit as soon as Cæsar.
> Now, in the names of all the gods at once,
> Upon what meat doth this our Cæsar feed,
> That he is grown so great?

And this exposition of the conspirators' cause in its highest
form is at the same time thrown into yet higher relief by a
background to the scene, in which the victim is presented at
his worst.   All through the conversation between Brutus and
Cassius, the shouting of the mob reminds of the scene which
from 182. is at the moment going on in the Capitol, while the conversation is interrupted for a time by the returning procession of
Cæsar.   In this action behind the scenes which thus mingles
with the main incident Cæsar is committing the one fault of
his life : this is the fault of 'treason,' which can be justified

only by being successful and so becoming 'revolution,' CHAP. IX.
whereas Cæsar is failing, and deserving to fail from the
vacillating hesitation with which he sins. Moreover, unfavourable as such incidents would be in themselves to our
sympathy with Cæsar, yet it is not the actual facts that we
are permitted to see, but they are further distorted by
the medium through which they reach us—the cynicism of
Casca which belittles and disparages all he relates.

Bru Tell us the manner of it, gentle Casca i. ii. 235.

Casca. I can as well be hanged as tell the manner of it: it was mere
foolery; I did not mark it I saw Mark Antony offer him a crown,—
yet' twas not a crown neither, 'twas one of these coronets :—and, as I
told you, he put it by once: but, for all that, to my thinking, he would
fain have had it. Then he offered it to him again; then he put it by
again: but, to my thinking, he was very loath to lay his fingers off it.
And then he offer'd it the third time; he put it the third time by: and
still as he refused it, the rabblement hooted and clapped their chapped
hands and threw up their sweaty night-caps and uttered such a deal of
stinking breath because Cæsar had refused the crown that it had almost
choked Cæsar; for he swounded and fell down at it. and, for mine own
part, I durst not laugh, for fear of opening my lips and receiving the
bad air. . . . When he came to himself again, he said, If he had done or
said anything amiss, he desired their worships to think it was his
infirmity. Three or four wenches, where I stood, cried, ' Alas, good
soul!' and forgave him with all their hearts, but there's no heed to be
taken of them; if Cæsar had stabbed their mothers they would have
done no less.

At the end of the scene Brutus is won, and we pass *Second*
immediately into the second stage of the action: the con- *stage: the*
conspiracy
spiracy is now formed and developing, and the emotional *formed and*
strain begins. The adhesion of Brutus has given us con- *developing.*
Passion-
fidence that the conspiracy will be effective, and we have *Strain be-*
only to *wait* for the issue. This mere notion of *waiting* is *gins*
i. iii–ii. ii.
itself enough to introduce an element of agitation into the *Suspense*
passion sufficient to mark off this stage of the action from *one element*
in the
the preceding. How powerful suspense is for this purpose we *strain of*
have expressed in the words of the play itself: *passion.*

Between the acting of a dreadful thing ii. i. 63.
And the first motion, all the interim is

Like a phantasma, or a hideous dream :
The Genius and the mortal instruments
Are then in council ; and the state of man,
Like to a little kingdom, suffers then
The nature of an insurrection.

The back-
ground of
tempest
and super-
natural
portents a
device for
increasing
the strain.

But besides the suspense there is a special device for
securing the agitation proper to this stage of the passion :
throughout there is maintained a Dramatic Background of
night, storm, and supernatural portents.

The conception of nature as exhibiting sympathy with
sudden turns in human affairs is one of the most fundamental instincts of poetry. To cite notable instances :
it is this which accompanies with storm and whirlwind the
climax to the *Book of Job*, and which leads Milton to make
the whole universe sensible of Adam's transgression :

Earth trembl'd from her entrails, as again
In pangs, and Nature gave a second groan ;
Sky lowr'd, and muttering thunder, some sad drops
Wept at completing of the mortal sin
Original.

So too the other end of the world's history has its appropriate
accompaniments : ‘ the sun shall be darkened and the moon
shall not give her light, and the stars shall be falling from
heaven.’ There is a *vagueness* of terror inseparable from
these outbursts of nature, so mysterious in their causes and
aims. They are actually the most mighty of forces—for
human artillery is feeble beside the earthquake—yet they are
invisible : the wind works its havoc without the keenest eye
being able to perceive it, and the lightning is never seen till
it has struck. Again, there is something weird in the feeling
that the most frightful powers in the material universe are all
soft things. The empty air becomes the irresistible wind ;
the fluid and yielding water wears down the hard and
massive rock and determines the shape of the earth ; im-
palpable fire that is blown about in every direction can be
roused till it devours the solidest constructions of human

skill; while the most powerful agencies of all, electricity and CHAP. IX.
atomic force, are imperceptible to any of the senses and are
known only by their results. This uncanny terror attaching
to the union between force and softness is the inspiration of
one of Homer's most unique episodes, in which the be-
wildered Achilles, struggling with the river-god, finds the
strength and skill of the finished warrior vain against the
ever-rising water, and bitterly feels the violation of the
natural order—

> That strong might fall by strong, where now weak water's luxury
> Must make my death blush.

To the terrible in nature are added portents of the super- i. iii; ii.
natural, sudden violations of the uniformity of nature, the ii, &c.
principle upon which all science is founded. The solitary
bird of night has been seen in the crowded Capitol; fire has
played around a human hand without destroying it; lions,
forgetting their fierceness, have mingled with men; clouds
drop fire instead of rain; graves are giving up their dead;
the chance shapes of clouds take distinctness to suggest
tumult on the earth. Such phenomena of nature and the
supernatural, agitating from their appeal at once to fear and
mystery, and associated by the fancy with the terrible in
human events, have made a deep impression upon primitive
thought; and the impression has descended by generations
of inherited tradition until, whatever may be the attitude of
the intellect to the phenomena themselves, their associations
in the emotional nature are of agitation. They thus become
appropriate as a Dramatic Background to an agitated passion
in the scenes themselves, calling out the emotional effect by
a vague sympathy, much as a musical note may set in vibra-
tion a distant string that is in unison with it.

   This device then is used by Shakespeare in the second
stage of the present play. We see the warning terrors
through the eyes of men of the time, and their force is

CHAP. IX. measured by the fact that they shake the cynical Casca into
eloquence.

i. iii. 3.

> Are not you moved, when all the sway of earth
> Shakes like a thing unfirm? O Cicero,
> I have seen tempests, when the scolding winds
> Have rived the knotty oaks, and I have seen
> The ambitious ocean swell and rage and foam,
> To be exalted with the threatening clouds:
> But never till to-night, never till now,
> Did I go through a tempest dropping fire.
> Either there is a civil strife in heaven,
> Or else the world, too saucy with the gods,
> Incenses them to send destruction.

And the idea thus started at the commencement is kept
before our minds throughout this stage of the drama by
compare perpetual allusions, however slight, to the sky and external
ii. i. 44, nature. Brutus reads the secret missives by the light of
101, 198, exhalations whizzing through the air; when some of the
221, 263; conspirators step aside, to occupy a few moments while the
ii. ii. rest are conferring apart, it is to the sky their thoughts
naturally seem to turn, and they with difficulty can make out
the East from the West; the discussion of the conspirators
includes the effect on Cæsar of the night's prodigies. Later
Portia remonstrates against her husband's exposure to the
raw and dank morning, to the rheumy and unpurged air;
even when daylight has fully returned, the conversation is of
Calpurnia's dream and the terrible prodigies.

i. iii. Against this background are displayed, first single figures
ii. i. 1-85. of Cassius and other conspirators; then Brutus alone in calm
ii. i. 86- deliberation: then the whole band of conspirators, their wild
228. excitement side by side with Brutus's immovable moderation.
ii. i, from Then the Conspiracy Scene fades in the early morning light
233. into a display of Brutus in his softer relations; and with
ii. ii. complete return of day changes to the house of Cæsar on
the fatal morning. Cæsar also is displayed in contact with
the supernatural, as represented by Calpurnia's terrors and
repeated messages of omens that forbid his venturing upon

public action for that day.   Cæsar faces all this with his usual loftiness of mind; yet the scene is so contrived that, as far as immediate effect is concerned, this very loftiness is made to tell against him.   The unflinching courage that overrides and interprets otherwise the prodigies and warnings seems presumption to us who know the reality of the danger. It is the same with his yielding to the humour of his wife. Why should he not? his is not the conscious weakness that must be firm to show that it is not afraid.   Yet when, upon Decius's explaining away the dream and satisfying Calpurnia's fears, Cæsar's own attraction to danger leads him to persevere in his first intention, this change of purpose seems to us, who have heard Decius's boast that he can o'ersway Cæsar with flattery, a confirmation of Cæsar's weakness.   So in accordance with the purpose that reigns through the first half of the play the victim is made to appear at his worst: the *passing* effect of the scene is to suggest weakness in Cæsar, while it is in fact furnishing elements which, upon reflection, go to build up a character of strength.   On the other hand, throughout this stage the justification of the conspirators' cause gains by their confidence and their high tone; in particular by the way in which they interpret to their own advantage the supernatural element.   Cassius feels the wildness of the night as in perfect harmony with his own spirit.

CHAP. IX.

Cæsar still seen at a disadvantage :

ii. ii. 8–56.

ii. i. 202.

and the justification of the conspirators still rising.

i. iii. 42–79.

> For my part, I have walk'd about the streets,
> Submitting me unto the perilous night,
> And, thus unbraced, Casca, as you see,
> Have bared my bosom to the thunder-stone ;
> And when the cross blue lightning seem'd to open
> The breast of heaven, I did present myself
> Even in the aim and very flash of it.

i. iii. 46.

And it needs only a word from him to communicate his confidence to his comrades.

> *Cassius.*   Now could I, Casca, name to thee a man
> Most like this dreadful night,
> That thunders, lightens, opens graves, and roars

i. iii. 72.

O 2

> As doth the lion in the Capitol,
> A man no mightier than thyself or me
> In personal action, yet prodigious grown
> And fearful, as these strange eruptions are—
>   *Casca.* 'Tis Cæsar that you mean; is it not, Cassius?

Third stage. The Crisis: the passion-strain rises to a Climax. ii. iii– iii. i. 121.

The third stage of the action brings us to the climax of the passion; the strain upon our emotions now rises to a height of agitation. The exact commencement of the crisis seems to be marked by the soothsayer's words at the opening of Act III. Cæsar observes on entering the Capitol the soothsayer who had warned him to beware of this very day.

> *Cæsar.* The ides of March are come.
> *Sooth.* Ay, Cæsar; but not gone.

Such words seem to measure out a narrow area of time in which the crisis is to work itself out. There is however no distinct break between different stages of a dramatic movement like that in the present play; and two short incidents have preceded this scene which have served as emotional devices to bring about a distinct advance in the intensification of the strain. In the first, Artemidorus appeared reading a letter of warning which he purposed to present to Cæsar on his way to the fatal spot. In the Capitol Scene he presents it, while the ready Decius hastens to interpose another petition to take off Cæsar's attention. Artemidorus conjures Cæsar to read his first for 'it touches him nearer'; but the imperial chivalry of Cæsar forbids:

Devices for working up the agitation. Artemidorus; ii. iii and iii. i. 3.

> What touches us ourself shall be last served.

Portia; ii. iv.

The momentary hope of rescue is dashed. In the second incident Portia has been displayed completely unnerved by the weight of a secret to the anxiety of which she is not equal; she sends messengers to the Capitol and recalls them as she recollects that she dare give them no message; her agitation has communicated itself to us, besides suggesting the fear that it may betray to others what she is anxious to conceal. Our sympathy has thus been tossed

from side to side, although in its general direction it still CHAP. IX.
moves on the side of the conspirators. In the crisis itself *Popilius*
the agitation becomes painful as the entrance of Popilius *Lena.*
Lena and his secret communication to Cæsar cause a panic iii. 1. 13.
that threatens to wreck the whole plot on the verge of its
success. Brutus's nerve sustains even this trial, and the way
for the accomplishment of the deed is again clear. Emotional
devices like these have carried the passion up to a climax of
agitation; and the conspirators now advance to present
their pretended suit and achieve the bloody deed. To the
last the double effect of Cæsar's demeanour continues.
Considered in itself, his unrelenting firmness of principle
exhibits the highest model of a ruler; yet to us, who know
the purpose lurking behind the hypocritical intercession of
the conspirators, Cæsar's self-confidence resembles the infatuation that goes before Nemesis. He scorns the fickle from 58.
politicians before him as mere wandering sparks of heavenly
fire, while he is left alone as a pole-star of true-fixed and
resting quality :—and in answer to his presumptuous boast
that he can never be moved come the blows of the assassins
which strike him down; while there is a flash of irony as he
is seen to have fallen beside the statue of Pompey, and the compare
marble seems to gleam in cold triumph over the rival at last 115.
lying bleeding at its feet. The assassination is accomplished,
the cause of the conspirators is won: pity notwithstanding
we are swept along with the current of their enthusiasm;
and the justification that has been steadily rising from the *The justifi-*
commencement reaches its climax as, their adversaries dis- *cation at*
persing in terror, the conspirators dip their hands in their *in the ap-*
victim's blood, and make their triumphant appeal to the *peal to all*
whole world and all time. *time.*

> *Cassius.* Stoop, then, and wash. How many ages hence   III.
>   Shall this our lofty scene be acted over
>   In states unborn and accents yet unknown!
> *Brutus.* How many times shall Cæsar bleed in sport,

That now on Pompey's basis lies along,
No worthier than the dust !

Cassius.　　　　　　　　　So oft as that shall be,
So often shall the knot of us be call'd
The men that gave their country LIBERTY !

Catas-
trophe, and
commence-
ment of the
Reaction.
iii. i, from
122.

　　　Enter a servant : this simple stage-direction is the 'catastrophe,' the turning-round of the whole action ; the arch has reached its apex and the Reaction has begun. So instantaneous is the change, that though it is only the servant of Antony who speaks, yet the first words of his message ring with the peculiar tone of subtly-poised sentences which are inseparably associated with Antony's eloquence ; it is like the first announcement of that which is to be a final theme in music, and from this point this tone dominates the scene to the very end.

125.

　　　　　　Thus he bade me say :
Brutus is noble, wise, valiant, and honest,
Cæsar was mighty, bold, royal, and loving,
Say I love Brutus, and I honour him ;
Say I fear'd Cæsar, honour'd him, and lov'd him.
If Brutus will vouchsafe that Antony
May safely come to him, and be resolv'd
How Cæsar hath deserved to lie in death,
Mark Antony shall not love Cæsar dead
So well as Brutus living.

In the whole Shakespearean Drama there is nowhere such a swift swinging round of a dramatic action as is here marked by this sudden up-springing of the suppressed individuality *ii. i. 165.* in Antony's character, hitherto so colourless that he has been spared by the conspirators as a mere limb of Cæsar. The tone of exultant triumph in the conspirators has in an *iii. i. 144.* instant given place to Cassius's 'misgiving' as Brutus grants Antony an audience ; and when Antony enters, Brutus's first *from 164.* words to him fall into the form of apology. The quick subtlety of Antony's intellect has grasped the whole situation, and with irresistible force he slowly feels his way towards using the conspirators' aid for crushing themselves

and avenging their victim. The bewilderment of the con- CHAP. IX.
spirators in the presence of this unlooked-for force is seen
in Cassius's unavailing attempt to bring Antony to the point, iii. i. 211,
as to what compact he will make with them. Antony, on compare
the contrary, reads his men with such nicety that he can 177.
indulge himself in sailing close to the wind, and grasps
fervently the hands of the assassins while he pours out a from 184.
flood of bitter grief over the corpse. It is not hypocrisy,
nor a trick to gain time, this conciliation of his enemies.
Steeped in the political spirit of the age, Antony knows, as
no other man, the mob which governs Rome, and is conscious of the mighty engine he possesses in his oratory to
sway that mob in what direction he pleases; when his bold
plan has succeeded, and his adversaries have consented to
meet him in contest of oratory, then ironical conciliation
becomes the natural relief to his pent-up passion.

> Friends am I with you all and love you all, 220
> *Upon this hope, that you shall give me reasons*
> Why and wherein Cæsar was dangerous.

It is as he feels the sense of innate oratorical power and of
the opportunity his enemies have given to that power, that
he exaggerates his temporary amity with the men he is
about to crush: it is the executioner arranging his victim
comfortably on the rack before he proceeds to apply the
levers. Already the passion of the drama has fallen under
the guidance of Antony. The view of Cæsar as an innocent victim is now allowed full play upon our sympathies
when Antony, left alone with the corpse, can drop the from 254.
artificial mask and give vent to his love and vengeance.
The success of the conspiracy had begun to decline as we 231–243.
marked Brutus's ill-timed generosity to Antony in granting
him the funeral oration; it crumbles away through the cold iii. ii, from
unnatural euphuism of Brutus's speech in its defence; it is 13.
hurried to its ruin when Antony at last exercises his spell iii. ii, from
upon the Roman people and upon the reader. The speech 78.

CHAP. IX.   of Antony, with its mastery of every phase of feeling, is a
——————   perfect sonata upon the instrument of the human emotions.
iii. ii. 78.   Its opening theme is sympathy with bereavement, against
which are working as if in conflict anticipations of future
95, 109,   themes, doubt and compunction.   A distinct change of
&c.
133.   movement comes with the first introduction of what is to be
the final subject, the mention of the will.   But when this new
movement has worked up from curiosity to impatience, there
177.   is a diversion : the mention of the victory over the Nervii
turns the emotions in the direction of historic pride, which
178.   harmonises well with the opposite emotions roused as the
orator fingers hole after hole in Cæsar's mantle made by the
daggers of his false friends, and so leads up to a sudden
200.   shock when he uncovers the body itself and displays the
popular idol and its bloody defacement.   Then the finale
243.   begins : the forgotten theme of the will is again started, and
from a burst of gratitude the passion quickens and inten-

The mob   sifies to rage, to fury, to mutiny.   The mob is won to the
won to the   Reaction ; and the curtain that falls upon the third Act rises
Reaction.
iii. iii.   for a moment to display the populace tearing a man to
pieces simply because he bears the same name as one of the
conspirators.

Last stage.   The final stage of the action works out the development
Develop-   of an inevitable fate.   The emotional strain now ceases,
ment of an
inevitable   and, as in the first stage, the passion is of the calmer order,
fate: pas-   the calmness in this case of pity balanced by a sense of
sion-strain
ceases.   justice.   From the opening of the fourth Act the decline in
the justification of the conspirators is intimated by the logic
of events.   The first scene exhibits to us the triumvirate that
now governs Rome, and shows that in this triumvirate
Acts iv, v.   Antony is supreme : with the man who is the embodiment
iv. i.   of the Reaction thus appearing at the head of the world,
the fall of the conspirators is seen to be inevitable.   The
decline of our sympathy with them continues in the following
iv. ii. 3.   scenes.   The Quarrel Scene shows how low the tone of

Cassius has fallen since he has dealt with assassination as a CHAP. IX.
political weapon; and even Brutus's moderation has hardened into unpleasing harshness. There is at this point iv. iii. 148, &c.
plenty of relief to such unpleasing effects: there is the
exhibition of the tender side of Brutus's character as shown iv. iii, from 239.
in his relations with his page, and the display of friendship iv. iii.
maintained between Brutus and Cassius amid falling fortunes.
But such incidents as these have a different effect upon us
from that which they would have had at an earlier period;
the justification of the conspirators has so far declined that
now attractive touches in them serve only to increase the
pathos of a fate which, however, our sympathy no longer
seeks to resist. We get a supernatural foreshadowing of the
end in the appearance to Brutus of Cæsar's Ghost, and the iv. iii. 275.
omen Cassius sees of the eagles that had consorted his army v. i. 80.
to Philippi giving place to ravens, crows, and kites on the
morning of battle: this lends the authority of the invisible
world to our sense that the conspirators' cause is doomed.
And judicial blindness overtakes them as Brutus's authority iv. iii. 196 -230.
in council overweighs in point after point the shrewder
advice of Cassius. Through the scenes of the fifth Act we
see the republican leaders fighting on without hope. The
last remnant of justification for their cause ceases as the *Justifica-tion entire-ly vanishes as the con-spirators recognise Cæsar's victory.*
conspirators themselves seem to acknowledge their error and
fate. Cassius as he feels his death-blow recognises the very
weapon with which he had committed the crime:

> Cæsar, thou art revenged,
> Even with the sword that kill'd thee.

v. iii. 45.

And at last even the firm spirit of Brutus yields:

> O Julius Cæsar, thou art mighty yet!
> Thy spirit walks abroad, and turns our swords
> In our own proper entrails.

v. v. 94.

X.

How Climax meets Climax in
the centre of Lear.

*A Study in more complex
Passion and Movement.*

CHAP. X.

*The plot
of Lear
highly
complex.*

IN *Julius Cæsar* we have seen how, in the case of a very simple play, a few simple devices are sufficient to produce a regular rise and fall in the passion. We now turn to a highly elaborate plot and trace how, notwithstanding the elaborateness, a similar concentration of the passion in the centre of the play can be secured. *King Lear* is one of the most complex of Shakespeare's tragedies ; its plot is made up of a number of separate actions, with their combinations accurately carried out, the whole impressing us with a sense of artistic involution similar to that of an elaborate musical fugue. Here, however, we are concerned only indirectly with the plot of the play : we need review it no further than may suffice to show what distinct interests enter into it, and enable us to observe how the separate trains of passion work toward a common climax at the centre.

Starting from the notion of pattern as a fundamental idea we have seen how Plot presents trains of events in human life taking form and shape as a crime and its nemesis, an oracle and its fulfilment, the rise and fall of an individual, or even as simply a story. The particular form of action under-

*The main
plot ex-
hibits the
Problem
form of*

lying the main plot of *King Lear* is different from any we have yet noticed. It may be described as a *Problem Action.* A mathematician in his problem assumes some unusual com-

bination of forces to have come about, and then proceeds to
trace its consequences: so the Drama often deals with *dramatic*
problems in history and life, setting up, before the com- *action.*
mencement of the play or early in the action, some peculiar
arrangement of moral relations, and then throughout the
rest of the action developing the consequences of these to the
personages involved. Thus the opening scene of *King Lear*
is occupied in bringing before us a pregnant and suggestive
state of affairs: imperiousness is represented as overthrowing
conscience and setting up an unnatural distribution of power.
A human problem has thus been enunciated which the re- *The prob-*
mainder of the play has to work out to its natural solution. *lem stated.*

Imperiousness seems to be the term appropriate to Lear's
conduct in the first scene. This is no case of dotage dividing
an inheritance according to public declarations of affection. The division had already been made according to
the best advice: in the case of two of the daughters 'equali- i. i. 3, &c.
ties had been so weighed that curiosity in neither could
make choice of either's moiety'; and if the portion of the
youngest and best loved of the three was the richest, this
is a partiality natural enough to absolute power. The
opening scene of the play is simply the court ceremony in
which the formal transfer is to be made. Lear is already 38.
handing to his daughters the carefully drawn maps which
mark the boundaries of the provinces, when he suddenly 49.
pauses, and, with the yearning of age and authority for tes-
timonies of devotion, calls upon his daughters for declarations
of affection, the easiest of returns for the substantial gifts he
is giving them, and which Goneril and Regan pour forth
with glib eloquence. Then Lear turns to Cordelia, and, 84.
thinking delightedly of the special prize he has marked out
for the pet of his old age, asks her:

> What can you say to draw
> A third more opulent than your sisters?

But Cordelia has been revolted by the fulsome flattery of the

CHAP. X. sisters whose hypocrisy she knows so well, and she bluntly refuses to be drawn into any declaration of affection at all. Cordelia might well have found some other method of separating herself from her false sisters, without thus flouting her father before his whole court in a moment of tenderness to herself; or, if carried away by the indignation of the moment, a sign of submission would have won her a ready pardon. But Cordelia, sweet and strong as her character is compare i. i. 131. in great things, has yet inherited a touch of her father's temper, and the moment's sullenness is protracted into obstinacy. Cordelia then has committed an offence of manner ; Lear's passion vents itself in a sentence proper only to a moral crime : now the punishment of a minute offence with wholly disproportionate severity simply because it is an offence against personal will is an exact description of imperiousness.

As Lear stands for imperiousness, so conscience is represented by Kent, who, with the voice of authority derived from lifelong intimacy and service, interposes to check the King's passion in its headlong course.

141–190.

Kent.   Royal Lear,
    Whom I have ever honour'd as my king,
    Loved as my father, as my master follow'd,
    As my great patron thought on in my prayers,—
Lear. The bow is bent and drawn, make from the shaft.
Kent. Let it fall rather, though the fork invade
    The region of my heart : be Kent unmannerly
    When Lear is mad. What wilt thou do, old man ?
    Think'st thou that duty shall have dread to speak,
    When power to flattery bows ? To plainness honour's bound,
    When majesty stoops to folly. Reverse thy doom . . .
Lear. Kent, on thy life, no more.
Kent. My life I never held but as a pawn
    To wage against thy enemies, nor fear to lose it,
    Thy safety being the motive . . .
Lear.   O, vassal ! miscreant !
                  [*Laying his hand on his sword.*

Albany. ⎫
Cornwall. ⎬ Dear sir, forbear.

Kent. Do:
 Kill thy physician, and the fee bestow
 Upon thy foul disease. Revoke thy doom;
 Or, whilst I can vent clamour from my throat,
 I'll tell thee thou dost evil.

In the banishment of this Kent, then, the resistance of Lear's conscience is overcome, and his imperious passion has full swing in transferring Cordelia's kingdom to her treacherous sisters.

The opening scene has put before us, not in words but figured i�)️ action, a problem in human affairs : the violation of moral equity has set up an unnatural arrangement of power—power taken from the good and lodged in the hands of the bad. Here is, so to speak, a piece of moral unstable equilibrium, and the rebound from it is to furnish the remainder of the action. The very structure of the plot corresponds with the simple structure of a scientific proposition. The latter consists of two unequal parts : a few lines are sufficient to enunciate the problem, while a whole treatise may be required for its solution. So in *King Lear* a single scene brings about the unnatural state of affairs, the consequences of which it takes the rest of the play to trace. The 'catastrophe,' or turning-point of the play at which the ultimate issues are decided, appears in the present case, not close to the end of the play, nor (as in *Julius Cæsar*) in the centre, but close to the commencement : at the end of the opening scene Lear's act of folly has in reality determined the issue of the whole action ; the scenes which follow are only working out a determined issue to its full realisation.

We have seen the problem itself, the overthrow of conscience by imperiousness and the transfer of power from the good to the bad : what is the solution of it as presented by the incidents of the play ? The consequences flowing from what Lear has done make up three distinct tragedies, which go on working side by side, and all of which are essential to the full solution of the problem. First, there is the nemesis

The solution of the problem in a triple tragedy.

CHAP. X. upon Lear himself—the double retribution of receiving nothing
(1) *Tragedy* but evil from those he has unrighteously rewarded, and
of Lear. nothing but good from her whom, he bitterly feels, he has
cruelly wronged. But the punishment of the wrong-doer is
(2) *Tragedy* only one element in the consequences of wrong; the inno-
of Cordelia cent also are involved, and we get a second tragedy in the
and Kent. sufferings of the faithful Kent and the loving Cordelia, who,
through Kent as her representative, watches over her father's
safety, until at the end she appears in person to follow up her
devotion to the death. When, however, the incidents making
up the sufferings of Lear, of Kent, and of Cordelia are taken
out of the main plot, there is still a considerable section left—
(3) *Tragedy* that which is occupied with the mutual intrigues of Goneril
of Goneril and Regan, intrigues ending in their common ruin. This
and Regan. constitutes a third tragedy which, it will be seen, is as necessary to the solution of our problem as the other two. To
place power in the hands of the bad is an injury not only to
others, but also to the bad themselves, as giving fuel to the
fire of their wickedness: so in the tragedy of Goneril and
Regan we see evil passions placed in improper authority
using this authority to work out their own destruction.

An under- To this main plot is added an underplot equally elaborate.
plot on the
same basis As in *The Merchant of Venice*, the stories borrowed from two
as the main distinct sources are worked into a common design; and the
plot. interweaving in the case of the present play is perhaps
Shakespeare's greatest triumph of constructive skill. The
two stories are made to rest upon the same fundamental idea—
compare that of undutifulness to old age: what Lear's daughters
1. i, fin. actually do is that which is insinuated by Edmund as his
false charge against his brother.

I. ii. 76, &c. I have heard him oft maintain it to be fit, that, sons at perfect age,
and fathers declining, the father should be as ward to the son, and the
son manage his revenue.

So obvious is this fundamental connection between the main
and the underplot, that our attention is called to it by a

personage in the play itself: 'he childed as I father'd,' is
Edgar's pithy summary of it when he is brought into contact
with Lear. But in this double tragedy, drawn from the *The main*
two families of Lear and of Gloucester, the chief bond *and under-*
plot parallel
between its two sides consists in the sharp contrast which *and con-*
extends to every detail of the two stories. In the main plot *trasted*
through-
we have a daughter, who has received nothing but harm from *out.*
her father, who has unjustly had her position torn from her
and given to undeserving sisters: nevertheless she sacrifices
herself to save the father who did the injury from the sisters
who profited by it. In the underplot we have a son, who has
received nothing but good from his father, who has, contrary
to justice, been advanced by him to the position of an elder
brother whom he has slandered: nevertheless, he is seeking
the destruction of the father who did him the unjust kindness,
when he falls by the hand of the brother who was wronged
by it. Thus as the main and underplot go on working side
by side, they are at every turn by their antithesis throwing up
one another's effect; the contrast is like the reversing of the
original subject in a musical fugue. Again, as the main *The under-*
plot an
plot consisted in the initiation of a problem and its solution, *Intrigue*
so the underplot consists in the development of an intrigue *Action*
and its consequences. The tragedy of the Gloucester family
will, if stated from the point of view of the father, correspond
in its parts with the tragedy in the family of Lear.
It must be remembered, however, that the position of the
father is different in the two cases; Gloucester is not, as Lear,
the agent of the crime, but only a deceived instrument in the
hands of the villain Edmund, who is the real agent; if the
proper allowance be made for this difference, it will be seen
that the three tragedies which make up the consequences of *involving*
Lear's error have their analogies in the three tragedies which *a triple*
tragedy
flow from the intrigue of Edmund. First, we have the *parallel*
with that
nemesis on Gloucester, and this, in analogy with the nemesis *of the main*
on Lear, consists in receiving nothing but evil from the son *plot.*

CHAP. X.

(1) *Tragedy of Gloucester.*

(2) *Tragedy of Edgar.*

(3) *Tragedy of Edmund.*

o

Complexity of plot not inconsistent with simplicity of movement.

he has so hastily advanced, and nothing but good from the other son whom, he comes gradually to feel, he has unintentionally wronged. In the next place we have the sufferings of the innocent Edgar. Then, as we before saw a third tragedy in the way in which the power conferred upon Goneril and Regan is used to work out their destruction, so in the underplot we find that the position which Edmund has gained involves him in intrigues, which by the development of the play are made to result in a nemesis upon his original intrigue. And it is a nemesis of exquisite exactness: for he meets his death in the very moment of his success, at the hands of the brother he has maligned and robbed, while the father he has deceived and sought to destroy is the means by which the avenger has been brought to the scene.

We have gone far enough into the construction of the plot to perceive its complexity and the principal elements into which that complexity can be analysed. Two separate systems, each consisting of an initial action and three resulting tragedies, eight actions in all, are woven together by common personages and incidents, by parallelism of spirit, and by movement to a common climax; not to speak of lesser Link Actions which assist in drawing the different stories closer together. As with plot generally, these separate elements are fully manifest only to the eye of analysis; in following the course of the drama itself, they make themselves felt only in a continued sense of involution and harmonious symmetry. It is with passion, not with plot, that the present study is concerned; and the train of passion which the common movement of these various actions calls out in the sympathy of the reader is as simple as the plot itself is intricate. In the case both of the main plot and the underplot the emotional effect rises in intensity; moreover at this central height of intensity the two merge in a common Climax. The construction of the play resembles, if such a comparison may be allowed, the patent gas-apparatus, which secures a high illuminating power by the simple CHAP. X. device of several ordinary burners inclined to one another at such an angle that the apexes of their flames meet in a point. So the present play contains a Centrepiece of some three *from ii. iv.* scenes, marked off (at least at the commencement) decisively, *290 to iii.* in which the main and underplot unite in a common Climax, *vi. with the* with special devices to increase its effect ; the diverse interests *interrup-* to which our sympathy was called out at the commencement, *tion of iii.* and which analysis can keep distinct to the end, are *focussed,* *iii, iii. v.* so far as passion is concerned, in this Centrepiece, in which *The differ-* human emotion is carried to the highest pitch of tragic *ent trains* agitation that the world of art has yet exhibited. *of passion focussed in a central Climax.*

The emotional effect of the main plot rises to a climax in *The pas-* the madness of Lear. This, as the highest form of human *sions of the* agitation, is obviously a climax to the story of Lear himself. *main plot* It is equally a climax to the story of Kent and Cordelia, who *gather to a* suffer solely through their devoted watching over Lear, and *common* to whom the bitterest point in their sufferings is that they feel *Climax in* over again all that their fallen master has to endure. Finally, *the madness* in the madness of Lear the third of the three tragedies, the *of Lear.* Goneril and Regan action, appears throughout in the background as the cause of all that is happening. If we keep our eye upon this madness of Lear the movement of the play assumes the form we have so often had to notice—the regular arch. The first half of the arch, or rise in emotional strain, we get in symptoms of mental disturbance preparing us for actual madness which is to come. It is important to note the difference between passion and madness: passion is a disease of the mind, madness is a disease extending to the mysterious linking of mind and body. At the commencement Lear is dominated by the passion of imperiousness, an imperiousness born of his absolute power as king and father; he has never learned from discipline restraint of his passion, but has been accustomed to fling himself upon obstacles and see them give way before him. Now the tragical situation is

P

CHAP. X. prepared for him of meeting with obstacles which will not give way, but from which his passion rebounds upon himself with a physical shock. As thus opposition follows opposition, we see *waves* of physical, that is of hysterical, passion, sweeping over Lear, until, as it were, a tenth wave lands him in the full disease of madness.

i. iv. The first case occurs in his interview with Goneril after that which is the first check he has received in his new life, the insolence shown to his retinue. Goneril enters his presence with a frown. The wont had been that Lear frowned and all cowered before him : and now he waits for his daughter to remember herself with a rising passion ill concealed under the forced calmness with which he enquires, 'Are you our daughter?' 'Doth any here know me?' But Goneril, on the contrary, calmly assumes the position of reprover, and details her unfounded charges of insolence against her father's sober followers, until at last he hears himself desired

> By her, that else will take the thing she begs,

to disquantity his train. Then Lear breaks out :

> Darkness and devils !
> Saddle my horses; call my train together.
> Degenerate bastard ! I'll not trouble thee :
> Yet have I left a daughter.

In a moment the thought of Cordelia's 'most small fault' and how it had been visited upon her occurs to condense into a single pang the whole sense of his folly; and here it is that the first of these waves of physical passion comes over Lear, its physical character marked by the physical action which accompanies it :

i. iv. 292.
> O Lear, Lear, Lear !
> Beat at this gate, that let thy folly in, [*Striking his head.*
> And thy dear judgement out.

It lasts but for a moment: but it is a wave, and it will
i. v. return. Accordingly in the next scene we see Lear on his journey from one daughter to the other. He is brooding

over the scene he is leaving behind, and he cannot disguise a CHAP. X.
shade of anxiety, in his awakened judgment, that some such
scene may be reserved for him in the goal to which he is
journeying. He is half listening, moreover, to the Fool, who
harps on the same thought, that the King is suffering what he
might have expected, that the other daughter will be like the
first :—until there comes another of these sudden outbursts of
passion, in which Lear for a moment half foresees the end to
which he is being carried.

> O, let me not be mad, not mad, sweet heaven !   i. v. 49.
> Keep me in temper. I would not be mad !

Imperiousness is especially attached to outward signs of
reverence : it is reserved for Lear when he arrives at Regan's ii. iv. 4.
palace to find the messenger he has sent on to announce him
suffering the indignity of the stocks. At first he will not believe that this has been done by order of his daughter and son.

Kent.   It is both he and she,
   Your son and daughter.
Lear. No.   13.
Kent. Yes.
Lear. No, I say.
Kent. I say, yea.
Lear. No, no, they would not
Kent. Yes, they have.
Lear. By Jupiter, I swear, no.
Kent. By Juno, I swear, ay.
Lear.   They durst not do't ;
   They could not, would not do't ; 'tis worse than murder,
   To do upon respect such violent outrage.

But he has to listen to a circumstantial account of the insult,
and, further, reminded by the Fool that

> Fathers that wear rags
> Do make their children blind,

he comes at last to realise it all,—and then there sweeps over
him a third and more violent wave of hysterical agitation.

> O, how this mother swells up toward my heart !   56.
> Hysterica passio, down, thou climbing sorrow,
> Thy element's below !

P 2

He has mastered the passion by a strong effort : but it is a wave, and it will return. He has mastered himself in order to confront the culprits face to face : his altered position is brought home to him when they refuse to receive him. And the refusal is made the worse by the well-meant attempt of Gloucester to palliate it, in which he unfortunately speaks of the ' fiery quality' of the duke.

> *Lear.* Vengeance ! plague ! death ! confusion !
> Fiery ? what quality ?

Nothing is harder than to endure what one is in the habit of inflicting on others ; it was Lear's own ' fiery quality' by which he had been accustomed to scorch all opposition out of his way ; now he has to hear another man's ' fiery quality' quoted to him. But this outburst is only momentary ; the very extremity of the case seems to calm Lear, and he begins himself to frame excuses for the duke, how sickness and infirmity neglect the ' office' to which health is bound—until his eye lights again upon his messenger sitting in the stocks, and the recollection of this deliberate affront brings back again the wave of passion.

122.   O me, my heart, my rising heart ! but, down !

Lear had a strange confidence in his daughter Regan. As we see the two women in the play, Regan appears the more cold-blooded ; nothing in Goneril is more cruel than Regan's

204.   I pray you, father, being weak, seem so ;

or her meeting Lear's ' I gave you all ' with the rejoinder,

253.   ●   And in good time you gave it.

But there was something in Regan's personal appearance that belied her real character ; her father says to her in this scene :

173.   Her eyes are fierce, but thine
       Do comfort and not burn.

Judas betrayed with a kiss, and Regan persecutes her father CHAP. X.
in tears. But Regan has scarcely entered her father's presence
when the trumpet announces the arrival of Goneril, and Lear 185.
has to see the Regan in whom he is trusting take Goneril's 197.
hand before his eyes in token that she is making common
cause with her. When following this the words 'indiscretion,'
'dotage,' reach his ear there is a momentary swelling of the
physical passion within :

O sides, you are too tough ;   200.
   Will you yet hold ?

He has mastered it for the last time : for now his whole
world seems to be closing in around him ; he has committed
his all to the two daughters standing before him, and they from 233.
unite to beat him down, from fifty knights to twenty-five,
from twenty-five to ten, to five, until the soft-eyed Regan
asks, 'What need one?' A sense of crushing oppression
stifles his anger, and Lear begins to answer with the same
calmness with which the question had been asked :

> O, reason not the need : our basest beggars
> Are in the poorest thing superfluous :
> Allow not nature more than nature needs,
> Man's life 's as cheap as beast's : thou art a lady ;
> If only to go warm were gorgeous,
> Why, nature needs not what thou gorgeous wear'st,
> Which scarcely keeps thee warm. But, for true need,—

He breaks off at finding himself actually pleading : and the
blinding tears come as he recognises that the kingly passion
in which he had found support at every cross has now
deserted him in his extremity. He appeals to heaven against
the injustice.

> You heavens, give me that patience, patience I need !
> You see me here, you gods, a poor old man,
> As full of grief as age ; wretched in both !
> If it be you that stir these daughters' hearts
> Against their father, fool me not so much

CHAP. X.

> To bear it tamely; touch me with noble anger,
> And let not women's weapons, water-drops,
> Stain my man's cheeks!

The prayer is answered; the passion returns in full flood, and at last brings Lear face to face with the madness which has threatened from a distance.

> No, you unnatural hags,
> I will have such revenges on you both,
> That all the world shall—I will do such things,—
> What they are, yet I know not; but they shall be
> The terrors of the earth. You think I'll weep;
> No, I'll not weep:
> I have full cause of weeping; but this heart
> Shall break into a hundred thousand flaws,
> Or ere I'll weep. O fool, I SHALL go mad!

ii. iv. 290.
The storm marks off the Centre-piece of the play

As Lear with these words rushes out into the night, we hear the first sound of the storm—the storm which here, as in *Julius Cæsar*, will be recognised as the dramatic background to the tempest of human emotions; it is the signal that we have now entered upon the mysterious Centrepiece of the play, in which the gathering passions of the whole drama are to be allowed to vent themselves without check or bound. And it is no ordinary storm: it is a night of bleak winds sorely ruffling, of cataracts and hurricanoes, of curled waters swelling above the main, of thought-executing fires and oak-cleaving thunderbolts; a night

iii. i. 12,
&c

> wherein the cub-drawn bear would couch,
> The lion and the belly-pinched wolf
> Keep their fur dry.

And all of it is needed to harmonise with the whirlwind of human passions which finds relief only in outscorning its fury. The purpose of the storm is not confined to this of marking the emotional climax: it is one of the agencies which assist in carrying it to its height. Experts in mental disease have noted amongst the causes which convert mere mental excitement into actual madness two leading ones, external physical shocks and imitation. Shakespeare has made use of both in

the central scenes of this play. For the first, Lear is exposed midwithout shelter to the pelting of the pitiless storm, and he
waxes wilder with its wildness. Again when all this is at its
height he is suddenly brought into contact with a half-naked
Tom o'Bedlam. This gives the final shock. So far he had
not gone beyond ungovernable rage; he had not lost self-
consciousness, and could say, 'My wits begin to turn';
but the sight of Edgar completely unhinges his mind, and
hallucinations set in; a moment after he has seen him the
spirit of imitation begins to work, and Lear commences to
strip off his clothes. Thus perfect is the regular arch of
effect which is connected with Lear's madness. We have its
gradual rise in the waves of hysterical passion which ebbed
after they had flowed, until, at the point separating the
Centrepiece from the rest of the play, Lear's 'O fool I *shall*
go mad' seems to mark a change from which he never goes
back. Through these central scenes exposure to the storm is
fanning his passion more and more irretrievably into madness; at the exact centre of all, imitation of Edgar comes to
make the insanity acute. After the Centrepiece Lear disappears for a time, and when we next see him agitation has
declined into what is more pathetic: the acute mania has
given place to the pitiful spectacle of a shattered intellect;
there is no longer sharp suffering, but the whole mind is
wrecked, gleams of coherence coming at intervals to mark
what a fall there has been; the strain upon our emotions
sinks into the calm of hopelessness.

CHAP. X
iii. i. 3;
iii. ii, &c
iii.iv,from
39.

iii iv. 66.

iii. ii 39.
*Decline
after the
Centrepiece
from vio-
lent mad-
ness to
shattered
intellect.*
iv. vi. 81.
compare
iv. vi. 178;
v. iii 314.

He hates him much
> That would upon the rack of this tough world
> Stretch him out longer.

But who is this madman with whom Lear meets at the
turning-point of the play? It is Edgar, the victim of the
underplot, whose life has been sought by his brother and
father until he can find no way of saving himself but the
disguise of feigned madness. This feigned madness of

*The pas-
sions of the
underplot
gather to a
common
Climax in
the madness
of Edgar.*

CHAP. X. Edgar, as it appears in the central scenes, serves as emotional climax to the underplot, just as the madness of Lear is the emotional climax of the main plot. Edgar's madness is obviously the climax to the tragedy of his own sufferings, but it is also a central point to the movement of the other two tragedies which with that of Edgar make up the underplot. One of these is the nemesis upon Gloucester, and this, we have seen, is double, that he receives good from the son he has wronged and evil from the son he has favoured. The

iii. iv. 170. turning-point of such a nemesis is reached in the Hovel Scene, where Gloucester says :

> I'll tell thee, friend,
> I am almost mad myself: I had a son,
> Now outlaw'd from my blood; he sought my life,
> But lately, very late: I loved him, friend:
> No father his son dearer: truth to tell thee,
> This grief hath crazed my wits !

He says this in the presence of the very Edgar, disguised under the form of the wretched idiot he hardly marks. Edgar now learns how his father has been deceived; in his heart he is re-united to him, and from this point of re-union springs the devotion he lavishes upon his father in the

compare affliction that presently falls upon him. On the other hand,
iii. iii. 15. that which brings Gloucester to this Hovel Scene, the attempt
iii. iii. 22; to save the King, is betrayed by Edmund, who becomes
iii. vii. thereby the cause of the vengeance which puts out his father's eyes. Thus from this meeting of the mad Edgar with the mad Lear there springs at once the final stroke in the misery Gloucester suffers from the son he has favoured, and the beginning of the forgiving love he is to experience from the son he has wronged: that meeting then is certainly the central climax to the double nemesis which makes up the Gloucester action. The remaining tragedy of the underplot embraces the series of incidents by the combination of which the success of Edmund's intrigue becomes gradually converted into the nemesis which punishes it. Now the

squalid wretchedness of a Bedlamite, together with the CHAP. X.
painful strain of supporting the assumed character amidst
the conflicting emotions which the unexpected meeting of
the Hovel Scene has aroused, represent the highest point to
which the misery resulting from the intrigue can rise. At
the same time the use Edgar makes of this madness after
hearing Gloucester's confession is to fasten himself in attend- iv. i, &c.
ance upon his afflicted father, and proves in the sequel the
means by which he is brought to be the instrument of the
vengeance that overtakes Edmund. The central climax of
a tragedy like this of intrigue and nemesis cannot be more
clearly marked than in the incident in which are combined
the summit of the injury and the foundation of the retribution. Thus all three tragedies which together make up
the resultant of the intrigue constituting the underplot reach
their climax of agitation in the scene in which Lear and
Edgar meet.

It appears, then, that the Centrepiece of the play is occupied *The Centre-*
with the contact of two madnesses, the madness of Lear and *piece a*
duet, or
the madness of Edgar; that of Lear gathering up into a *by the ad-*
climax trains of passion from all the three tragedies of the *dition of*
the Fool,
main plot, and that of Edgar holding a similar position to the *a trio of*
three tragedies of the underplot. Further, these madnesses *madness*
do not merely go on side by side; as they meet they
mutually affect one another, and throw up each other's
intensity. By the mere sight of the Bedlamite, Lear, already
tottering upon the verge of insanity, is driven really and
incurably mad; while in the case of Edgar, the meeting with
Lear, and through Lear with Gloucester, converts the burden
of feigning idiocy from a cruel stroke of unjust fate into a
hardship voluntarily undergone for the sake of ministering to
a father now forgiven and pitied. And so far as the general
effect of the play is concerned this central Climax presents a
terrible *duet of madness,* the wild ravings and mutual inter-
workings of two distinct strains of insanity, each answering

CHAP. X. and outbidding the other. The distinctness is the greater as the two are different in kind. In Lear we have the madness of passion, exaggeration of ordinary emotions; Edgar's is the madness of idiocy, as idiocy was in early ages when the cruel neglect of society added physical hardship to mental affliction. In Edgar's frenzy we trace rapid irrelevance with gleams of unexpected relevance, just sufficient to partly answer a question and go off again into wandering; a sense of ill-treatment and of being an outcast; remorse and thoughts as to close connection of sin and retribution; visions of fiends as in bodily presence; cold, hunger: these alternating with mere gibberish, and all perhaps within the compass of a few lines.

iii. iv. 51. Who gives anything to poor Tom? whom the foul fiend hath led through fire and through flame, and through ford and whirlipool, o'er bog and quagmire; that hath laid knives under his pillow, and halters in his pew; set ratsbane by his porridge; made him proud of heart, to ride on a bay trotting-horse over four-inched bridges, to course his own shadow for a traitor. Bless thy five wits! Tom's a-cold,—O, do de, do de, do de. Bless thee from whirlwinds, star-blasting, and taking! Do poor Tom some charity, whom the foul fiend vexes: there could I have him now,—and there,—and there again, and there.

But this is not all. When examined more closely this Centrepiece exhibits not a duet but <u>a *trio of madness*</u>; with <u>the other two there mingles a third form of what may be</u> <u>called madness, the professional madness of the court fool.</u>

Institution of the court fool. This court fool or jester is an institution of considerable interest. It seems to rest upon three mediæval and ancient notions. The first is the barbarism of enjoying personal defects, illustrated in the large number of Roman names derived from bodily infirmities, Varus the bandy-legged, Balbus the stammerer, and the like; this led our ancestors to find fun in the incoherence of natural idiocy, and finally made the imitation of it a profession. A second notion underlying the institution of a jester is the connection to the ancient mind between madness and inspiration; the same

Greek word *entheos* stands for both, and to this day the idiot of a Scotch village is believed in some way to see further than sane folk. A third idea to be kept in mind is the mediæval conception of wit. With us wit is weighed by its intrinsic worth; the old idea, appearing repeatedly in Shakespeare's scenes, was that wit was a mental game, a sort of battledore and shuttlecock, in which the jokes themselves might be indifferent since the point of the game lay in keeping it up as smartly and as long as possible. The fool, whose title and motley dress suggested the absence of ordinary sense or propriety, combines in his office all three notions : from the last he was bound to keep up the fire of badinage, even though it were with witless nonsense ; from the second he was expected at times to give utterance to deep truths; and in virtue of the first he had license to make hard · hits under protection of the ' folly ' which all were supposed to enjoy.

> He that hath a fool doth very wisely hit,
> Doth very foolishly, although he smart,
> Not to seem senseless of the bob.

The institution, if it has died out as a personal office attached *The institution adapted to kings or nobles, has perhaps been preserved by the nation *tution as a whole in a form analogous to other modern institutions: *modern the all-embracing newspaper has absorbed this element of *times in Punch.* life, and Mr. Punch is the national jester. His figure and face are an improvement on the old motley habit; his fixed number of pages have to be filled, if not always with wit, yet with passable padding: no one dare other than enjoy the compliment of his notice, under penalty of showing that ' the cap has fitted ' ; and certainly Mr. Punch finds ways of conveying to statesmen criticisms to which the proprieties of parliament would be impervious. The institution of the court fool is eagerly utilised by Shakespeare, and is the source of some of his finest effects : he treats it as a sort of chronic Comedy, the function of which may be described as that of translating deep truths of human nature into the language of laughter.

In applying, then, this general view of the court fool to the present case we must avoid two opposite errors. We must not pass over all his utterances as unmeaning folly, nor, on the other hand, must we insist upon seeing a meaning in everything that he says: what truth he speaks must be expected to make its appearance amidst a cloud of nonsense. *The function of the Fool in Lear is to keep before us the original problem:* Making this proviso we may lay down that the function of the Fool in *King Lear* is to keep vividly before the minds of the audience (as well as of his master) the idea at the root of the main plot—that unstable moral equilibrium, that unnatural distribution of power which Lear has set up, and of which the whole tragedy is the rebound. In the first scene *i. iv.* in which he appears before us he is, amid all his nonsense, harping upon the idea that Lear has committed the folly of trusting to the gratitude of the ungrateful, and is reaping the inevitable consequences. As he enters he hands his coxcomb, the symbol of folly, to the King, and to Kent for taking the King's part. His first jingling song,

> Have more than thou showest,
> Speak less than thou knowest,
> Lend less than thou owest, &c.,

is an expansion of the maxim, Trust nobody. And however irrelevant he becomes, he can in a moment get back to this root idea. They tell him his song is nothing:

Fool. Then 'tis like the breath of an unfee'd lawyer; you gave me nothing for 't. Can you make no use of nothing, nuncle?
Lear. Why, no, boy; nothing can be made out of nothing.
Fool [to Kent]. Prithee, tell him, so much the rent of his land comes to : he will not believe a fool.

i. i. 92. 'Nothing will come of nothing' had been the words Lear had used to Cordelia; now he is bidden to see how they have become the exact description of his own fortune. No wonder Lear exclaims, ' A bitter fool!'

Fool. Dost thou know the difference, my boy, between a bitter fool and a sweet one?

Lear. No, lad; teach me

Fool.
              That lord that counsell'd thee
                  To give away thy land,
              Come place him here by me,
                  Do thou for him stand:
              The sweet and bitter fool
                  Will presently appear;
              The one in motley here.
              The other found out there

Lear. Dost thou call me fool, boy?

Fool. All thy other titles thou hast given away, that thou wast born with.

Again and again he turns to other topics and comes suddenly back to the main thought.

Fool. Prithee, nuncle, keep a schoolmaster that can teach thy fool i. iv 195. to lie: I would fain learn to lie

Lear. An you lie, sirrah, we'll have you whipped.

Fool. I marvel what kin thou and thy daughters are: they'll have me whipped for speaking true, thou'lt have me whipped for lying; and sometimes I am whipped for holding my peace. I had rather be any kind o' thing than a fool: and yet I would not be thee, nuncle; thou hast pared thy wit o' both sides, and left nothing i' the middle: here comes one o' the parings.

It is Goneril who enters, and who proceeds to state her case i. iv. 207. in the tone of injury, detailing how the order of her household state has been outraged, but ignoring the source from which she has received the power to keep up state at all: what she has omitted the Fool supplies in parable, as if continuing her sentence—

              For, you trow, nuncle,
        The hedge-sparrow fed the cuckoo so long,
        That it's had it head bit off by it young,

and then instantly involves himself in a cloud of irrelevance,

        So, out went the candle, and we were left darkling.

In the scene which follows, the Fool is performing a variation i. v. on the same theme: the sudden removal from one sister

CHAP. X. to the other is no real escape from the original foolish
situation.

i. v. 8

> *Fool.* If a man's brains were in 's heels, were 't not in danger of
> kibes?
> *Lear.* Ay, boy,
> *Fool.* Then, I prithee, be merry; thy wit shall ne'er go slip-shod.

To say that Lear is in no danger of suffering from brains in
his heels is another way of saying that his flight is folly. He
goes on to insist that the other daughter will treat her father
'kindly,' that 'she 's as like this as a crab 's like an apple.'
His laying down that the reason why the nose is in the
middle of the face is to keep the eyes on either side of the
nose, and that the reason why the seven stars are no more
than seven is 'a pretty reason—because they are not eight,'
suggests (if it be not pressing it too far) that we must not
look for depth where there is only shallowness—the mistake
Lear has made in trusting to the gratitude of his daughters.
And the general thought of Lear's original folly he brings
out, true to the fool's office, from the most unlikely be-
ginnings.

i. v. 26.

> *Fool.* Canst tell how an oyster makes his shell?
> *Lear.* No.

'Nor I neither,' answers the Fool, with a clown's impudence;
'but,' he adds, 'I can tell why a snail has a house.'

> *Lear.* Why?
> *Fool.* Why, to put his head in; not to give it away to his daughters.

ii. iv. 1–
128.

All through the scene in front of the stocks the Fool is harping on the folly of expecting gratitude from such as Goneril
and Regan. It is fathers who bear bags that see their children
kind; the wise man lets go his hold on a great wheel running
down hill, but lets himself be drawn after by the great wheel
that goes up the hill; he himself, the Fool hints, is a fool for
staying with Lear; to cry out at Goneril and Regan's behaviour is as unreasonable as for the cook to be impatient
with the eels for wriggling; to have trusted the two

daughters with power at all .was like the folly of the man that, CHAP. X.
'in pure kindness to his horse, buttered his hay.'

The one idea, then, stationary amidst all the Fool's gyrations
of folly is the idea of Lear's original sin of passion, from the
consequences of which he can never escape ; only the idea is *but in an*
put, not rationally, but translated into an emotional form *emotional form as*
which makes it fit to mingle with the agitation of the central *adapted to*
scenes. The emotional form consists partly in the irrelevance *the agita-*
amid which the idea is brought out, producing continual *Centre-*
shocks of surprise. But more than this an emotional form is *piece.*
given to the utterances of the Fool by his very position with
reference to Lear. There is a pathos that mingles with his iii. 1 16 ;
humour, where the Fool, a tender and delicate youth, is found iii. ii. 10, 25, 68 ; iii.
the only attendant who clings to Lear amid the rigour of the iv 80, 150
storm, labouring with visibly decreasing vigour to out-jest
his master's heart-struck injuries, and to keep up holiday
abandon amidst surrounding realities. Throughout he is i. iv. 107 ;
Lear's best friend, and epithets of endearment are continually iii. ii 68, 72, &c
passing between them : he has been Cordelia's friend (as
Touchstone was the friend of Rosalind), and pined for Cor- i. iv. 79.
delia after her banishment. Nevertheless he is the only one
who can deliver hard thrusts at Lear, and bring home to him,
under protection of his double relation to wisdom and folly,
Lear's original error and sin. So faithful and so severe, the
Fool becomes an outward conscience to his master : he keeps
before Lear the unnatural act from which the whole tragedy
springs, but he converts the thought of it into the emotion of
self-reproach.

Our total result then is this. The intricate drama of *King* *Summary.*
Lear has a general movement which centres the passion of
the play in a single Climax. Throughout a Centrepiece of a
few scenes, against a background of storm and tempest is
thrown up a tempest of human passion—a madness trio, or
mutual play of three sorts of madness, the real madness of
passion in Lear, the feigned madness of idiocy in Edgar, and

CHAP. X. the professional madness of the court fool.   When the elements of this madness trio are analysed, the first is found to gather up into itself the passion of the three tragedies which form the main plot; the second is a similar climax to the passion of the three tragedies which make up the underplot; the third is an expression, in the form of passion, of the original problem out of which the whole action has sprung. Thus intricacy of plot has been found not inconsistent with simplicity of movement, and from the various parts of the drama the complex trains of passion have been brought to a focus in the centre.

PART SECOND.

SURVEY OF

DRAMATIC CRITICISM

AS AN INDUCTIVE SCIENCE.

XI.

TOPICS OF DRAMATIC CRITICISM.

CHAP. XI.

*Purpose·
'o survey
Dramatic
Criticism
as an in-
ductive
science.*

IN the Introduction to this book I pleaded that a regular inductive science of literary criticism was a possibility. In the preceding ten chapters I have endeavoured to exhibit such a regular method at work on the dramatic analysis of leading points in Shakespeare's plays. The design of the whole work will not be complete without an attempt to present our results in complete form, in fact to map out a Science of Dramatic Art. I hope this may not seem too pretentious an undertaking in the case of a science yet in its infancy; while it may be useful at all events to the young student to have suggested to him a methodical treatment with which he may exercise himself on the literature he studies. Moreover the reproach against literary criticism is, not that there has not been plenty of inductive work done in this department, but that the assertion of its inductive character has been lacking; and I believe a critic does good service by throwing his results into a formal shape, however imperfectly he may be able to accomplish his task. It will be understood that the survey of Dramatic Science is here attempted only in the merest outline: it is a glimpse, not a view, of a new science that is proposed. Not even a survey would be possible within the limits of a few short chapters except by confining the matter introduced to that previously laid before the reader in a different form. The leading features of Dramatic Art have already been explained in the application of them to particular plays: they are now included in a single view,

CHAP. XI. so arranged that their mutual connection may be seen to be building up this singleness of view. Such a survey, like a microscopic lens of low power, must sacrifice detail to secure a wider field. Its compensating gain will consist in what it can contribute to the orderly product of methodised enquiry which is the essence of science, and the interest in which becomes associated with the interest of curiosity when the method has been applied in a region not usually acknowledging its reign.

Definition of Dramatic Criticism·   The starting-point in the exposition of any science is naturally its definition. But this first step is sufficient to divide inductive criticism from the treatment of literature mostly in vogue. I have already protested against the criticism which starts with the assumption of some 'object' or 'fundamental purpose' in the Drama from which to deduce binding canons. Such an all-embracing definition, if it is possible at all, will come as the final, not the first, step of investigation. Inductive criticism, on the contrary, will seek

as to its field and its method.   its point of departure from outside. On the one hand it will consider the relation of the matter which it proposes to treat to other matter which is the subject of scientific enquiry; on the other hand it will fix the nature of the treatment it proposes to apply by a reference to scientific method in general. That is to say, its definition will be based upon differentiation of matter and development in method.

Stages of development in inductive method.   To begin with the latter. There are three well-marked stages in the development of sciences. The first consists in the mere observation of the subject-matter. The second is distinguished by arrangement of observations, by analysis and classification. The third stage reaches systematisation—the wider arrangement which satisfies our sense of explanation, that curiosity as to causes which is the instinct specially developed by scientific enquiry. Astronomy remained for long ages in the first stage, while it was occupied with the observation of the heavenly bodies and the naming of the constellations. It would pass into the second stage with Chap. XI. division of labour and the study of solar, lunar, planetary, and cometary phenomena separately. But by such discoveries as that of the laws of motion, or of gravitation, the great mass of astronomical knowledge was bound together in a system which at the same time satisfied the sense of causation, and astronomy was fully developed as an inductive science. Or to take a more modern instance: comparative philology has attained completeness in our own day. Philology was in its first stage at the Renaissance, when 'learning' meant the mere accumulation of detailed knowledge connected with the Classical languages; Grimm's Law may illustrate the second stage, a classification comprehensive but purely empiric; the principle of phonetic decay with its allied recuperative processes has struck a unity through the laws of philology which stamps it as a full-grown science. Applying this to our *Dramatic* present subject, I do not pretend that Literary Criticism has *Criticism in the in-* reached the third of these three stages: but materials are *termediate* ready for giving it a secure place in the second stage. In time, no doubt, literary science must be able to explain the modus operandi of literary production, and show how different classes of writing come to produce their different effects. But at present such explanation belongs mostly to the region of speculation; and before the science of criticism is ripe for this final stage much work has to be done in the way of methodising observation as to literary matter and form.

Dramatic Criticism, then, is still in the stage of provisional arrangement. Its exact position is expressed by the technical *or 'topical'* term 'topical.' Where accumulation of observations is great *stage.* enough to necessitate methodical arrangement, yet progress is insufficient to suggest final bases of arrangement which will crystallise the whole into a system, science takes refuge in 'topics.' These have been aptly described as intellectual pigeon-holes—convenient headings under which materials may be digested, with strict adherence to method, yet only as

sentation one of the departments of the science; but we shall be only following the law of differentiation if we separate the two. This is especially appropriate in the case of the Shakespearean Drama. The Puritan Revolution, which has played such a part in its history, was in effect an attack rather on the Theatre than on the Drama itself. No doubt when the movement became violent the two were not discriminated, and the Drama was made a 'vanity' as well as the Stage. Still the one interest was never so thoroughly dropped by the nation and was more readily taken up again than the other; so that from the point of view of the Stage our continuity with the Elizabethan age has been severed, from the point of view of the literary Drama it has not. The Shakespearean Drama has made a field for itself as a branch of literature quite apart from the Stage; and, however we may regret the severance and look forward to a completer appreciation of Shakespeare, yet it can hardly be doubted that at the present moment as earnest and comprehensive an interest in our great dramatist is to be found in the study as in the theatre.

Dramatic Criticism, then, is to be separated, on the one side, from the wider Literary Criticism which must include a review of language, ethics, philosophy, and general art; and, on the other hand, from the companion art of Stage-Representation. But here caution is required; for all these are so closely and so organically connected with the Drama that *Topics* there cannot but exist a mutual reaction. Thus we have *common to* already had to treat of topics which belong to the Drama *Drama* only as a part of literature and art in general. In the first *general.* chapter we had occasion to notice how even the raw material out of which the Shakespearean Drama is constructed itself forms another species in literature. When we proceeded to watch the process of working up this Story into dramatic form we were led on to what was common ground between Drama and the other arts. In such process we saw illus-

trated the 'hedging,' or double process which leaves monstrosity to produce its full impression and yet provides by
special means against any natural reaction; the reduction
of improbabilities, by which difficulties in the subject-matter
are evaded or met; the utilisation of mechanical details to
assist more important effects; the multiplication and interweaving of different interests by which each is made to assist
the rest. Such points of Mechanical Construction, together
with the general principles of balance and symmetry, are not
special to any one branch of art: in all alike the artist will
contrive not wholly to conceal his processes, but by occasional glimpses will add to higher effects the satisfaction of
our sense of neat workmanship.

Similarly, it may be convenient to make Literary Drama *Drama and*
and Stage-Representation separate branches of enquiry: it is *its Repre-*
sentation
totally inadmissible and highly misleading to divorce the two *separate in*
in idea. The literary play must be throughout read *relatively* *exposition,*
not in idea.
to its representation. In actual practice the separation of the
two has produced the greatest obstacles in the way of sound
appreciation. Amongst ordinary readers of Shakespeare
Character-Interest, which is largely independent of performance, has swallowed up all other interests; and most of the
effects which depend upon the connection and relative force
of incidents, and on the compression of the details into a
given space, have been completely lost. Shakespeare is
popularly regarded as supreme in the painting of human
nature, but careless in the construction of Plot: and, worst
of all, Plot itself, which it has been the mission of the
English Drama to elevate into the position of the most
intellectual of all elements in literary effect, has become
degraded in conception to the level of a mere juggler's
mystery. It must then be laid down distinctly at the outset
of the present enquiry that the Drama is to be considered
throughout relatively to its acting. Much of dramatic effect
that is special to Stage-Representation will be here ignored:

CHAP. XI. the whole mechanism of elocution, effects of light, colour and
costume, the greater portion of what constitutes *mise-en-scène.*
But in dealing with any play the fullest scope is assumed
for ideal acting. The interpretation of a character must
include what an actor can put into it; in dealing with
effects regard must be had to surroundings which a reader
might easily overlook, but which would be present to the eye
of a spectator; and no conception of the movement of a
drama will be adequate which has not appreciated the rapid
sequence of incidents that crowds the crisis of a life-time or
a national revolution into two or three hours of actual time.
The relation of Drama to its acting will be exactly similar to
that of music to its performance, the two being perfectly
separable in their exposition, but never disunited in idea.

Funda-mental di-vision of Dramatic Criticism into Hu-man Inter-est and Ac-tion.   Dramatic Art, then, as thus defined, is to be the field of
our enquiry, and its method is to be the discovery and
arrangement of topics. For a fundamental basis of such
analysis we shall naturally look to the other arts. Now all
the arts agree in being the union of two elements, abstract
and concrete. Music takes sensuous sounds, and adds a
purely abstract element by disposing these sounds in har-
monies and melodies; architecture applies abstract design
to a concrete medium of stone and wood; painting gives
us objects of real life arranged in abstract groupings: in
dancing we have moving figures confined in artistic bonds of
rhythm; sculpture traces in still figures ideas of shape and
attitude. So Drama has its two elements of Human Interest
and Action: on the one hand life *presented in action*—so the
word 'Drama' may be translated; on the other hand the
action, itself, that is, the concurrence of all that is presented
in an abstract unity of design. The two fundamental
divisions of dramatic interest, and consequently the two fundamental divisions of Dramatic Criticism, will thus be
Human Interest and Action. But each of these has its
different sides, the distinction of which is essential before we

can arrive at an arrangement of topics that will be of practical CHAP. XI.
value in the methodisation of criticism. The interest of the *Twofold*
life presented is twofold. There is our interest in the *division of*
separate personages who enter into it, as so many varieties *Human*
of the *genus homo* : this is Interest of *Character.* There is *Interest.*
again our interest in the experience these personages are
made to undergo, their conduct and fate : technically, Interest
of *Passion.*

$$\text{Human Interest} \begin{cases} \text{Character.} \\ \text{Passion.} \end{cases}$$

It is the same with the other fundamental element of art, the *Threefold*
working together of all the details so as to leave an impres- *division of*
sion of unity : while in practice the sense of this unity, say *Action.*
in a piece of music or a play, is one of the simplest of
instincts, yet upon analysis it is seen to imply three separate
mental impressions. The mind, it implies, must be conscious
of a unity. It must also be conscious of a complexity of
details without which the unity could not be perceptible.
But the mere perception of unity and of complexity would
give no art-pleasure unless the unity were seen to be *developed*
out of the complexity, and this brings in a third idea of progress and gradual *Movement.*

$$\text{Action} \begin{cases} \text{Unity.} \\ \text{Complexity.} \\ \text{Development or Movement.} \end{cases}$$

Now if we apply the threefold idea involved in Action to the *Applica-*
twofold idea involved in Human Interest we shall get the *tion of the*
natural divisions of dramatic analysis. One element of *threefold*
Human Interest was Character : looking at this in the three- *division of*
fold aspect which is given to it when it is connected with *Action to*
Action we shall have to notice the interest of single charac- *the twofold*
ters, or *Character-Interpretation,* the more complex interest *division of*
of *Character-Contrast,* and in the third place *Character-De-* *Human*
velopment. Applying a similar treatment to the other side of *Interest.*
Human Interest, Passion, we shall review single elements of

CHAP. XI. Passion, that is to say, *Incidents and Effects*; the mixture of various passions to express which the term *Passion-Tones* will be used ; and again *Passion-Movement.* But Action has an interest of its own, considered in the abstract and as separate from Human Interest. This is *Plot*; and it will lend itself to the same triple treatment, falling into the natural divisions of *Single Action, Complex Action,* and that development of Plot which constitutes dramatic *Movement* in the most important sense. At this point it is possible only to name these leading topics of Dramatic Criticism : to explain each, and to trace them further into their lesser ramifications will be the work of the remaining three chapters.

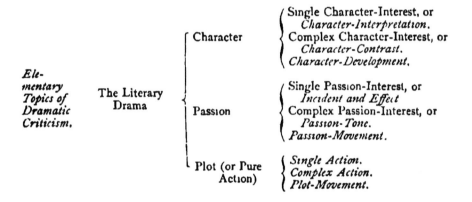

Ele-mentary Topics of Dramatic Criticism. — The Literary Drama

Character
- Single Character-Interest, or *Character-Interpretation.*
- Complex Character-Interest, or *Character-Contrast.*
- *Character-Development.*

Passion
- Single Passion-Interest, or *Incident and Effect*
- Complex Passion-Interest, or *Passion-Tone.*
- *Passion-Movement.*

Plot (or Pure Action)
- *Single Action.*
- *Complex Action.*
- *Plot-Movement.*

XII.

INTEREST OF CHARACTER.

OF the main divisions of dramatic interest Character stands first for consideration: and we are to view it under the three aspects of unity, complexity, and movement. The application of the idea unity to the idea character suggests at once our interest in single personages. This interest becomes more defined when we take into account the medium through which the personages are presented to us: characters in Drama are not brought out by abstract discussion or description, but are presented to us concretely, self-pourtrayed by their own actions without the assistance of comments from the author.

Accordingly, the leading interest of character is *Interpretation*, the mental process of turning from the concrete to the abstract: from the most diverse details of conduct and impression Interpretation extracts a unity of conception which we call a character. Interpretation when scientifically handled must be, we have seen, of the nature of an hypothesis, the value of which depends upon the degree in which it explains whatever details have any bearing upon the character. Such an hypothesis may be a simple idea: and we have seen at length how the whole portraiture of Richard precipitates into the notion of Ideal Villainy, ideal on the subjective side in an artist who follows crime for its own sake, and on the objective side in a success that works by fascination. But the student must beware of the temptation to grasp at epigrammatic labels as

CHAP. XII. sufficient solutions of character; in the great majority of
cases Interpretation can become complete only by recognising and harmonising various and even conflicting elements.

Canons of   Incidentally we have noticed some of the principles govern-
Interpre-
tation.   ing careful Interpretation.   One of these principles is that it
It must be must take into consideration all that is presented of a per-
exhaustive. sonage.   It is unscientific on the face of it to say (as is
repeatedly said) that Shakespeare is ' inconsistent' in ascrib-
ing deep musical sympathies to .so thin a character as
Lorenzo.   Such allegation of inconsistency means that the
process of Interpretation is unfinished ; it can be paralleled
only by the astronomer who should complain of eclipses as
' inconsistent' with his view of the moon's movements.   In
the particular case we found no difficulty in harmonising the
apparent conflict : the details of Lorenzo's portraiture fit
in well with the not uncommon type of nature that is so
deeply touched by art sensibilities as to have a languid interest in life outside art.   Again : Interpretation must look
It must take for *indirect* evidence of character, such as the impression a
in indirect
evidence ; personage seems to have made on other personages in the
story, or the effect of action outside the field of view.   It is
impatient induction to pronounce Bassanio unworthy of
Portia merely from comparison of the parts played by the
two in the drama itself.   It happens from the nature of the
story that the incidents actually represented in the drama
are such as always display Bassanio in an exceptional and
dependent position ; but we have an opportunity of getting
to the other side of our hero's character by observing the
attitude held to him by others in the play, an attitude
founded not on the incidents of the drama alone, but upon
the sum total of his life and behaviour in the Venetian
world.   This gives a very different impression ; and when we
take into consideration the force with which his personality
sways all who approach him, from the strong Antonio and

the intellectual Lorenzo to giddy Gratiano and the rough common sense of Launcelot, then the character comes out in its proper scale. As a third principle, it is perhaps too obvious to be worth formulating that Interpretation must *and the de-* allow for the degree to which the character is displayed by *gree to which the* the action : that Brutus's frigid eloquence at the funeral of *character is* Cæsar means not coldness of feeling but stoicism of public *displayed.* demeanour. It is a less obvious principle that the very *Interpre-* details which are to be unified into a conception of cha- *tation re-* racter may have a different complexion given to them when *acting on* they are looked at in the light of the whole. It has been *the details.* noticed how Richard seems to manifest in some scenes a slovenliness of intrigue that might be a stumbling-block to the general impression of his character. But when in our view of him as a whole we see what a large part is played by the invincibility that is stamped on his very demeanour, it becomes clear how this slovenliness can be interpreted by the analyst, and represented by the actor, not as a defect of power, but as a trick of bearing which measures his own sense of his irresistibility. Principles like these flow naturally from the fundamental idea of character and its unity. Their practical use however will be mainly that of tests for suggested interpretations : to the actual reading of character in Drama, as in real life, the safest guide is sympathetic insight.

The second element underlying all dramatic effect was *Complexity* complexity ; when complexity is applied to Character we *applied to* get Character-Contrast. In its lowest degree this appears in *Character.* the form of *Character-Foils* : by the side of some prominent *Character-* character is placed another of less force and interest but cast *Foils.* in the same mould, or perhaps moulded by the influence of its principal, just as by the side of a lofty mountain are often to be seen smaller hills of the same formation. Thus beside Portia is placed Nerissa, beside Bassanio Gratiano, beside Shylock Tubal ; Richard's villainy stands out by

CHAP. XII. comparison with Buckingham, Hastings, Tyrrel, Catesby, any one of whom would have given blackness enough to an ordinary drama. It is quite possible that minute examination may find differences between such companion figures: but the general effect of the combination is that the lesser serves as foil to throw up the scale on which the other is framed. The more pronounced effects of Character-Contrast depend upon differences of kind as distinguished from differences of degree. In this form it is clear how *Cha-*

Character-Contrast. *racter-Contrast* is only an extension of Character-Interpretation: it implies that some single conception explains, that is, gives unity to, the actions of more than one person. A whole chapter has been devoted to bringing out such contrast in the case of Lord and Lady Macbeth: to accept these as types of the practical and inner life, cast in such an age and involved in such an undertaking, furnishes a conception sufficient to make clear and intelligible all that the

Duplica-tion. two say and do in the scenes of the drama. Character-Contrast is especially common amongst the minor effects in a Shakespearean drama. In the case of personages demanded by the necessities of the story rather than introduced for their own sake Shakespeare has a tendency to double the number of such personages for the sake of getting effects of contrast. We have two unsuccessful suitors in *The Merchant of Venice* bringing out, the one the unconscious pride of royal birth, the other the pride of intense self-consciousness; two wicked daughters of Lear, Goneril with no shading in her harshness, Regan who is in reality a degree more calculating in her cruelty than her sister, but conceals it under a charm of manner, 'eyes that comfort and not burn.' Of

iii. i. the two princes in *Richard III* the one has a gravity beyond his years, while York overflows with not ungraceful pertness. Especially interesting are the two murderers in that play. The first is a dull, 'strong-framed' man, without

i. iv, from 84. any better nature. The second has had culture, and been

accustomed to reflect; his better nature has been vanquished CHAP. XII.
by love of greed, and now asserts itself to prevent his
sinning with equanimity. It is the second murderer whose
conscience is set in activity by the word 'judgment'; and he 110.
discourses on conscience, deeply, yet not without humour, as 124-157.
he recognises the power of the expected reward over the oft-
vanquished compunctions. He catches, as a thoughtful
man, the irony of the duke's cry for wine when they are 167.
about to drown him in the butt of malmsey. Again, instead
of hurrying to the deed while Clarence is waking he cannot 165.
resist the temptation to argue with him, and so, as a man
open to argument, he feels the force of Clarence's unex- 263.
pected suggestion:

He that set you on
To do this deed will hate you for the deed.

Thus he exhibits the weakness of all thinking men in a
moment of action, the capacity to see two sides of a
question; and, trying at the critical moment to alter his
course, he ends by losing the reward of crime without 284
escaping the guilt.

Character-Contrast is carried forward into *Character-* *Character-*
Grouping when the field is still further enlarged, and a single *Grouping.*
conception is found to give unity to more than two per-
sonages of a drama. A chapter has been devoted to showing how the same antithesis of outer and inner life which
made the conception of Macbeth and his wife intelligible
would serve, when adapted to the widely different world of
Roman political life, to explain the characters of the leading
conspirators in *Julius Cæsar*, of their victim and of his
avenger: while, over and above the satisfaction of Interpretation, the Grouping of these four figures, so colossal and so
impressive, round a single idea is an interest in itself. The *Dramatic*
effect is carried a stage further still when some single phase *Colouring.*
of human interest tends, in a greater or less degree, to give
a common feature to all the personages of a play; the

R

whole dramatic field is *coloured* by some idea, though of course the interpretative significance of such an idea is weakened in proportion to the area over which it is distributed. The five plays to which our attention is confined do not afford the best examples of Dramatic Colouring. It is a point, however, of common remark how the play of *Macbeth* is coloured by the superstition and violence of the Dark Ages. The world of this drama seems given over to powers of darkness who can read, if not mould, destiny; witchcraft appears as an instrument of crime and ghostly agency of punishment. We have rebellion without any suggestion of cause to ennoble it, terminated by executions without the pomp of justice; we have a long reign of terror in which massacre is a measure of daily administration and murder is a profession. With all this there is a total absence of relief in any picture of settled life: there is no rallying-point for order and purity. The very agent of retribution gets the impulse to his task in a reaction from a shock of bereavement that has come down upon him as a natural punishment for an act of indecisive folly.

compare
iv. iii. 26;
iv. ii. 1–22.

There are, then, three different effects that arise when complexity enters into Character-Interest. The complexity is one never separable from the unity which binds it together: in the first effect the diversity is stronger than the unity, and the whole manifests itself as Character-Contrast; in Character-Grouping the contrast of the separate figures is an equal element with the unity which binds them all into a group; in the third case the diversity is lost in the unity, and a uniformity of colouring is seized by the dramatic sense as an effect apart from the individual varieties without which such colouring would not be remarkable.

Movement applied to Character: Character-Development.

When to Character-Interpretation, the formation of a single conception out of a multitude of concrete details, the further idea of growth and progress is added, we get the third variety of Character-Interest—*Character-Development.*

In the preceding chapters this has received only negative CHAP. XII. notice, its absence being a salient feature in the portraiture of Richard.   For a positive illustration no better example could be desired than the character of Macbeth.   Three features, we have seen, stand out clear in the general conception of Macbeth.   There is his eminently practical nature, which is the key to the whole.   And the absence in him of the inner life adds two special features : one is his helplessness under suspense, the other is the activity of his imagination with its susceptibility to supernatural terrors.   Now, if we fix our attention on these three points they become three threads of development as we trace Macbeth through the stages of his career.   His practical power developes as capacity for crime.   Macbeth undertook his first crime only after a protracted and terrible struggle; the murder of the grooms was a crime of impulse ;   the murder of Banquo appears a thing of contrivance, in which Macbeth is a deliberate planner directing the agency of others, while his dark hints to his wife suggest the beginning of a relish for iii. ii. 40, such deeds.   This capacity for crime continues to grow, &c until slaughter becomes an end in itself :

> Each new morn   iv. iii. 4.
> New widows howl, new orphans cry:

and then a mania :

> Some say he's mad; others that lesser hate him   v. ii. 13.
> Do call it valiant fury.

We see a parallel development in Macbeth's impatience of suspense.   Just after his first temptation he is able to brace himself to suspense for an indefinite period :

> If chance will have me king, why, chance may crown me,   i. iii. 143.
> Without my stir.

On the eve of his great crime the suspense of the few hours i. vii. that must intervene before the banquet can be despatched and Duncan can retire becomes intolerable to Macbeth, and

he is for abandoning the treason. In the next stage it is
the suspense of a single moment that impels him to stab the
grooms. From this point suspense no longer comes by fits
III. ii. 13, and starts, but is a settled disease : his mind is as scorpions ;
36, &c. it is tortured in restless ecstasy. Suspense has undermined
his judgment and brought on him the gambler's fever—the
haunting thought that just one more venture will make him
safe ; in spite of the opposition of his reason—which his
III. ii 45. unwillingness to confide the murder of Banquo to his wife
betrays—he is carried on to work the additional crime which
unmasks the rest. And finally suspense intensifies to a panic,
and he himself feels that his deeds —

III. iv. 140.   must be acted ere they may be scann'd.

The third feature in Macbeth is the quickening of his sensitiveness to the supernatural side by side with the deadening
of his conscience. Imagination becomes, as it were, a pictorial conscience for one to whom its more rational channels
have been closed : the man who ' would jump the world to
come ' accepts implicitly every word that falls from a witch.
Now this imagination is at first a restraining force in Mac-
I. iii. 134. beth : the thought whose image unfixes his hair leads him to
abandon the treason. When later he has, under pressure,
delivered himself again to the temptation, there are still signs
that imagination is a force on the other side that has to be
overcome :

I. iv. 50.   Stars, hide your fires ;
                Let not light see my black and deep desires :
                The eye wink at the hand.

Once passed the boundary of the accomplished deed he becomes an absolute victim to terrors of conscience in super-
II. ii. 22– natural form. In the very first moment they reach so near
46. the boundary that separates subjective and objective that a
real voice appears to be denouncing the issue of his crime :

Macbeth. Methought I heard a voice cry 'Sleep no more.' . . .
Lady M. Who was it that thus cried?

In the reaction from the murder of Banquo the supernatural C<small>HAP</small> XII.
appearance—which no eye sees but his own—appears more iii. iv
real to him than the real life around him   And from this
point he *seeks* the supernatural, forces it to disclose its iv. L 48.
terrors, and thrusts himself into an agonised vision of generations that are to witness the triumph of his foes.

XIII.

INTEREST OF PASSION.

HUMAN Interest includes not only varieties of human nature, or Character, but also items of human experience, or Passion. Passion is the second great topic of Dramatic Criticism. It is concerned with the life that is lived through the scenes of the story, as distinguished from the personages who live it; not treating this with the abstract treatment that belongs to Plot, but reviewing it in the light of its human interest; it embraces conduct still alive with the motives which have actuated it—fate in the process of forging. The word 'passion' signifies primarily what is suffered of good or bad; secondarily the emotions generated by suffering, whether in the sufferer or in bystanders. Its use as a dramatic term thus suggests how in Drama an experience can be grasped by us through our emotional nature, through our sympathy, our antagonism, and all the varieties of emotional interest that lie between. To this Passion we have to apply the threefold division of unity, complexity, and movement.

When unity is applied to Passion we get a series of details bound together into a singleness of impression as an Incident, a Situation, or an Effect. The distinction of the three rests largely on their different degrees of fragmentariness.

Incidents are groups of continuous details forming a complete interest in themselves as ministering to our sense of story. The suit of Shylock against Antonio in the course of which fate swings right round; the murder of Clarence with its long-drawn agony; Richard and Buckingham with the

Lord Mayor and Citizens exhibiting a picture of political
manipulation in the fifteenth century; the startling sight of a
Lady Anne wooed beside the bier of her murdered husband's murdered father, by a murderer who rests his suit on
the murders themselves; Banquo's Ghost appearing at the
feast at which Banquo's presence had been so vehemently
called for; Lear's faithful Gloucester so brutally blinded
and so instantly avenged:—all these are complete stories
presented in a single view, and suggest how Shakespeare's
dramas are constructed out of materials which are themselves dramas in miniature. In *Situation*, on the other hand, *Situation.*
a series of details cohere into a single impression without
losing the sense of incompleteness. The two central personages of *The Merchant of Venice*, around whom brightness
and gloom have been revolving in such contrast, at last
brought to face one another from the judgment-seat and the
dock; Lorenzo and Jessica wrapped in moonlight and
music, with the rest of the universe for the hour blotted out
into a background for their love; Margaret like an apparition of the sleeping Nemesis of Lancaster flashed into the
midst of the Yorkist courtiers while they are bickering
through very wantonness of victory; Shylock pitted against
Tubal, Jew against Jew, the nature not too narrow to mix
affection with avarice, mocked from passion to passion by the
nature only wide enough to take in greed; Richard waking
on Bosworth morning, and miserably piecing together the
wreck of his invincible will which a sleeping vision has
shattered; Macbeth's moment of rapture in following the
airy dagger, while the very night holds its breath, to break out
again presently into voices of doom; the panic mist of
universal suspicion amidst which Malcolm blasts his own
character to feel after the fidelity of Macduff; Edgar from
his ambush of outcast idiocy watching the sad marvel of his
father's love restored to him:—all these brilliant Situations are
fragments of dramatic continuity in which the fragmentari-

CH. XIII. ness is a part of the interest.   Just as the sense of sculpture might seek to arrest and perpetuate a casual moment in the evolutions of a dance, so in Dramatic Situation the mind is conscious of isolating something from what precedes and what follows so as to extract out of it an additional impression ; the morsel has its purpose in ministering to a complete process of digestion, but it gets a sensation of its own by momentary delay in contact with the palate.

Effect.   Of a still more fragmentary nature is *Dramatic Effect*— Effect strictly so called, and as distinguished from the looser use of the term for dramatic impressions in general.   Such Effect seems to attach itself to single momentary details, though in reality these details owe their impressiveness to their connection with others : the final detail has completed an electric circle and a shock is given.   No element of the Drama is of so miscellaneous a character and so defies analysis : all that can be done here is to notice three special *Irony as* Dramatic Effects. *Dramatic Irony* is a sudden appearance of *an Effect.* double-dealing in surrounding events : a dramatic situation accidentally starts up and produces a shock by its bearing upon conflicting states of affairs, both known to the audience, but one of them hidden from some of the parties to the scene. This is the special contribution to dramatic effect of Greek tragedy.   The ancient stage was tied down in its subject-matter to stories perfectly familiar to the audience as sacred legends, and so almost excluding the effect of surprise : in Irony it found some compensation.   The ancient tragedies harp upon human blindness to the future, and delight to ex-hibit a hero speculating about, or struggling with, or perhaps in careless talk stumbling upon, the final issue of events which the audience know so well—Œdipus, for example, through great part of a play moving heaven and earth to pierce the mystery of the judgment that has come upon his city, while according to the familiar sacred story the offender can be none other than himself.   Shakespeare has used to

almost as great an extent as the Greek dramatists this effect   CH. XIII.
of Irony.   His most characteristic handling of it belongs to
the lighter plays; yet in the group of dramas dealt with in
this work it is prominent amongst his effects.   It has been
pointed out how *Macbeth* and *Richard III* are saturated
with it.   There are casual illustrations in *Julius Cæsar*, as
when the dictator bids his intended murderer

> Be near me, that I may remember you;   ii. ii. 123.

or in *Lear*, when Edmund, intriguing guiltily with Goneril, in
a chance expression of tenderness unconsciously paints the
final issue of that intrigue:

> Yours in the ranks of death!   iv. ii. 25.

A comic variety of Irony occurs in the Trial Scene of *The
Merchant of Venice*, when Bassanio and Gratiano in their iv 1 282
distracted grief are willing to sacrifice their new wives if this
could save their friend—little thinking these wives are so near
to record the vow.   The doubleness of Irony is one which
attaches to a situation as a whole: the effect however is
especially keen when a scene is so impregnated with it that iii. ii 60–
the very language is true in a double sense.   73.

> *Catesby.*   'Tis a vile thing to die, my gracious lord,
>   When men are unprepared and look not for it.
> *Hastings.*   O monstrous, monstrous! and so falls it out
>   With Rivers, Vaughan, Grey: *and so 'twill do*
>   *With some men else, who think themselves as safe*
>   *As thou and I.*

Nemesis, though usually extending to the general movement *Nemesis as*
of a drama, and so considered below, may sometimes be only *an Effect.*
an effect of detail—a sign connecting very closely retribution
with sin or reaction with triumph.   Such a Nemesis may be
seen where Cassius in the act of falling on his sword recog- v. iii. 45.
nises the weapon as the same with which he stabbed Cæsar.
Another special variety of effect is *Dramatic Foreshadow-* *Dramatic*
ing—mysterious details pointing to an explanation in the *Fore-*
shadowing.
sequel, a realisation in action of the saying that coming

Cн. XIII. events cast their shadows before them.   The unaccountable

i. i. 1.   'sadness' of Antonio at the opening of *The Merchant of Venice* is a typical illustration.   Others will readily suggest

iii. i. 68. themselves—the Prince's shuddering aversion to the Tower

i. i. 39. in *Richard III*, the letter G that of Edward's heirs the

v. i. 77–90. murderer should be, the crows substituted for Cassius's eagles on the morning of the final battle.   A more elaborate example is seen in *Julius Cæsar*, where the soothsayer's

i. ii. 18. vague warning 'Beware the Ides of March'—a solitary voice that could yet arrest the hero through the shouting of the crowd — is later on found, not to have become dissipated, but to have gathered definiteness as the moment comes nearer :

iii. i. 1.

> *Cæsar.* The Ides of March are come.
>
> *Soothsayer.* Ay, Cæsar ; but not gone.

These three leading Effects may be sufficient to illustrate a branch of dramatic analysis in which the variety is endless.

Complexity applied to Passion.   We are next to consider the application of complexity to Passion, and the contrasts of passion that so arise.   Here care is necessary to avoid confusion with a complexity of passion that hardly comes within the sphere of dramatic

iii. i. criticism.   In the scene in which Shylock is being teased by Tubal it is easy to note the conflict between the passions of greed and paternal affection: such analysis is outside dramatic criticism and belongs to psychology.   In its dramatic sense Passion applies to experience, not decomposed into its emotional elements, but grasped as a whole by our emotional nature : there is still room for complexity of such passion in the appeal made *to different sides of our emotional nature, the*

Passion-Tone.   *serious and the gay.*   In dealing with this element of dramatic effect a convenient technical term is *Tone.*   The deep insight of metaphorical word-coining has given universal sanction to the expression of emotional differences by analogies of music : our emotional nature is exalted with mirth and de-

pressed with sorrow, we speak of a chord of sympathy, a
strain of triumph, a note of despair; we are in a serious
mood, or pitch our appeal in a higher key.　These expressions are clearly musical, and there is probably a half
association of music in many others, such as a theme of
sorrow, acute anguish and profound despair, response of
gratitude, or even the working of our feelings.　Most exactly
to the purpose is a phrase of frequent occurrence, the 'gamut
of the passions,' which brings out with emphasis how our
emotional nature in its capacity for different kinds of impressions suggests a *scale* of passion-contrasts, not to be *Scale of*
sharply defined but shading off into one another like the *Passion-*
tones of a musical scale—Tragic, Heroic, Serious, Elevated, *Tones.*
Light, Comic, Farcical.　It is with such complexity of tones
that Dramatic Passion is concerned.

　Now the mere *Mixture of Tones* is an effect in itself. *Mixture of*
For the present I am not referring to the combination of one *Tones.*
tone with another in the same incident (which will be treated
as a distinct variety): I apply it more widely to the inclusion of
different tones in the field of the same play.　Such mixture is
best illustrated by music, which gives us an adagio and an
allegro, a fantastic scherzo and a pompous march, within
the same symphony or sonata, though in separate movements.　In *The Merchant of Venice*, as often in plays of
Shakespeare, every tone in the scale is represented.　When **iv. i.**
Antonio is enduring through the long suspense, and triumphant malignity is gaining point after point against helpless
friendship, we have travelled far into the Tragic; the woman-
nature of Portia calling Venetian justice from judicial murder **iv. i. 184.**
to the divine prerogative of mercy throws in a touch of the
Heroic; a great part of what centres around Shylock, when
he is crushing the brightness out of Jessica or defying the **ii. v　iii.**
Christian world, is pitched in the Serious strain; the incidents ¹' &c.
of the unsuccessful suitors, the warm exuberance of Oriental **ii. i, vii;**
courtesy and the less grateful loftiness of Spanish family pride, **ii. ix.**

Ch. XIII.

i. i, &c.
i. ii.

ii. ii, iii;
iii. v, &c.

ii. ii, from
34.

*a distinc-
tion of the
modern
Drama.*

might be a model for the Elevated drama of the English Restoration; the infinite nothings of Gratiano, prince of diners-out, the more piquant small talk of Portia and Nerissa when they criticise the man-world from the secrecy of a maiden-bower—these throw a tone of Lightness over their sections of the drama; Launcelot is an incarnation of the conventional Comic serving-man, and his Comedy becomes broad Farce where he teases the sand-blind Gobbo and draws him on to bless his astonishing beard. How distinct an effect is this mere Mixture of Tones within the same play may be seen in the fact that the Classical Drama found it impossible. The exclusive and uncompromising spirit of antiquity carried caste into art itself, and their Tragedy and Comedy were kept rigidly separate, and indeed were connected with different rituals. The spirit of modern life is marked by its comprehensiveness and reconciliation of opposites; and nothing is more important in dramatic history than the way in which Shakespeare and his contemporaries created a new departure in art, by seizing upon the rude jumble of sport and earnest which the mob loved, and converting it into a source of stirring passion-effects. For a new faculty of mental grasp is generated by this harmony of tones in the English Drama. If the artist introduces every tone into the story he thereby gets hold of every tone in the spectators' emotional nature; the world of the play is presented from every point of view as it works upon the various passions, and the difference this makes is the difference between simply looking down upon a surface and viewing a solid from all round:—the mixture of tones, so to speak, makes passion of three dimensions. Moreover it brings the world of fiction nearer to the world of nature, which has never yet evolved an experience in which brightness was dissevered from gloom: half the pleasure of the world is wrung out of others' pain; the two jostle in the street, house together under every roof, share every stage

of life, and refuse to be sundered even in the mysteries of CH. XIII.
death.

Quite a distinct class of effects is produced when the con-
trasting tones are not only included in the same drama but
are further brought into immediate contact and made to react
upon each other. *Tone-Play* is made by simple variety and *Tone-Play.*
alternation of light and serious passions. It has been pointed
out in a previous chapter what a striking example of this is
The Merchant of Venice, in which scene by scene two stories
of youthful love and of deadly feud alternate with one
another as they progress to their climaxes, until from the
rapture of Portia united to Bassanio we drop to the full iii. ii. 221.
realisation of Antonio in the grasp of Shylock ; and again the
cruel anxiety of the trial and its breathless shock of deliverance are balanced by the mad fun of the ring trick and the joy iv. i. 408.
of the moonlight scene which Jessica feels is too deep for mer- v. i.
riment. A slight variation of this is *Tone-Relief*: in an action *Tone-Re-*
which is cast in a uniform tone the continuity is broken by a *lief.*
brief spell of a contrary passion, the contrast at once relieving and intensifying the prevailing tone. One of the best
examples (notwithstanding its coarseness) is the introduction
in *Macbeth* of the jolly Porter, who keeps the impatient nobles ii. iii. 1.
outside in the storm till his jest is comfortably finished,
making each furious knock fit in to his elaborate conceit of
Hell-gate. This tone of broad farce, with nothing else like it
in the whole play, comes as a single ray of common daylight
to separate the agony of the dark night's murder from the
agony of the struggle for concealment. The mixture of
tones goes a stage further when opposing tones of passion
clash in the same incident and are *fused* together. These *Tone-*
terms are, I think, scarcely metaphorical: as a physiological *Clash.*
fact we see our physical susceptibility to pleasurable and
painful emotions drawn into conflict with one another in the
phenomena of hysteria ; and their mental analogues must be
capable of much closer union. As examples of these effects

CH. XIII.

resting upon an appeal to opposite sides of our emotional nature at the same time may be instanced the flash of comic irony, already referred to more than once, that starts up in

iv. i. 288, &c.

the most pathetic moment of Antonio's trial by his friend's allusion to his newly wedded wife. Of the same double nature are the strokes of pathetic humour in this play; as

iii. iii. 32.

where Antonio describes himself so worn with grief that he will hardly spare a pound of flesh to his bloody creditor; or again his pun,

iv. i. 280.

> For if the Jew do cut but deep enough
> I'll pay it presently with all my heart!

Shakespeare is very true to nature in thus borrowing the language of word-play to express suffering so exquisite as to leave sober language far behind. Finally Tone-Clash rises

Tone-Storm.

into *Tone-Storm* in such rare climaxes as the centrepiece of *Lear*, where against a tempest of nature as a fitting back-

iii. i–vi.

ground we have the conflict of three madnesses, passion, idiocy, and folly, bidding against one another, and inflaming each other's wildness into an inextricable whirl of frenzy.

Movement applied to Passion.

The idea of movement has next to be applied to Passion. Passion is experience as grasped by our emotional nature: this will be sensitive not only to isolated fragments of experience, but equally to the succession of incidents. The movement of events will produce a corresponding movement in our emotional nature as this is variously affected by them; and as the succession of incidents seems to take direction so the play of our sympathies will seem to take form. Again, events cannot succeed one another without suggesting causes at work and controlling forces: when such causes and forces are of a nature to work upon our sympathy another element of Passion will appear. Under Passion-Movement then are

Motive Form and Motive Force.

comprehended two things—*Motive Form* and *Motive Force*. The first of these is a thing in which two of the great elements of Drama, Passion, and Plot, overlap, and it will be best con-

page 278.

sidered in connection with Plot which takes in dramatic

form as a whole. Here we have to consider the Motive Forces
of dramatic passion. The dramatist is, as it were, a God in
his universe, and disposes the ultimate issues of human experience at his pleasure : what then are the principles which
are found to have governed his ordering of events? to
personages in a drama what are the great determinants of
fate?

The first of the great determinants of fate in the Drama is *Poetic Jus-*
Poetic Justice. What exactly is the meaning of this term? It *tice a form*
of art-
is often understood to mean the correction of justice, as if *beauty.*
justice in poetry were more just than the justice of real life.
But this is not supported by the facts of dramatic story. An
English judge and jury would revolt against measuring out to
Shylock the justice that is meted to him by the court of
Venice, though the same persons beholding the scene in a
theatre might feel their sense of Poetic Justice satisfied;
unless, indeed, which might easily happen, the confusion of
ideas suggested by this term operated to check their acquiescence in the issue of the play. A better notion of Poetic
Justice is to understand it as the modification of justice by
considerations of art. This holds good even where justice
and retribution do determine the fate of individuals in the
Drama; in these cases our dramatic satisfaction still rests,
not on the high degree of justice exhibited, but on the artistic
mode in which it works. A policeman catching a thief with
his hand in a neighbour's pocket and bringing him to
summary punishment affords an example of complete justice,
yet its very success robs it of all poetic qualities; the same
thief defeating all the natural machinery of the law, yet overtaken after all by a questionable ruse would be to the poetic
sense far more interesting.

Treating Poetic Justice, then, as the application of art to *Nemesis as*
morals, its most important phase will be *Nemesis*, which we *a dramatic*
motive.
have already seen involves an artistic link between sin and retribution. The artistic connection may be of the most varied

CH. XIII.
Varieties of Nemesis.
compare
iii. i. 118
and 165.

description. There is a Nemesis of perfect equality, Shylock reaping measure for measure as he has sown. When Nemesis overtook the Roman conspirators it was partly its suddenness that made it impressive: within fifty lines of their appeal to all time they have fallen into an attitude of deprecation. For Richard, on the contrary, retribution was delayed to the last moment: to have escaped to the eleventh hour is shown to be no security.

> Jove strikes the Titans down
> Not when they first begin their mountain piling,
> But when another rock would crown their work.

Nemesis may be emphasised by repetition and multiplication; in the world in which Richard is plunged there appears to be no event which is not a nemesis. Or the point may be the unlooked-for source from which the nemesis comes; as when upon the murder of Cæsar a colossus of energy and resource starts up in the time-serving and frivolous Antony, whom the ii. i. 165. conspirators had spared for his insignificance. Or again, retribution may be made bitter to the sinner by his tracing in it his own act and deed: from Lear himself, and from no other source, Goneril and Regan have received the power they use to crush his spirit. Nay, the very prize for which the sinner has sinned turns out in some cases the nemesis fate has provided for him; as when Goneril and Regan use their ill-gotten power for the state intrigues which work their death. And most keenly pointed of all comes the nemesis that is combined with mockery: Macbeth, if he had not iii. i. 49. essayed the murder of Banquo as an *extra* precaution, might have enjoyed his stolen crown in safety; his expedition iv. iii. 219. against Macduff's castle slays all *except* the fate-appointed avenger; Richard disposes of his enemies with flawless iv. ii. 46. success until *the last*, Dorset, escapes to his rival.

Such is Nemesis, and such are some of the modes in which the connection between sin and retribution may be made artistically impressive. Poetic Justice, however, is a

wider term than Nemesis. The latter implies some offence, CH. XIII.
as an occasion for the operation of judicial machinery. But, *Poetic*
apart from sin, fate may be out of accord with character, and *Justice*
the correction of this ill distribution will satisfy the dramatic *other than Nemesis.*
sense. But here again the practice of dramatic providence
appears regulated, not with a view to abstract justice, but to
justice modified by dramatic sympathy: Poetic Justice extends to the exhibition of fate moving in the interests of those
with whom we sympathise and to the confusion of those
with whom we are in antagonism. Viewed as a piece of
equity the sentence on Shylock—a plaintiff who has lost his iv i. 346–
suit by an accident of statute-law—seems highly question- 363.
able. On the other hand, this sentence brings a fortune to
a girl who has won our sympathies in spite of her faults;
it makes provision for those for whom there is a dramatic
necessity of providing; above all it is in accord with our
secret liking that good fortune should go with the bright and
happy, and sever itself from the mean and sordid. Whether
this last is justice, I will not discuss: it is enough that it is
one of the instincts of the imagination, and in creative literature justice must pay tribute to art.

But however widely the term be stretched, justice is only *Pathos as a*
one of the determinants of fate in the Drama: confusion on *dramatic motive.*
this point has led to many errors of criticism. The case of
Cordelia is in point. Because she is involved in the ruin of
Lear it is felt by some commentators that a consideration of
justice must be sought to explain her death: they find it
perhaps in her original resistance to her father; or the
ingenious suggestion has been made that Cordelia, in her
measures to save her father, invades England, and this breach
of patriotism needs atonement. But this is surely twisting
the story to an explanation, not extracting an explanation
from the details of the story. It would be a violation of all
dramatic proportion, needing the strongest evidence from the
details of the play, if Cordelia's 'most small fault' betrayed

S

CH. XIII. her to dramatic execution.   And as to the sin against

iv. iv. 27. patriotism, the whole notion of it is foreign to the play itself,

ii. ii. 170– in which the truest patriots, such as Kent and Gloucester,

177*; iii. are secretly confederate with Cordelia and look upon her as

i, v. the hope of their unhappy country; while even Albany him-

iv. ii. 2– self, however necessary he finds it to repel the invader, yet

10 (com- distinctly feels that justice is on the other side.   The fact is

pare 55, that in Cordelia's case, as in countless other cases, motives

95); v. i. determine fate which have in them no relation to justice;

21–27. fiction being in this matter in harmony with real life,

where in only a minority of instances can we recognise

any element of justice or injustice as entering into the

fates of individuals.   When in real life a little child

dies, what consideration of justice is there that bears

on such an experience?   Nevertheless there is an irre-

---

* The text in this passage is regarded as difficult by many editors, and
is marked in the Globe Edition as corrupt.   I do not see the difficulty
of taking it as it stands, if regard be had to the general situation, in
which (as Steevens has pointed out) Kent is reading the letter in disjointed snatches by the dim moonlight.   Commentators seem to me to
have increased the obscurity by taking 'enormous' in its rare sense of
'irregular,' 'out of order,' and making it refer to the state of England.
Surely it is used in its ordinary meaning, and applies to France; the
clause in which it occurs being part of the *actual words* of Cordelia's
letter, who naturally uses 'this' of the country from which she writes.
Inverted commas would make the connection clear.

> Approach, thou beacon to this under globe,
> That by thy comfortable beams I may
> Peruse this letter!—'Nothing almost sees miracles'—
> 'But misery'—I know 'tis from Cordelia,
> Who hath 'most fortunately been inform'd'
> Of my 'obscured course, and shall find time
> From this enormous state '—' seeking to give
> Losses their remedies,' &c.

I. e. Cordelia promises she will find leisure from the oppressive cares of
her new kingdom to remedy the evils of England.   Kent gives up the
attempt to read; but enough has been brought out for the dramatist's
purpose at that particular stage, viz. to hint that Kent was in correspondence with Cordelia, and looked to her as the deliverer of England.

sistible sense of beauty in the idea of the fleeting child-life
arrested while yet in its completeness, before the rude hand
of time has begun to trace lines of passion or hardness; the
parent indeed may not feel this in the case of his own child,
but in art, where there is no mist of individual feeling to
blind, the sense of beauty comes out stronger than the sense
of loss. It is the mission of the Drama thus to interpret the
beauty of fate: it seeks, as Aristotle puts it, to purify our
emotions by healthy exercise. The Drama does with human
experience what Painting does with external nature. There
are landscapes whose beauty is obvious to all; but it is one of
the privileges of the artist to reveal the charm that lies in the
most ordinary scenery, until the ideal can be recognised
everywhere, and nature itself becomes art. Similarly there
are striking points in life, such as the vindication of justice,
which all can catch: but it is for the dramatist, as the artist
in life, to arrange the experience he depicts so as to bring
out the hidden beauties of fate, until the trained eye sees a
meaning in all that happens;—until indeed the word 'suffering' itself has only to be translated into its Greek equivalent,
and *pathos* is recognised as a form of beauty. Accumulation
of Pathos then must be added to Poetic Justice as a determinant of fate in the Drama. And our sensitiveness to this
form of beauty is nowhere more signally satisfied than when
we see Cordelia dead in the arms of Lear: fate having mys-
teriously seconded her self-devotion, and nothing, not even
her life, being left out to make her sacrifice complete.

There remains a third great determinant of fate in the *The Super-*
Drama—the Supernatural. I have in a former chapter *natural as*
a dramatic
pointed out how in relation to this topic the modern Drama *motive.*
stands in a different position from that of ancient Tragedy.
In the Drama of antiquity the leading motive forces were
supernatural, either the secret force of Destiny, or the inter-
position of supernatural beings who directly interfered with
human events. We are separated from this view of life by a

Ch. XIII.

*The Super-
natural
rational-
ised in
modern
Drama.*

revolution of thought which has substituted Providence for Destiny as the controller of the universe, and absorbed the supernatural within the domain of Law. Yet elements that had once entered so deeply into the Drama would not be easily lost to the machinery of Passion-Movement; supernatural agency has a degree of recognition in modern thought, and even Destiny may still be utilised if it can be stripped of antagonism to the idea of a benevolent Providence. To begin with the latter: the problem for a modern dramatist is to reconcile Destiny with Law. The characteristics which made the ancient conception of fate dramatically impressive—its irresistibility, its unintelligibility, and its suggestion of personal hostility—he may still insinuate into the working of events: only the destiny must be rationalised, that is, the course of events must at the same time be explicable by natural causes.

*As an ob-
jective force
in Irony.*

First: Shakespeare gives us Destiny acting objectively, as an external force, in the form of *Irony*, already discussed in connection with the standard illustration of it in *Macbeth.* In the movement of this play Destiny appears in the most pronounced form of mockery: every difficulty and check being in the issue converted into an instrument for furthering the course of events. Yet this mockery is wholly without any suggestion of malignity in the governing power of the universe; its effect being rather to measure the irresistibility of righteous retribution. This Irony makes just the difference between the ordinary operations of Law or Providence and the suggestion of Destiny: yet each step in the action is sufficiently explained by rational considerations. What more

i. iv. 37.

natural than that Duncan should proclaim his son heir-apparent to check any hopes that too successful service might excite? Yet what more natural than that this loss of

i. iv. 48.

Macbeth's remote chance of the crown should be the occasion of his resolve no longer to be content with chances?

ii. iii. 141.

What more natural than that the sons of the murdered king

should take flight upon the revelation of a treason useless to Ch XIII.
its perpetrator as long as they were living? Yet what again
more natural than that the momentary reaction consequent
upon this flight should, in the general fog of suspicion and ii. iv 21–
terror, give opportunity to the object of universal dread 41.
himself to take the reins of government? The Irony is
throughout no more than a garb worn by rational history.

Or, again, Destiny may be exhibited as a subjective force *As a sub-*
in *Infatuation*, or *Judicial Blindness:* 'whom the gods *jective*
would destroy they first blind.' This was a conception *force in In-*
fatuation.
specially impressive to ancient ethics; the lesson it gathered
from almost every great fall was that of a spiritual darkening
which hid from the sinner his own danger, obvious to every
other eye, till he had been tempted beyond the possibility of
retreat.

> Falling in frenzied guilt, he knows it not;
>   So thick the blinding cloud
> That o'er him floats; and Rumour widely spread
> With many a sigh repeats the dreary doom,
>   A mist that o'er the house
>   In gathering darkness broods.

Such Infatuation is very far from being inconsistent with the
idea of Law; indeed, it appears repeatedly in the strong
figures of Scriptural speech, by which the ripening of sin to
its own destruction—a merciful law of a righteously-ordered
universe—is suggested as the direct act of Him who is the
founder of the universe and its laws. By such figures God
is represented as hardening Pharaoh's heart; or, again, an
almost technical description of Infatuation is put by the
fervour of prophecy into the mouth of God:

Make the heart of this people fat, and make their ears heavy, and shut
their eyes; lest they see with their eyes, and hear with their ears, and
understand with their heart, and convert, and be healed.

In the case of Macbeth the judicial blindness is maintained to the last moment, and he pauses in the final combat v. viii. 13.
to taunt Macduff with certain destruction. Yet, while we

CH. XIII. thus get the full dramatic effect of Infatuation, it is so far rationalised that we are allowed to see the machinery by which the Infatuation has been brought about: we have heard

iii. v. 16. the Witches arrange to deceive Macbeth with false oracles. A very dramatic, but wholly natural, example of Infatuation appears at the turning-point of Richard's career, where, when he has just discovered that Richmond is the point from which the storm of Nemesis threatens to break upon him,

iv. ii. 98, &c. prophecies throng upon his memory which might have all his life warned him of this issue, had he not been blind

i. iii. 131. to them till this moment. Again, Antonio's challenge to Shylock to do his worst is, as I have already pointed out, an outburst of *hybris,* the insolence of Infatuation: but this is no more than a natural outcome of a conflict between two implacable temperaments. In Infatuation, then, as in all its other forms, Destiny is exhibited by Shakespeare as harmonised with natural law.

Super-natural agencies.   Besides Destiny the Shakespearean Drama admits direct supernatural agencies—witches, ghosts, apparitions, as well as portents and violations of natural law. It appears to me idle to contend that these in Shakespeare are not really supernatural, but must be interpreted as delusions of their victims. There may be single cases, such as the appearance of Banquo to Macbeth, where, as no eye sees it but his own, the apparition may be resolved into an hallucination. But to determine Shakespeare's general practice it is enough to point to the Ghost in *Hamlet,* which, as seen by three persons at once and on separate occasions, is indisputably objective: and a single instance is sufficient to establish the assumption in the Shakespearean Drama of supernatural beings with a real existence. Zeal for Shakespeare's rationality is a main source of the opposite view; but for the assumption of such supernatural existences the responsibility lies not with Shakespeare, but with the opinion of the age he is pourtraying. A more important question is how far Shakespeare uses such

supernatural agency as a motive force in his plays; how far CH. XIII.
does he allow it to enter into the working of events, for the
interpretation of which he is responsible? On this point
Shakespeare's usage is clear and subtle : he uses the agency
of the supernatural to intensify and to illuminate human
action, not to determine it.

Supernatural agency intensifying human action is illus- *Intensify-*
trated in *Macbeth*. No one can seriously doubt the objective ^*ing human* *action.*
existence of the Witches in this play, or that they are en-
dowed with superhuman sources of knowledge. But the
question is, do they in reality turn Macbeth to crime? In
one of the chapters devoted to this play I have dwelt on the
importance of the point that Macbeth has been already meditating treason in his heart when he meets the Witches on
the heath. His secret thoughts—which he betrays in his
guilty start—have been an invitation to the powers of evil, i. iii. 51
and they have obeyed the summons : Macbeth has already
ventured a descent, and they add an impulse downward. To
bring this out the more clearly, Shakespeare keeps Banquo
side by side with Macbeth through the critical stages of the
temptation : Banquo has made no overtures to temptation,
and to him the tempters have no mission. It is noticeable
that where the two warriors meet the Witches on the heath
it is Banquo who begins the conversation. i. iii. 38–
50.

> *Banquo.* How far is 't called to Forres?

No answer. The silence attracts his attention to those he is
addressing.

> What are these
> So wither'd and so wild in their attire,
> That look not like the inhabitants o' the earth,
> And yet are on 't?

Still no answer.

> Live you? or are you aught
> That man may question?

They signify in dumb show that they may not answer

> You seem to understand me,
> By each at once her chappy finger laying
> Upon her skinny lips: you should be women,
> And yet your beards forbid me to interpret
> That you are so.

Still he can draw no answer. At last Macbeth chimes in:

> Speak, if you can: what are you?

The tamperer with temptation has spoken, and in a moment they break out, 'All hail, Macbeth!' and ply their supernatural task. Later on in the scene, when directly challenged by Banquo, they do respond and give out an oracle for him. But into his upright mind the poison-germs of insight into the future fall harmlessly; it is because Macbeth is already tainted that these breed in him a fever of crime. In the second incident of the Witches, so far from their being the tempters, it is Macbeth who seeks them and forces from them knowledge of the future. Yet, even here, what is the actual effect of their revelation upon Macbeth? It is, like that of his air-drawn dagger, only to marshal him along the way that he is going. They bid him beware Macduff: he answers, 'Thou hast harp'd my fear aright.' They give him preternatural pledges of safety: are these a help to him in enjoying the rewards of sin? On the contrary, as a matter of fact we find Macbeth, in panic of suspicion, seeking security by means of daily butchery; the oracles have produced in him confidence enough to give agony to the bitterness of his betrayal, but not such confidence as to lead him to dispense with a single one of the natural bulwarks to tyranny. The function of the Witches throughout the action of this play is exactly expressed by a phrase Banquo uses in connection with them: they are only 'instruments of darkness,' assisting to carry forward courses of conduct initiated independently of them. Macbeth has made the destiny which the Witches reveal.

Again, supernatural agency is used to illuminate human

57.

iii. v and iv. i.

iv. i. 74.

iv. iii. 4, &c.

i. iii. 124.

action: the course of events in a drama not ceasing to obey
natural causes, but becoming, by the addition of the super- *Illuminat-*
natural agency, endowed with a new art-beauty. The great *ing human*
action
example of this is the *Oracular Action*. This important *The Ora-*
element of dramatic effect—how it consists in the working *cular Ac-*
tion.
out of Destiny from mystery to clearness, and the different
forms it assumes—has been discussed at length in a former
chapter. The question here is, how far do we find such
superhuman knowledge used as a force in the movement of
events? As Shakespeare handles oracular machinery, the
conditions of natural working in the course of events are
not in the least degree altered by the revelation of the
future. The actor's belief (or disbelief) in the oracle may be
one of the circumstances which have influenced his action—
as it would have done in the real life of the age—but to the
spectator, to whom the Drama is to reveal the real governing forces of the world, the oracular action is presented not
as a force but as a light. It gives to a course of events the
illumination that can be in actual fact given to it by History,
the office of which is to make each detail of a story interesting in the light of the explanation that comes when all the
details are complete. Only it uses the supernatural agency to
project this illumination into the midst of the events themselves, which History cannot give till they are concluded;
and also it carries the art-effect of such illumination a stage
further than History could carry it, by making it progressive
in intelligibility, and making this progress keep pace with the
progress of the events themselves. Fate will allow none but
Macduff to be the slayer of Macbeth. True: but Macduff
(who moreover knows nothing of his destiny) is the most
deeply injured of Macbeth's subjects, and as a fact we find
it needs the news of his injury to rouse him to his task; as **iv.** iii.
he approaches the battle he feels that the ghosts of his wife **v.** vii. **15.**
and children will haunt him if he allows any other to be the
tyrant's executioner. Thus far the interpretation of History

Cʜ. XIII. might go: but the oracular machinery introduced points dimly to Macduff before the first breath of the King's suspicion has assailed him, and the suggestiveness becomes clearer and clearer as the convergence of events carries the action to its climax. The natural working of human events has been undisturbed: only the spectator's mind has been endowed with a special illumination for receiving them.

The Super-
natural as
Dramatic
Back-
ground.

In another and very different way we have supernatural agency called in to throw a peculiar illumination over human events. In dealing with the movement of *Julius Cæsar* I have described at length the *Supernatural Background* of storm, tempest, and portent, which assist the emotional agitation throughout the second stage of the action. These are clearly supernatural in that they are made to suggest a mystic sympathy with, and indeed prescience of, mutations in human life. Yet their function is simply that of illumination: they cast a glow of emotion over the spectator as he watches the train of events, though all the while the action of these events remains within the sphere of natural causes. In narrative and lyric poetry this endowment of nature with human sympathies becomes the commonest of poetic devices, personification; and here it never suggests anything supernatural because it is so clearly recognised as belonging to expression. But 'expression' in the Drama extends beyond language, and takes in presentation; and it is only a device in presentation that tumult in nature and tumult in history, each perfectly natural by itself, are made to have a suggestion of the supernatural by their coincidence in time. After all there is no real meaning in storm any more than in calm weather, only that contemplative observers have transferred their own emotions to particular phases of nature: it would seem, then, a very slight and natural reversal of the process to call in this humanised nature to assist the emotions which have created it.

In these various forms Shakespeare introduces super-

natural agency into his dramas. In my discussion of them
it will be understood that I am not in the least endeavouring
to explain away the reality of their supernatural character.
My purpose is to show for how small a proportion of his
total effect Shakespeare draws on the supernatural, allowing it
to carry further or to illustrate, but not to mould or determine
a course of events. It will readily be granted that he brings
effect enough out of a supernatural incident to justify the use
of it to our rational sense of economy.

XIV.

INTEREST OF PLOT.

WE now come to the third great division of Dramatic Criticism—Plot, or the purely intellectual side of action. Action itself has been treated above as the mutual connection and interweaving of all the details in a work of art so as to unite in an impression of unity. But we have found it impossible to discuss Character and Passion entirely apart from such action and interworking : the details of human interest become dramatic by being permeated with action-force. When however this mutual relation of all the parts is looked at by itself, as an abstract interest of design, the human life being no more than the material to which this design is applied, then we get the interest of Plot. So defined, I hope Plot is sufficiently removed from the vulgar conception of it as sensational mystery, which has done so much to lower this element of dramatic effect in the eyes of literary students. If Plot be understood as the extension of design to the sphere of human life, threads of experience being woven into a symmetrical pattern as truly as vari-coloured threads of wool are woven into a piece of wool-work, then the conception of it will come out in its true dignity. What else is such reduction to order than the meeting-point of science and art? Science is engaged in tracing rhythmic movements in the beautiful confusion of the heavenly bodies, or reducing the bewildering variety of external nature to regular species and nice gradations of life. Similarly, art continues the work of creation in calling ideal

order out of the chaos of things as they are. And so the
tangle of life, with its jumble of conflicting aspirations, its
crossing and twisting of contrary motives, its struggle and
partnership of the whole human race, in which no two individuals are perfectly alike and no one is wholly independent of the rest—this has gradually in the course of ages been
laboriously traced by the scientific historian into some such
harmonious plan as evolution. But he finds himself long
ago anticipated by the dramatic artist, who has touched
crime and seen it link itself with nemesis, who has transformed passion into pathos, who has received the shapeless
facts of reality and returned them as an ordered economy of
design. This application of form to human life is Plot:
and Shakespeare has had no higher task to accomplish than
in his revolutionising our ideas of Plot, until the old critical
conceptions of it completely broke down when applied to
his dramas. The appreciation of Shakespeare will not be
complete until he is seen to be as subtle a weaver of plots as
he is a deep reader of the human heart.

We have to consider Plot in its three aspects of unity, *Unity ap-*
complexity, and development. The simplest element of *plied to Plot.*
Plot is the *Single Action*, which may be defined as any train *The Single*
of incidents in a drama which can be conceived as a separate *Action.*
whole. Thus a series of details bringing out the idea of a
crime and its nemesis will constitute a Nemesis Action, an
oracle and its fulfilment will make up an Oracular Action, a
problem and its solution a Problem Action. Throughout
the treatment of Plot the root idea of *pattern* should be
steadily kept in mind: in the case of these Single Actions—
the units of Plot—we have as it were the lines of a geometrical design, made up of their details as a geometrical
line is made up of separate points. The *Form* of a dramatic *Forms of*
action—the shape of the line, so to speak—will be that *Dramatic Action.*
which gives the train of incidents its distinctiveness: the
nemesis, the oracle, the problem. An action may get its

distinctiveness from its tone as a Comic Action or a Tragic Action; or it may be a Character Action, when a series of details acquire a unity in bringing out the character of Hastings or Lady Macbeth; an action may be an Intrigue, or the Rise and Fall of a person, or simply a Story like the Caskets Story. Finally, an action may combine several different forms at the same time, just as a geometrical line may be at once, say, an arch and a spiral. The action that traces Macbeth's career has been treated as exhibiting a triple form of Nemesis, Irony, and Oracular Action; further, it is a Tragic Action in tone, it is a Character Action in its contrast with the career of Lady Macbeth, and it stands in the relation of Main Action to others in the play.

Complexity applied to Action: a distinction of Modern Drama. Now what I have called Single Action constituted the whole conception of Plot in ancient Tragedy; in the Shakespearean Drama it exists only as a unit of Complex Action. The application of complexity to action is rendered particularly easy by the idea of pattern, patterns which appeal to the eye being more often made up of several lines crossing and interweaving than of single lines. Ancient tragedy clung to 'unity of action,' and excluded such matter as threatened to set up a second interest in a play. Modern Plot has a unity of a much more elaborate order, perhaps best expressed by the word *harmony*—a harmony of distinct actions, each of which has its separate unity. The illustration of harmony is suggestive. Just as in musical harmony each part is a melody of itself, though one of them leads and is *the* melody, so a modern plot draws together into a common system a Main Action and other inferior yet distinct actions. Moreover the step from melody alone to melody harmonised, or that from the single instruments of the ancient world to the combinations of a modern orchestra, marks just the difference between ancient and modern art which we find reflected in the different conception of Plot held by Sophocles and by Shakespeare. Shakespeare's

plots are federations of plots: in his ordering of dramatic
events we trace a common self-government made out of
elements which have an independence of their own, and at
the same time merge a part of their independence in common action.

The foundation of critical treatment in the matter of Plot *Analysis of*
is the *Analysis* of Complex Action into its constituent Single * *Action.*
Actions.   This is easy in such a play as *The Merchant of
Venice.*   Here two of the actions are stories, a form of
unity readily grasped, and which in the present case had an
independent existence outside the play.   These identified and
separated, it is easy also to see that Jessica constitutes a
fresh centre of interest around which other details gather
themselves; that the incidents in which Launcelot and
Gobbo are concerned are separable from these; while the
matter of the rings constitutes a distinct episode of the
Caskets Story: already the junction of so many separate
stories in a common working gratifies our sense of design.
In other plays where the elements are not stories the individuality of the Single Actions will not always be so positive: all would readily distinguish the Lear Main plot from
the Underplot of Gloucester, but in the subdivision of these
difference of opinion arises.   In an Appendix to this
chapter I have suggested schemes of Analysis for each of
the five plays treated in this work: I may here add four *Canons of*
remarks.   (1) Any series of details which can be collected *Analysis.*
from various parts of a drama to make up a common in- *Analysis*
terest may be recognised in Analysis as a separate action. *tentative*
It follows from this that there may be very different modes *not posi-*
of dividing and arranging the elements of the same plot: *tive.*
such Analysis is not a matter in which we are to look for
right or wrong, but simply for better or worse.   No scheme
will ever exhaust the wealth of design which reveals itself in

---

* See note on page 74.

a play of Shakespeare ; and the value of Analysis as a critical process is not confined to the scheme it produces, but includes also the insight which the mere effort to analyse a drama gives into the harmony and connection of its parts. (2) The essence of Plot being design, that will be the best scheme of Analysis which best brings out the idea of symmetry and design. (3) Analysis must be exhaustive : every detail in the drama must find a place in some one of the actions. (4) The constituent actions will of course not be mutually exclusive, many details being common to several actions : these details are so many meeting-points, in which the lines of action cross one another.—With these sufficiently obvious principles I must leave the schemes of analysis in the Appendix to justify themselves.

Design as the test of Analysis.

Analysis exhaustive.

The elementary actions not mutually exclusive.

The Enveloping Action.

In the process of analysis we are led to notice special forms of action : in particular, the *Enveloping Action.* This interesting element of Plot may be described as the fringe, or border, or frame, of a dramatic pattern. It appears when the personages and incidents which make up the essential interest of a play are more or less loosely involved with some interest more wide-reaching than their own, though more vaguely presented. It is seen in its simplest form where a story occupied with private personages connects itself at points with public history : homely life being thus wrapped round with life of the great world; fiction having reality given to it by its being set in a frame of accepted fact. We are familiar enough with it in prose fiction. Almost all the Waverley Novels have Enveloping Actions, Scott's regular plan being to entangle the fortunes of individuals, which are to be the main interest of the story, with public events which make known history. Thus in *Woodstock* a Cavalier maiden and her Puritan lover become, as the story proceeds, mixed up in incidents of the Commonwealth and Restoration ; or again, the plot of *Redgauntlet,* which consists in the separate adventures of a pair of Scotch

friends, is brought to an issue in a Jacobite rising in which Ch. XIV.
both become involved. The Enveloping Action is a favourite element in Shakespeare's plots. In the former part of
the book I have pointed out how the War of the Roses
forms an Enveloping Action to *Richard III*; how its connection with the other actions is close enough for it to catch
the common feature of Nemesis; and how it is marked
with special clearness by the introduction of Queen Margaret
and the Duchess of York to bring out its opposite sides.
In *Macbeth* there is an Enveloping Action of the supernatural centring round the Witches: the human workings
of the play are wrapped in a deeper working out of destiny,
with prophetic beings to keep it before us. *Julius Cæsar*,
as a story of political conspiracy and political reaction, is
furnished with a loose Enveloping Action in the passions of
the Roman mob: this is a vague power outside recognised
political forces, appearing at the beginning to mark that uncertainty in public life which can drive even good men to conspiracy, while from the turning-point it furnishes the force
the explosion of which is made to secure the conspirators'
downfall. A typical example is to be found in *Lear*, all the
more typical from the fact that it is by no means a prominent interest in the play. The Enveloping Action in this
drama is the French War. The seeds of this war are sown
in the opening incident, in which the French King receives
his wife from Lear with scarcely veiled insult: it troubles i. i. 265.
Gloucester in the next scene that France is 'in choler parted.' i. ii. 23.
Then we get, in the second Act, a distant hint of rupture
from the letter of Cordelia read by Kent in the stocks. In ii. ii. 172.
the other scenes of this Act the only political question is of
'likely wars toward' between the English dukes; but at the ii. i. 11.
beginning of the third Act Kent directly connects these
quarrels of the dukes with the growing chance of a war with iii. i. 19–
France: the French have had intelligence of the 'scattered 34.
kingdom,' and have been 'wise in our negligence.' In this

T

Act Gloucester confides to Edmund the feeler he has received from France, and his trustfulness is the cause of his downfall; Edmund treacherously reveals the confidence to Cornwall, and makes it the occasion of his rise. Gloucester's measures for the safety of Lear have naturally a connection with the expected invasion, and he sends him to Dover to find welcome and protection. The final scene of this Act, devoted to the cruel outrage on Gloucester, shows from its very commencement the important connection of the Enveloping Action with the rest of the play: the French army has landed, and it is this which is felt to make Lear's escape so important, and which causes such signal revenge to be taken on Gloucester. Throughout the fourth Act all the threads of interest are becoming connected with the invading army at Dover; if this Act has a separate interest of its own in Edmund's intrigues with both Goneril and Regan at once,

yet these intrigues are possible only because Edmund is hurrying backwards and forwards between the princesses in the measures of military preparation for the battle. The fifth Act has its scene on the battlefield, and the double issue of the battle stamps itself on the whole issue of the play: the death of Lear and Cordelia is the result of the French defeat, while, on the other hand, all who were to

reap the fruits of guilt die in the hour of victory. Thus this French War is a model of Enveloping Action—outside the main issues, yet loosely connecting itself with every phase of the movement; originating in the incident which is the origin of the whole action; the possibility of it developed by the progress of the Main story, alike by the cruelty shown to Lear and by the rivalry between his daughters; the fear of it playing a main part in the tragic side of the Underplot, and the preparation for it serving as occasion for the remaining interest of intrigue; finally, breaking out as a reality in which the whole action of the play merges.

From Analysis we pass naturally to *Economy*. Considered

in the abstract, as a phase of plot-beauty, Economy may be
defined as that perfection of design which lies midway be- *Economy*
tween incompleteness and waste. Its formula is that a play *supple-*
mentary to
must be seen to contain all the details necessary to the *Analysis.*
unity, no detail superfluous to the unity, and each detail
expanded in exact proportion to its bearing on the unity.
In practice, as a branch of treatment in Shakespeare-
Criticism, Economy, like Analysis, deals with complexity of
plot. The two are supplementary to one another. The one
resolves a complexity into its elements, the other traces the
unity running through these elements. Analysis distinguishes
the separate actions which make up a plot, while Economy
notes the various bonds between these actions and the way
in which they are brought into a common system : it being
clear that the more the separateness of the different interests
can be reduced the richer will be the economy of design.

It will be enough to note three Economic Forms. The *Economic*
Forms.
first is simple *Connection* : the actual contact of action *Connection*
with action, the separate lines of the pattern meeting at
various points. In other words, the different actions have
details or personages in common. Bassanio is clearly a
bond between the two main stories of *The Merchant of*
Venice, in both of which he figures so prominently ; and it has
been pointed out that the scene of Bassanio's successful choice
is an incident with which all the stories which enter into the
action of the play connect themselves. There are *Link and Link-*
ing.
Personages, who have a special function so to connect
stories, and similarly *Link Actions* : Gloucester in the play
of *Lear* and the Jessica Story in *The Merchant of Venice* are
examples. Or Connection may come by the interweaving
of stories as they progress : they alternate, or fill, so to
speak, each other's interstices. Where the Story of the *from ii. i. to*
Jew halts for a period of three months, the elopement of *iii. ii. 319.*
Jessica comes to occupy the interval ; or again, scenes
from the tragedy of the Gloucester family separate scenes

CH. XIV. from the tragedy of Lear, until the two tragedies have become mutually entangled. Envelopment too serves as a kind of Connection : the actions which make up such a play as *Richard III* gain additional compactness by their being merged in a common Enveloping Action.

Depend-ence.

Another Form of Economy is *Dependence.* This term expresses the relation between an underplot and main plot, or between subactions and the actions to which they are subordinate. The fact that Gloucester is a follower of

compare i. i. 35, 191.

Lear—he would appear to have been his court chamberlain—makes the story of the Gloucester family seem to spring out of the story of the Lear family; that we are not called upon to initiate a fresh train of interest ministers to our sense of Economy.

Symmetry.

But in the Shakespearean Drama the most important Economic Form is *Symmetry* : between different parts of a design symmetry is the closest of bonds. A simple form of

Balance.

Symmetry is the *Balance* of actions, by which, as it were, the mass of one story is made to counterpoise that of another. If the Caskets Story, moving so simply to its goal of success, seems over-weighted by the thrilling incidents of the Jew Story, we find that the former has by way of compensation the Episode of the Rings rising out of its close, while the elopement of Jessica and her reception at Belmont transfers a whole batch of interests from the Jew side of the play to the Christian side. Or again, in a play such as *Macbeth*, which traces the Rise and Fall of a personage, the Rise is accompanied by the separate interest of Banquo till he falls a victim to its success; to balance this we have in the Fall Macduff, who becomes important only after Banquo's death, and from that point occupies more and more of the field of view until he brings the action to a close. Similarly in *Julius Cæsar* the victim himself dominates the first half; Antony, his avenger, succeeds to his position for the second half. More important than Balance

as forms of Symmetry are *Parallelism* and *Contrast* of Cᴜ. XIV.
actions.   Both are, to a certain extent, exemplified in the *Parallel-*
plot of *Macbeth* : the triple form of Nemesis, Irony, and Ora- *ism and*
cular binding together all the elements of the plot down to *Contrast.*
the Enveloping Action illustrates Parallelism, and Contrast
has been shown to be a bond between the interest of Lady
Macbeth and of her husband.   But Parallelism and Contrast
are united in their most typical forms in *Lear*, which is at
once the most intricate and the most symmetrical of Shakespearean dramas.   A glance at the scheme of this plot shows
its deep-seated parallelism.   A Main story in the family of
Lear has an Underplot in the family of Gloucester.   The
Main plot is a problem and its solution, the Underplot is an
intrigue and its nemesis.   Each is a system of four actions :
there is the action initiating the problem with the three
tragedies which make up its solution, there is again the
action generating the intrigue and the three tragedies
which constitute its nemesis.   The threefold tragedy in
the Main plot has its elements exactly analogous, each to
each, to the threefold tragedy of the Underplot : Lear and
Gloucester alike reap a double nemesis of evil from the
children they have favoured, and good from the children they
have wronged; the innocent Cordelia has to suffer like the
innocent Edgar ; alike in both stories the gains of the
wicked are found to be the means of their destruction.   Even
in the subactions, which have only a temporary distinctness
in carrying out such elaborate interworking, the same
Parallelism manifests itself.   They run in pairs : where Kent e. g. i. iv.
has an individual mission as an agency for good, Oswald 85–104;
runs a course parallel with him as an agency for evil ; of the ii. ii, &c.
two heirs of Lear, Albany, after passively representing the e. g. iv. ii.
good side of the Main plot, has the function of presiding 29;
over the nemesis which comes on the evil agents of the v. iii, from
Underplot, while Cornwall, who is active in the evil of the 59.
Main plot, is the agent in bringing suffering on the good iii. vii.

CH. XIV.

iv. ii; iv.
v; v. iii.
238.

victims of the Underplot; once more from opposite sides
of the Lear story Goneril and Regan work in parallel intrigues to their destruction. Every line of the pattern runs
parallel to some distant line. Further, so fundamental is the
symmetry that we have only to shift the point of view and
the Parallelism becomes Contrast. If the family histories
be arranged around Cordelia and Edmund, as centres of
good and evil in their different spheres, we perceive a sharp
antithesis between the two stories extending to every detail:
though stated already in the chapter on *Lear*, I should like
to state it again in parallel columns to do it full justice.

In the MAIN PLOT a	In the UNDERPLOT a
Daughter,	Son,
Who has received nothing but Harm from her father,	Who has received nothing but Good from his father,
Who has had her position unjustly torn from her and given to her undeserving elder Sisters,	Who has, contrary to justice, been advanced to the position of an innocent elder Brother he had maligned,
Nevertheless sacrifices herself to save the Father who *did* the injury from the Sisters who *profited* by it.	Nevertheless is seeking the destruction of the Father who *did* him the unjust kindness, when he falls by the hand of the Brother who *was wronged* by it.

The play of *Lear* is itself sufficient to suggest to the critic
that in the analysis of Shakespeare's plots he may safely ex-
pect to find symmetry in proportion to their intricacy.

*Movement
applied to
Plot: Mo-
tive Form.*

*Simple
Movement:
the Line of*

Movement applied to Plot becomes *Motive Form* : without
its being necessary to take the play to pieces Motive Form is
the impression of design left by the succession of incidents
in the order in which they actually stand. The succession
of incidents may suggest progress to a goal, as in the

Caskets Story. This is preeminently Simple * Movement: Сн XIV.
the Line of Motion becomes a straight line. We get the *Motion a*
next step by the variation that is made when a curved line is *straight line*
substituted for a straight line: in other words, when the *Compli-*
succession of incidents reaches its goal, but only after a *cated Move-*
diversion. This is what is known as *Complication and Reso-* *ment · the Line of*
lution. A train of events is obstructed and diverted from *Motion a*
what appears its natural course, which gives the interest *curve.*
of Complication: after a time the obstruction is removed
and the natural course is restored, which is the Resolution
of the action: the Complication, like a musical discord,
having existed only for the sake of being resolved. No
clearer example could be desired than that of Antonio,
whose career when we are introduced to it appears to be
that of leading the money-market of Venice and extending
patronage and protection all around; by the entanglement
of the bond this career is checked and Antonio turned into
a prisoner and bankrupt; then Portia cuts the knot and
Antonio becomes all he has been before. Or again, the
affianced intercourse of Portia and Bassanio begins with an iii ii 173.
exchange of rings; by the cross circumstances connected with
Antonio's trial one of them parts with this token, and the result iv. ii.
is a comic interruption to the smoothness of lovers' life, until
by Portia's confession of the ruse the old footing is restored. v. i. 266.

Such Complicated Movement belongs entirely to the *Action-*
Action side of dramatic effect. It rests upon design and *Movement distin-*
the interworking of details; its interest lies in obstacles in- *guished*
terposed to be removed, doing for the sake of undoing, en- *from Pas-sion-Move-*
tanglement for its own sake; in its total effect it ministers to *ment.*
a sense of intellectual satisfaction, like that belonging to a
musical fugue, in which every opening suggested has been
sufficiently followed up. We get a movement of quite a
different kind when the sense of design is inseparable from
effects of passion, and the movement is, as it were, traced in

* See note on page 74.

CH. XIV.

our emotional nature.   In this case a growing strain is put upon our sympathy which is not unlike Complication.   But no Resolution follows : the rise is made to end in fall, the progress leads to ruin ; in place of the satisfaction that comes from restoring and unloosing is substituted a fresh appeal to our emotional nature, and from agitation we pass only to the calmer emotions of pity and awe.   There is thus a *Passion-Movement* distinct from *Action-Movement*; and, analogous to the Complication and Resolution of the latter, Passion-Movement has its *Strain and Reaction*.   The Line of Passion has its various forms.   A chapter has been devoted to illustrating one form of Passion-Movement, which may be called the *Regular Arch*—if we may found a technical term on the happy illustration of Gervinus.   The example was taken from the play of *Julius Cæsar*, the emotional effect in which was shown to pass from calm interest to greater and greater degree of agitation, until after culminating in the centre it softens down and yields to the different calmness of pity and acquiescence.   The movement of *Richard III* and many other dramas more resembles the form of an *Inclined Plane*, the turn in the emotion occurring long past the centre of the play.   Or again, there is the *Wave Line* of emotional distribution, made by repeated alternations of strain and relief.   This is a form of Passion-Movement that nearly approaches Action-Movement, and readily goes with it in the same play ; in *The Merchant of Venice* the union of the two stories gives such alternate Strain and Relief, and the Episode of the Rings comes as final Relief to the final Strain of the trial.

The Line of Passion a Regular Arch,

an Inclined Plane

IV. ii. 46.

or a Wave Line.

For 'Comedy,' 'Tragedy,' substitute, in the case of Shakespeare,

The distinction between Action-Movement and Passion-Movement is of special importance in Shakespeare-Criticism, inasmuch as it is the real basis of distinction between the two main classes of Shakespearean dramas.   Every one feels that the terms Comedy and Tragedy are inadequate, and indeed absurd, when applied to Shakespeare.   The dis-

tinction these terms express is one of Tone, and they were
quite in place in the ancient Drama, in which the comic
and tragic tones were kept rigidly distinct and were not
allowed to mingle in the same play.   Applied to a branch of
Drama of which the leading characteristic is the complete
Mixture of Tones the terms necessarily break down, and the
so-called 'Comedies' of *The Merchant of Venice* and *Measure
for Measure* contain some of the most tragic effects in
Shakespeare.   The true distinction between the two kinds
of plays is one of Movement, not Tone.   In *The Merchant
of Venice* the leading interest is in the complication of Antonio's fortunes and its resolution by the device of Portia.
In all such cases, however perplexing the entanglement of
the complication may have become, the ultimate effect of
the whole lies in the resolution of this complication ; and
this is an intellectual effect of satisfaction.   In the plays
called Tragedies there is no such return from distraction to
recovery : our sympathy having been worked up to the emotion of agitation is relieved only by the emotion of pathos or
despair.   Thus in these two kinds of dramas the impression
which to the spectator overpowers all other impressions, and
gives individuality to the particular play, is this sense of intellectual or of emotional unity in the movement :—is, in other
words, Action-Movement or Passion-Movement.   The two *'Action-*
may be united, as remarked above in the case of *The Mer- Drama,'*
chant of Venice; but one or the other will be predominant *Drama.'*
and will give to the play its unity of impression.   The distinction, then, which the terms Comedy and Tragedy fail
to mark would be accurately brought out by substituting for
them the terms Action-Drama and Passion-Drama.

  With complexity of action comes complexity of movement. *Compound*
Compound Movement takes in the idea of the relative motion *Movement.*
amongst the different actions into which a plot can be
analysed.   A play of Shakespeare presents a system of wheels
within wheels, like a solar system in motion as a whole

while the separate members of it have their own orbits to follow. The nature of Compound Movement can be most simply brought out by describing its three leading Modes of Motion. In *Similar Motion* the actions of a system are moving in the same form. The plot of *Richard III*, for example, is a general rise and fall of Nemesis made up of elements which are themselves rising and falling Nemeses. Such Similar Motion is only Parallelism looked at from the side of movement. A variation of it occurs when the form of one action is distributed amongst the rest : the main action of *Julius Cæsar* is a Nemesis Action, the two sub-actions are the separate interests of Cæsar and Antony, which put together amount to Nemesis.

In *Contrary Motion* the separate actions as they move on interfere with one another, that is, each acts as complicating force to the other, turning it out of its course ; in reality they are helping one another's advance, seeing that complication is a step in dramatic progress. *The Merchant of Venice* furnishes an example. The Caskets Story progresses without check to its climax ; in starting it complicates the Jew action—for before Bassanio can get to Belmont he borrows of Antonio the loan which is to entangle him in the meshes of the Jew's revenge; then the Caskets Story as a result of its climax resolves this complication in the Story of the Jew—for the union of Portia with Bassanio provides the deliverer for Bassanio's friend. But in thus resolving the Story of the Jew the Caskets Story, in the new phase of it that has commenced with the exchange of betrothal rings, itself suffers complication—the circumstances of the trial offering the suggestion to Portia to make the demand for Bassanio's ring. Thus of the two actions moving on side by side the one interferes with and diverts the other from its course, and again in restoring it gets itself diverted. This mutual interference makes up Contrary Motion.

A third mode of Compound movement is *Convergent Motion,*

by which actions, or systems of actions, at first separate,
become drawn together as they move on, and assist one
another's progress. Once more the play of *Lear* furnishes
a typical example. This play, it will be recollected, includes
two distinct systems of actions tracing the story of two
separate families. Moreover the main story after its opening incident presents, so far as movement is concerned, three
different sides, according as its incidents centre around Lear,
Goneril, or Regan. The first link between these diverse
actions is Gloucester, the central personage of the whole
plot. Gloucester has been the King's chamberlain and his i. i. 35, 191.
close friend, the King having been godfather to his son. ii. i. 93.
Accordingly, in the highly unstable political condition of a
kingdom divided equally between two unprincipled sisters,
Gloucester represents a third party, the party of Lear: he
holds the balance of power, and the effort to secure him
draws the separate interests together. Thus as soon as
Lear and Goneril have quarrelled Lear sends Kent to Glou- i. v. i
cester, and our actions begin to approach one another.
Before this messenger can arrive we hear of ' hints and ear- ii. i. 9
kissing arguments ' as to rupture between the dukes, and
we see Regan and her husband making a hasty journey—
' out of season threading dark-eyed night '—in order to be ii. i. 121.
the first at Gloucester's castle; when Goneril in self-defence ii. iv. 192.
follows, all the separate elements of the main plot have
found a meeting-point. But this castle of Gloucester in
which they meet is the seat of the underplot, and the two
systems become united in the closest manner by this central
linking. Regan arrives in time to use her authority in fur- ii. i. 88–
thering the intrigue against Edgar as a means of recom- 131, esp.
mending herself to the deceived Gloucester; the other in- 112.
trigue of the underplot, that against Gloucester himself, is iii. v, &c.
promoted by the same means when Edmund has betrayed
to Regan his father's protection of Lear; while the meeting
of both sisters with Edmund lays the foundation of the

mutual intriguing which forms the further interest of the entanglement between underplot and main story. All the separate lines of action have thus moved to a common centre, and their concentration in a common focus gives opportunity for the climax of passion which forms the centre-piece of the play. Then the Enveloping Action comes in as a further binding force, and it has been pointed out above how throughout the fourth and fifth Acts all the separate actions, whatever their immediate purpose, have an ultimate reference to Dover as the landing-place of the invading army: in military phrase Dover is the common *objective* on which all the separate trains of interest are concentrating. In this way have the actions of this intricate plot, so numerous and so separate at first, been found to converge to a common centre and then move together to a common *dénouement*.

Turning-points.   The distinction of movement from the other elements of Plot leads also to the question of *Turning-points*, an idea equally connected with movement and with design. In the movement of every play a Turning-point is implied: movement could not have dramatic interest unless there were a change in the direction of events, and such change implies a point at which the change becomes apparent. Changes of a kind may be frequent through the progress of a play, but one notable point will stand out at which the ultimate issues present themselves as decided, the line of motion changing from complication to resolution, the line of passion from strain to reaction. Such a point is technically a *Catas-*

The Cata-strophe: or Focus of Movement.   *trophe*: a word whose etymological meaning suggests a turning round so as to come down. In Shakespeare's dramatic

The Centre of Plot.   practice we find a not less important Turning-point in relation to the design of the plot. This is always at the exact centre—the middle of the middle Act—and serves as a balancing-point about which the plot may be seen to be symmetrical: it is a *Centre of Plot* as the Catastrophe is a Focus of Movement. The Catastrophe of *The Merchant of*

Venice is clearly Portia's judgment in the Trial Scene, by Сн. XIV.
which in a moment the whole entanglement is resolved. In iv. i. 305.
an earlier chapter it has been pointed out how the union of
Portia and Bassanio—at the exact centre of the play—is the iii. ii.
real determinant of the whole plot, uniting the complicating
and resolving forces, and constituting a scene in which all
the four stories find a meeting-point. In *Richard III*, while
the Catastrophe comes in the hero's late recognition of his iv. ii. 45.
own nemesis, yet there has been, before this and in the
exact centre, a turn in the Enveloping Action, which includes all the rest, shown by the recognition that Margaret's iii iu 15.
curses have now begun to be fulfilled. The exact centre of
Macbeth, as pointed out above, marks the hero's passage iii. iv. 20.
from rise to fall, that is from unbroken success to unbroken
failure : the corresponding Catastrophe in this play is double,
a first appearance of Nemesis in Banquo's ghost, its final iii. iv. 49;
stroke in the revelation of Macduff's secret of birth. *Julius* v. viii. 13.
Cæsar presents the interesting feature of the Catastrophe
and Central Turning-point exactly coinciding, in the trium- iii i. 122
phant appeal of the conspirators to future history. *Lear*,
according to the scheme of analysis suggested in this work,
has its Catastrophe at the close of the initial scene, by
which time the problem in experience has been set up in
action, and the tragedies arising out of it thenceforward
work on without break to its solution. A Centre of Plot is
found for this play where, in the middle Scene of the middle iii. iv. 45.
Act, the third of the three forms of madness is brought into
contact with the other two and makes the climax of passion
complete. This regular union by Shakespeare of a marked
catastrophe, appealing to every spectator, with a subtle
dividing-point, interesting to the intellectual sense of analysis, illustrates the combination of force with symmetry,
which is the genius of the Shakespearean Drama : it throughout presents a body of warm human interest governed by a
mind of intricate design.

Conclusion. The plan laid down for this work has now been followed to its completion. The object I have had in view throughout has been the *recognition* of inductive treatment in literary study. For this purpose it was first necessary to distinguish the inductive method from other modes of treatment founded on arbitrary canons of taste and comparisons of merit, so natural in view of the popularity of the subject-matter, and to which the history of Literary Criticism has given an unfortunate impetus. This having been done in the Introduction, the body of the work has been occupied in applying the inductive treatment to some of the masterpieces of Shakespeare. The practical effect of such exposition has been, it may be hoped, to intensify the reader's appreciation of the poet, and also to suggest that the detailed and methodical analysis which in literary study is usually reserved for points of language is no less applicable to a writer's subject-matter and art. But to entitle Dramatic Criticism to a place in the circle of the inductive sciences it has further appeared necessary to lay down a scheme for the study as a whole, that should be scientific both in the relation of its parts to one another, and in the attainment of a completeness proportioned to the area to which the enquiry was limited and the degree of development to which literary method has at present attained. The proper method for the nascent science was fixed as the enumeration and arrangement of topics; and by analogy with the other arts a simple scheme for Dramatic Criticism was found, in which all the results of the analysis performed in the first part of the book could be readily distributed under one or other of the main topics—Character, Passion, and Plot. Incidentally the discussion of Shakespeare has again and again reminded us of just that greatness in the modern Drama which judicial criticism with its inflexibility of standard so persistently missed. Everywhere early criticism recognised our poet's grasp of human nature, yet its almost universal verdict of him was that he was both irregular in his art as a whole, and in particular careless in the construction of his plots. We have seen, on the contrary, that Shakespeare has elevated the whole conception of Plot, from that of a mere unity of action obtained by reduction of the amount of matter presented, to that of a harmony of design binding together concurrent actions from which no degree of complexity was excluded. And, finally, instead of his being a despiser of law, we have had suggested to us how Shakespeare and his brother artists of the Renaissance form a point of departure in legitimate Drama, so important as amply to justify the instinct of history which named that age the Second Birth of literature.

TABULAR DIGEST OF THE PRINCIPAL TOPICS IN DRAMATIC SCIENCE.

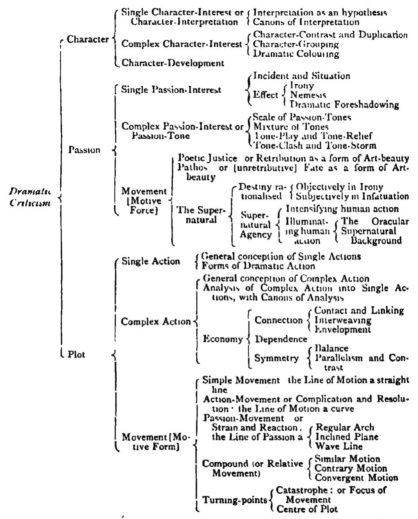

To which may be added { Mechanical Construction [belonging to Art in general]
Story as Raw Material [belonging to Literary History]

APPENDIX TO CHAPTER XIV.

·

TECHNICAL ANALYSIS OF THE PLOT
OF THE FIVE PLAYS.

U

THE MERCHANT OF VENICE.

An Action-Drama.

Scheme of Actions.

Main Plot.
{
  First Main **Cross Nemesis** Action : Story of the Jew : complicated and resolved.

  Sub-Action to First Main, also Link Action : Jessica and Lorenzo : simple movement.

  Comic Relief Action : Launcelot : stationary[1].

  Sub-Action to Second Main : Episode of the Rings : complicated and resolved.
} Under-plot.

Second Main **Problem** Action : Caskets Story : simple movement.

External Circumstance[2] : The (rumoured) Shipwrecks.

Economy.

Two Main Actions connected by Common Personage [Bassanio] and by Link Action [Jessica].

General Interweaving.

Balance. The First Main Action, which is complicated, balances the Second, which is simple, by the additions to the latter of the Jessica interest transferred to it, and the Episode of the Rings generated out of it. [Pages 82, 88.]

Movement.

Action-Movement : with Contrary Motion between the two Main Actions. The First Main complicated and resolved by the Second

---

[1] Stationary, as having no place in the movement of the plot : its separateness from the rest of the Jessica Action only for purposes of Tone-effect, as Comic Relief.

[2] 'External' as not included in any Action, 'Circumstance' because it presents itself as a single detail instead of the series of details necessary to make up an Action. An External Circumstance is analogous to an Enveloping Action : outside the other Actions, yet in contact with them at certain points.

Main [hero of Second, Bassanio, is Complicating Force ; heroine of Second, Portia, is Resolving Force], the Complication assisted by the External Circumstance of the Shipwrecks—in process of resolving the First generates a Complication to the Second in the form of the Episode of the Rings, which is self-resolved. [Pages 66, 282.]

Passion-Movement in the background : Wave-Line of Strain and Relief by alternation of the two main Stories ; the Episode of the Rings is Final Relief to the Final Strain of the Trial.

Turning-points.

Centre of Plot : Scene of Bassanio's Choice (iii. ii.) in which the Complicating and Resolving Forces are united and all the Four Actions meet. [Pages 67-8.]

Catastrophe : Portia's Judgment in the Trial (iv. i, from 299).

RICHARD THE THIRD.

A Passion-Drama.

Scheme of Actions.

Main **Nemesis** Action : Life and Death of Richard.

Underplot : System of **Cross Nemesis** Actions connecting Main with YORK side of Enveloping Action.

⌈ CLARENCE has betrayed the Lancastrians for the sake of the House of York :

He falls by a treacherous death from the KING of the House of York. — To this the QUEEN and her kindred have been assenting parties [ii. ii. 62–5] :

The shock of Clarence's death as announced by Gloster kills the King (ii. i. 131), leaving the Queen and her kindred at the mercy of their enemies. — Unseemly Exultation of their great enemy HASTINGS :

The same treachery step by step overtakes Hastings in his Exultation [iii. iv. 15–95]. — In this treacherous casting off of Hastings when he will no longer support them BUCKINGHAM has been a prime agent [iii. i, from 157, iii. ii. 114] :

By precisely similar treachery Buckingham himself is cast off when he hesitates to go further with Richard [iv. ii. and v. i]

Link **Nemesis** Action connecting Main with LANCASTER side of
Enveloping Action : Marriage of Richard and Anne (p. 113).

Enveloping **Nemesis** Action : The War of the Roses [the Duchess
of York introduced to mark the York side, Queen Margaret to
mark the Lancastrian side].

Economy.

All the Actions bound together by the Enveloping Action of which
they make up a phase.

Parallelism : the common form of Nemesis.

Central Personage : Richard.

Movement.

Passion-Movement, with Similar Motion [form Nemesis repeated
throughout (page 282)].

Turning-points.

Centre of Plot : Realisation of Margaret's Curses [turn of Enveloping Action] in iii. iii. 15.

Catastrophe : Realisation of Nemesis in the Main Action : iv. ii,
from 45.

MACBETH.

A PASSION-DRAMA.

Scheme of Actions.

> { Main **Character** Action : Rise and Fall of Macbeth.
> { **Character** Counter-Action : Lady Macbeth.

> > { **Character** Sub-Action : covering and involved in the Rise :
> > Banquo.
> > { **Character** Sub-Action : covering and involving the Fall :
> > Macduff. [Pages 129, 142.]

> Enveloping **Supernatural** Action : The Witches.

Economy.

> Parallelism : Triple form of Nemesis, Irony and Oracular Action
> extending to the Main Action, to its parts the Rise and Fall
> separately, and through to the Enveloping Action.
> Contrast as a bond between the Main and Counter-Action.
> Balance : the Rise by the Fall, the Sub-Action to the Rise by the
> Sub-Action to the Fall. [Page 276.]

Movement.

> Passion Movement, with Similar Motion between all.

Turning-points.

> Centre of Plot : Change from unbroken success to unbroken
> failure : iii. iii. 18. [Page 127.]
> Catastrophe : Divided : First Shock of Nemesis ; Appearance of
> Banquo's Ghost : iii. iv.
> > Final Accumulation of Nemesis : Revela-
> > tion of Macduff's birth : v. viii. 12.

JULIUS CÆSAR.

A Passion-Drama.

Scheme of Actions.

Main **Nemesis** Action: Rise and Fall of the Republican Conspirators.

{ Sub-Action to the Rise [**Character-decline**]: The Victim
Cæsar.
Sub-Action to the Fall [**Character-rise**]: The Avenger An-
tony.

Enveloping Action: the Roman Mob.

Economy.

Balance about the Centre: the Rise by the Fall, the Sub-Action to
the Rise by the Sub-Action to the Fall.

Movement.

Passion-Movement, with Similar Motion between the Main and
Sub-Actions. [The form of the Main is distributed between the
two Sub-Actions: compare page 282.]

Turning-points.

The Centre of Plot and Catastrophe coincide: iii. i. between 121
and 122.

KING LEAR.

A Passion-Drama.

Scheme of Actions.

Main Plot: a **Problem** Action: Family of Lear: falling into

Generating Action: [the Problem].	Lear's unstable settlement of the kingdom, power transferred from the good to the bad.
System of Tragedies [the Solution].	⌈**Double Nemesis** Action: Lear receiving good from the injured and evil from the favoured children. **Tragic** Action: Cordelia: Suffering of the innocent. **Tragic** Action: Goneril and Regan: Evil passions endowed with power using it ⌊ to work their own destruction.

Underplot: an **Intrigue** Action: Family of Gloucester: falling into

Generating Action: [the Intrigue].	Gloucester deceived into reversing the positions of Edgar and Edmund.
System of Tragedies [its Nemesis].	⌈**Double Nemesis** Action: Gloucester receiving good from the injured and evil from the favoured child. **Tragic** Action: Edgar: Suffering of the innocent. **Tragic** Action: Edmund: Power gained by intrigue used for the destruction of ⌊ the intriguer.

Central Link Personage between Main Plot and Underplot: Gloucester (page 283).

Sub-Actions, linking Main and Underplot, or different elements of the Main together.

First Pair:
- From the good side of the Main: Kent.
- From the evil side of the Main: Oswald.

Crossing & complicating one another.

Second Pair:
- From the good side of the Main assisting Nemesis on Evil Agent of the Underplot: Albany.
- From the evil side of the Main assisting Nemesis on Good Victim of the Underplot: Cornwall.

Third Pair: Cross Intrigues between the Evil sides of Main and Underplot
- Goneril and Edmund
- Regan and Edmund
culminating in destruction of all three (v. iii. 96, 221-7, and compare 82 with 160).

Farcical Relief Action: The Fool: Stationary.

Enveloping Action: The French War: originating ultimately in the Initial Action and becoming the Objective of the *Dénouement.* [Page 273.]

Economy.

The Underplot dependent to the Main (page 276).

Especially: Parallelism and Contrast (page 277).

Central Linking by Gloucester.

Interweaving: Linking by Sub-Actions, &c., and movement to a common Objective.

Envelopment in Common Enveloping Action.

Movement.

Passion-Movement, with Convergent Motion between the Main and Underplot, and their parts: the Lear and Gloucester systems by the visit to Gloucester's Castle drawn to a Central Focus and then moving towards a common Objective in the Enveloping Action. [Page 282.]

Turning-points.

Catastrophe: at the end of the Initial Action, the Problem being set up in practical action. [Page 205.]

Centre of Plot: the summit of emotional agitation when three madnesses are brought into contact (page 223).

INDEXES.

GENERAL INDEX.

dern conception 138-9—connected with Oracular Action 139—combined with Nemesis 256—as an objective presentation of Destiny 260-1   Dramatic Irony as example of mixed Passion 73—as a mode of emphasising Nemesis 115–119, 120—as one of the triple Forms of Action in *Macbeth* 139–42—as a Dramatic Effect 248-9—this a contribution of the Greek Stage 248—Dramatic Irony extended to the language of a scene 249—Comic Irony 249.

Illustrations in *Merchant of Venice* 73, 249; *Richard III* 115-19, 120, 121, 249, 256, *Macbeth* 139-142, 256, Macduff 143; Banquo 142; the Witches Action 143; proclamation of Cumberland 260; *Julius Cæsar* 249, 197; *King Lear* 249; Story of Œdipus 248.

Jeffrey 12.
Jester 218. [*See* King Lear: Fool]
Jew, Story of: 44, &c. [*See* Story.] —Feud of Jew and Gentile 60—Jews viewed as social outcasts 83.
Job, Book of: its conclusion as an example of Dramatic Background of Nature 192
Johnson, Dr.: on Shakespeare 10-11, 20—on Milton's minor poems 11—on Blank Verse 14—on Metaphysical Poetry 16—on Addison's *Cato* 19—on the Unities 20.
Jonson, Ben: 2-4—his Dramatic Satires 3—his Blank Verse 13—his *Catiline* 17.
Journalism: its influence on critical method 5—place of Reviewing in literary classification 21-2.
Judicial Blindness 201, 261. [*See* Infatuation.]

Julius Cæsar, Play of: 168-201, Chapters VIII and IX. As an example of Character-Grouping

168 and Chapter VIII, 241—example of Enveloping Action 273—Balance 276—Regular Arch Movement 280—Similar Motion 282—Turning-points 285—Technical Analysis 296.
Julius Cæsar, Characters in: Antony balances Cæsar 129—spared by the Conspirators 171—contrasted by Cæsar with Cassius 179-80—his general character 182-3—its culture 179-80—self-seeking 182—affection for Cæsar 183, 199—his position in the group of characters 183, 184—peculiar tone of his oratory 198—dominant spirit of the reaction 198—upspringing of a character in him 198—his ironical conciliation of the conspirators 199—his oration 199-200—Antony's servant 198.   Artemidorus 196.

Brutus: general character 171-6—its equal balance 171-5—its force 171 softness 173—this concealed under Stoicism 173, 174-5, 239—his culture 173—relations with his Page 173-4—with Portia 173, 174—with Cæsar 175—slays Cæsar for what he might become 175—position in the State 176—relations with Cassius 172, 173, 182—overrules Cassius in council 172—his general position in the Grouping 183.

Cæsar: a balance to Antony 129—general discussion of his character 176-81—its difficulty and contradictions 176-8—his vacillation 176-7—explained by the antithesis of Practical and Inner Life 178—Cæsar pre-eminently the Practical man 178-9—strong side of his character 176-7—lacking in the Inner Life 178-9—compared with Macbeth 178—a change in Cæsar and his world 180-1—his superstition 180-1—position in the Grouping 183—different effect of his personality in the earlier and later half of the play 188, 195, 197.   Calpur-

* The reader will remember that 'Single' is used as antithetical to 'Complex,' and 'Simple' to 'Complicated.' See note to page 74.

INDEX OF SCENES

ILLUSTRATED IN THE FOREGOING CHAPTERS.

₊ *Clarendon type is used where the passage referred to approaches the character of an analysis of the scene.*

Clarendon Press, Oxford

A SELECTION OF

BOOKS

SHED FOR THE UNIVERSITY BY

IENRY FROWDE,

AT THE   ₹D UNIVERSITY PRESS WAREHOUSE,

AMEN CORNER, LONDON.

ALSO TO BE HAD AT THE

CLARENDON PRESS DEPOSITORY, OXFORD.

[*Every book is bound in cloth, unless otherwise described.*]

LEXICONS, GRAMMARS, &c.

(See also Clarendon Press Series, pp. 14, 18, 21, 24, 25.)

ANGLO-SAXON.—*An Anglo-Saxon Dictionary*, based on the MS. Collections of the late Joseph Bosworth, D.D., Professor of Anglo-Saxon, Oxford. Edited and enlarged by Prof T. N. Toller, M A. (To be completed in four parts.) Parts I and II. A—HWISTLIAN (pp. vi, 576). 1882. 4to. 15s. each.

CHINESE.—*A Handbook of the Chinese Language.* Parts I and II, Grammar and Chrestomathy. By James Summers. 1863. 8vo. half bound, 1l. 8s.

ENGLISH.—*A New English Dictionary, on Historical Principles:* founded mainly on the materials collected by the Philological Society. Edited by James A. H. Murray, LL D., President of the Philological Society: with the assistance of many Scholars and men of Science. Part I. A—ANT (pp. xvi, 352). Imperial 4to. 12s. 6d.

—— *An Etymological Dictionary of the English Language.* By W. W. Skeat, M.A. *Second Edition.* 1884. 4to. 2l. 4s.

——Supplement to the First Edition of the above. 1884. 4to. 2s. 6d.

—— *A Concise Etymological Dictionary of the English Language.* By W. W. Skeat, M.A. *Second and Revised Edition.* 1885. Crown 8vo. 5s. 6d.

GREEK.—*A Greek-English Lexicon,* by Henry George Liddell, D.D., and Robert Scott, D.D. Seventh Edition, Revised and Augmented throughout. 1883. 4to. 1l. 16s.

—— *A Greek-English Lexicon,* abridged from Liddell and Scott's 4to. edition, chiefly for the use of Schools. Twenty-first Edition. 1884. Square 12mo. 7s. 6d.

[9]   B

GREEK.—*A copious Greek-English Vocabulary*, compiled from the best authorities. 1850. 24mo. 3*s*.

—— *A Practical Introduction to Greek Accentuation*, by H. W. Chandler, M.A. Second Edition. 1881. 8vo. 10*s*. 6*d*.

HEBREW.—*The Book of Hebrew Roots*, by Abu 'l-Walîd Marwân ibn Janâh, otherwise called Rabbî Yônâh. Now first edited, with an Appendix. by Ad. Neubauer. 1875. 4to. 2*l*. 7*s*. 6*d*.

—— *A Treatise on the use of the Tenses in Hebrew*. By S. R. Driver, M.A. Second Edition, Revised and Enlarged. 1881. Extra fcap. 8vo. 7*s*. 6*d*.

—— *Hebrew Accentuation of Psalms, Proverbs, and Job*. By William Wickes, D.D. 1881. Demy 8vo. stiff covers, 5*s*.

ICELANDIC.—*An Icelandic-English Dictionary*, based on the MS. collections of the late Richard Cleasby. Enlarged and completed by G. Vigfússon. M.A. With an Introduction, and Life of Richard Cleasby, by G. Webbe Dasent, D.C.L. 1874 4to. 3*l* 7*s*.

—— *A List of English Words the Etymology of which is illustrated by comparison with Icelandic*. Prepared in the form of an APPENDIX to the above. By W. W. Skeat, M.A. 1876. stitched, 2*s*.

—— *An Icelandic Prose Reader*, with Notes, Grammar and Glossary. by Dr. Gudbrand Vigfússon and F. York Powell, M.A. 1879. Extra fcap. 8vo. 10*s*. 6*d*.

LATIN.—*A Latin Dictionary*, founded on Andrews' edition of Freund's Latin Dictionary, revised, enlarged, and in great part rewritten by Charlton T Lewis, Ph.D, and Charles Short, LL.D. 1879. 4to. 1*l*. 5*s*.

SANSKRIT.—*A Practical Grammar of the Sanskrit Language*, arranged with reference to the Classical Languages of Europe, for the use of English Students, by Monier Williams, M A. Fourth Edition, 1877. 8vo. 15*s*.

—— *A Sanskrit-English Dictionary*, Etymologically and Philologically arranged, with special reference to Greek, Latin, German, Anglo-Saxon, English, and other cognate Indo-European Languages. By Monier Williams, M.A. 1872. 4to. 4*l*. 14*s*. 6*d*.

—— *Nalopákhyánam*. Story of Nala, an Episode of the Mahá-Bhárata: the Sanskrit text, with a copious Vocabulary, and an improved version of Dean Milman's Translation, by Monier Williams, M.A. Second Edition, Revised and Improved. 1879. 8vo. 15*s*.

—— *Sakuntalá*. A Sanskrit Drama, in Seven Acts. Edited by Monier Williams, M.A. Second Edition, 1876. 8vo. 21*s*.

SYRIAC.—*Thesaurus Syriacus*: collegerunt Quatremère, Bernstein. Lorsbach, Arnoldi, Agrell, Field, Roediger: edidit R. Payne Smith, S.T.P. Fasc. I-VI. 1868-83. sm. fol. each, 1*l*. 1*s*. Vol. I, containing Fasc. I-V, sm. fol. 5*l*. 5*s*.

—— *The Book of Kalîlah and Dimnah*. Translated from Arabic into Syriac. Edited by W. Wright, LL.D., Professor of Arabic in the University of Cambridge. 1884. 8vo. 21*s*.

GREEK CLASSICS, &c.

Aristophanes: A Complete Concordance to the Comedies and Fragments. By Henry Dunbar, M.D. 4to. 1*l.* 1*s.*

Aristotle: The Politics, translated into English, with Introduction, Marginal Analysis, Notes, and Indices, by B. Jowett, M.A. Medium 8vo *Nearly ready.*

Heracliti Ephesii Reliquiae. Recensuit I. Bywater, M.A. Appendicis loco additae sunt Diogenis Laertii Vita Heracliti, Particulae Hippocratei De Diaeta Libri Primi, Epistolae Heracliteae. 1877. 8vo. 6*s.*

Homer: A Complete Concordance to the Odyssey and Hymns of Homer; to which is added a Concordance to the Parallel Passages in the Iliad, Odyssey, and Hymns. By Henry Dunbar, M D. 1880. 4to. 1*l.* 1*s.*

—— *Scholia Graeca in Iliadem.* Edited by Professor W. Dindorf, after a new collation of the Venetian MSS. by D. B. Monro, M.A., Fellow of Oriel College.
      Vols. I. II 1875. 8vo 24*s.*
      Vols III IV. 1877 8vo 26*s.*
      Vols. V. VI. *In the Press.*

—— *Scholia Graeca in Odysseam.* Edidit Guil. Dindorfius Tomi II. 1855. 8vo. 15*s.* 6*d.*

Plato: Apology, with a revised Text and English Notes, and a Digest of Platonic Idioms, by James Riddell, M.A. 1878. 8vo. 8*s.* 6*d.*

—— *Philebus,* with a revised Text and English Notes, by Edward Poste, M.A. 1860. 8vo. 7*s.* 6*d.*

—— *Sophistes and Politicus,* with a revised Text and English Notes, by L. Campbell, M.A. 1867. 8vo. 18*s.*

—— *Theaetetus,* with a revised Text and English Notes, by L. Campbell, M.A. Second Edition. 8vo. 10*s.* 6*d.*

—— *The Dialogues,* translated into English, with Analyses and Introductions, by B. Jowett, M.A. A new Edition in 5 volumes, medium 8vo. 1875. 3*l.* 10*s.*

—— *The Republic,* translated into English, with an Analysis and Introduction, by B. Jowett, M A. Medium 8vo. 12*s.* 6*d.*

—— *Index to.* Compiled for the Second Edition of Professor Jowett's Translation of the Dialogues. By Evelyn Abbott, M.A. 1875. 8vo. paper covers, 2*s.* 6*d.*

Thucydides: Translated into English, with Introduction, Marginal Analysis, Notes, and Indices. By B. Jowett, M.A. 2 vols. 1881. Medium 8vo. 1*l.* 12*s.*

THE HOLY SCRIPTURES, &c.

ENGLISH.—*The Holy Bible in the earliest English Versions*, made from the Latin Vulgate by John Wycliffe and his followers: edited by the Rev. J. Forshall and Sir F. Madden. 4 vols. 1850. Royal 4to 3*l*. 3*s*.

[**Also reprinted from the above, with Introduction and Glossary by W. W. Skeat, M.A.**

—— *The Books of Job, Psalms, Proverbs, Ecclesiastes, and the Song of Solomon*: according to the Wycliffite Version made by Nicholas de Hereford, about A.D. 1381, and Revised by John Purvey, about A.D. 1388. Extra fcap 8vo. 3*s*. 6*d*.

—— *The New Testament in English*, according to the Version by John Wycliffe, about A.D 1380, and Revised by John Purvey, about A.D. 1388. Extra fcap. 8vo. 6*s*.]

—— *The Holy Bible*: an exact reprint, page for page, of the Authorised Version published in the year 1611. Demy 4to. half bound, 1*l*. 1*s*.

—— *The Psalter, or Psalms of David, and certain Canticles*, with a Translation and Exposition in English, by Richard Rolle of Hampole. Edited by H. R. Bramley, M A, Fellow of S. M Magdalen College, Oxford. With an Introduction and Glossary. Demy 8vo 1*l*. 1*s*.

GOTHIC.—*The Gospel of St. Mark in Gothic*, according to the translation made by Wulfila in the Fourth Century. Edited with a Grammatical Introduction and Glossarial Index by W. W. Skeat, M.A. Extra fcap. 8vo. 4*s*.

GREEK.—*Vetus Testamentum* ex Versione Septuaginta Interpretum secundum exemplar Vaticanum Romae editum. Accedit potior varietas Codicis Alexandrini. Tomi III. Editio Altera. 18mo. 18*s*.

—— *Origenis Hexaplorum* quae supersunt; sive, Veterum Interpretum Graecorum in totum Vetus Testamentum Fragmenta. Edidit Fridericus Field, A.M. 2 vols. 1875. 4to. 5*l*. 5*s*.

—— *The Book of Wisdom*: the Greek Text, the Latin Vulgate, and the Authorised English Version; with an Introduction, Critical Apparatus, and a Commentary. By William J. Deane, M.A. Small 4to. 12*s*. 6*d*.

—— *Novum Testamentum Graece*. Antiquissimorum Codicum Textus in ordine parallelo dispositi. Accedit collatio Codicis Sinaitici. Edidit E. H. Hansell, S. T. B. Tomi III. 1864. 8vo. half morocco, 2*l*. 12*s*. 6*d*.

—— *Novum Testamentum Graece*. Accedunt parallela S. Scripturae loca, necnon vetus capitulorum notatio et canones Eusebii. Edidit Carolus Lloyd, S. T. P. R. 18mo. 3*s*.

The same on writing paper, with large margin, 10*s*.

GREEK.—*Novum Testamentum Graece* juxta Exemplar Millia-
num. 18mo. 2s. 6d.

> The same on **writing paper,** with large margin, 9s.

—— *Evangelia Sacra Graece.* Fcap. 8vo. limp, 1s. 6d.

—— *The Greek Testament*, with the Readings adopted by
the Revisers of the Authorised Version:—

> (1) Pica type, with Marginal References. Demy 8vo. 10s. 6d.

> (2) Long Primer type. Fcap. 8vo. 4s. 6d.

> (3) The same, on writing paper, with wide margin, 15s.

—— *The Parallel New Testament*, Greek and English ; being
the Authorised Version, 1611 ; the Revised Version, 1881 ; and the Greek
Text followed in the Revised Version 8vo. 12s 6d.

The Revised Version is the joint property of the Universities of Oxford and Cambridge.

—— *Canon Muratorianus:* the earliest Catalogue of the
Books of the New Testament. Edited with Notes and a Facsimile of the
MS. in the Ambrosian Library at Milan, by S. P. Tregelles, LL.D. 1867.
4to., 10s. 6d.

—— *Outlines of Textual Criticism applied to the New Testament.* By C. E Hammond, M.A. Fourth Edition. Extra fcap. 8vo. 3s. 6d.

HEBREW, etc.—*The Psalms in Hebrew without points.* 1879.
Crown 8vo. 3s. 6d.

—— *A Commentary on the Book of Proverbs.* Attributed
to Abraham Ibn Ezra. Edited from a MS. in the Bodleian Library by
S. R. Driver, M.A. Crown 8vo. paper covers, 3s. 6d.

—— *The Book of Tobit.* A Chaldee Text, from a unique
MS. in the Bodleian Library ; with other Rabbinical Texts, English Transla-
tions, and the Itala. Edited by Ad. Neubauer, M.A. 1878. Crown 8vo. 6s.

—— *Horae Hebraicae et Talmudicae*, a J. Lightfoot. A new
Edition, by R. Gandell, M.A. 4 vols 1859. 8vo. 1l. 1s.

LATIN.—*Libri Psalmorum* Versio antiqua Latina, cum Para-
phrasi Anglo-Saxonica. Edidit B. Thorpe, F.A.S. 1835. 8vo. 10s. 6d.

—— *Old-Latin Biblical Texts: No. I.* The Gospel according
to St Matthew from the St. Germain MS. (g₁). Edited with Introduction
and Appendices by John Wordsworth, M.A. Small 4to., stiff covers, 6s.

OLD-FRENCH.—*Libri Psalmorum* Versio antiqua Gallica e
Cod MS. in Bibl. Bodleiana adservato, una cum Versione Metrica aliisque
Monumentis pervetustis. Nunc primum descripsit et edidit Franciscus Michel,
Phil. Doc. 1860. 8vo. 10s. 6d.

FATHERS OF THE CHURCH, &c.

St. Athanasius: Historical Writings, according to the Bene-
dictine Text. With an Introduction by William Bright, D.D. 1881. Crown
8vo. 10s. 6d.

—— *Orations against the Arians.* With an Account of his
Life by William Bright, D.D. 1873. Crown 8vo. 9s.

St. Augustine: Select Anti-Pelagian Treatises, and the Acts
of the Second Council of Orange. With an Introduction by William Bright,
D.D. Crown 8vo. 9s.

Canons of the First Four General Councils of Nicaea, Con-
stantinople, Ephesus, and Chalcedon. 1877. Crown 8vo. 2s. 6d.

—— *Notes on the Canons of the First Four General Councils.*
By William Bright, D.D. 1882. Crown 8vo. 5s. 6d.

Cyrilli Archiepiscopi Alexandrini in XII Prophetas. Edidit
P. E. Pusey, A.M. Tomi II. 1868. 8vo. cloth, 2l. 2s.

—— *in D. Joannis Evangelium.* Accedunt Fragmenta varia
necnon Tractatus ad Tiberium Diaconum duo. Edidit post Aubertum P.
E. Pusey, A.M. Tomi III. 1872. 8vo. 2l. 5s.

—— *Commentarii in Lucae Evangelium* quae supersunt
Syriace. E MSS. apud Mus. Britan. edidit R. Payne Smith, A.M. 1858.
4to. 1l. 2s.

—— Translated by R. Payne Smith, M.A. 2 vols. 1859.
8vo. 14s.

Ephraemi Syri, Rabulae Episcopi Edesseni, Balaei, aliorum-
que Opera Selecta. E Codd. Syriacis MSS. in Museo Britannico et Bibliotheca
Bodleiana asservatis primus edidit J. J. Overbeck. 1865. 8vo. 1l. 1s.

Eusebius' Ecclesiastical History, according to the text of
Burton, with an Introduction by William Bright, D.D. 1881. Crown 8vo.
8s. 6d.

Irenaeus: The Third Book of St. Irenaeus, Bishop of Lyons,
against Heresies. With short Notes and a Glossary by H. Deane, B.D.
1874. Crown 8vo. 5s. 6d.

Patrum Apostolicorum, S. Clementis Romani, S. Ignatii,
S Polycarpi, quae supersunt. Edidit Guil. Jacobson, S.T.P.R. Tomi II.
Fourth Edition, 1863. 8vo. 1l. 1s.

Socrates' Ecclesiastical History, according to the Text of
Hussey, with an Introduction by William Bright, D.D. 1878. Crown 8vo.
7s. 6d.

ECCLESIASTICAL HISTORY, BIOGRAPHY, &c.

Ancient Liturgy of the Church of England, according to the uses of Sarum, York, Hereford, and Bangor, and the Roman Liturgy arranged in parallel columns, with preface and notes. By William Maskell, M.A. Third Edition. 1882. 8vo. 15*s.*

Baedae Historia Ecclesiastica. Edited, with English Notes, by G. H. Moberly, M.A. 1881. Crown 8vo 10*s.* 6*d.*

Bright (W.). Chapters of Early English Church History. 1878. 8vo. 12*s.*

Burnet's History of the Reformation of the Church of England. A new Edition. Carefully revised, and the Records collated with the originals, by N. Pocock, M A. 7 vols. 1865. 8vo. *Price reduced to 1£ 10s.*

Councils and Ecclesiastical Documents relating to Great Britain and Ireland. Edited, after Spelman and Wilkins, by A. W. Haddan, B.D, and W. Stubbs, M.A. Vols. I. and III. 1869-71. Medium 8vo. each 1*l.* 1*s.*

> Vol. II. Part I. 1873. Medium 8vo. 10*s* 6*d.*

> Vol. II. Part II. 1878. Church of Ireland; Memorials of St. Patrick. Stiff covers, 3*s.* 6*d.*

Hamilton (John, Archbishop of St. Andrews). The Catechism of. Edited, with Introduction and Glossary, by Thomas Graves Law. With a Preface by the Right Hon. W E Gladstone. 8vo. 12*s.* 6*d.*

Hammond (C. E.). Liturgies, Eastern and Western. Edited, with Introduction, Notes, and Liturgical Glossary. 1878. Crown 8vo. 10*s.* 6*d.*

An Appendix to the above. 1879. Crown 8vo paper covers, 1*s.* 6*d.*

John, Bishop of Ephesus. The Third Part of his Ecclesiastical History. [In Syriac.] Now first edited by William Cureton, M.A. 1853. 4to. 1*l.* 12*s.*

—— Translated by R. Payne Smith, M.A. 1860. 8vo. 10*s.*

Leofric Missal, The, as used in the Cathedral of Exeter during the Episcopate of its first Bishop, A.D. 1050-1072; together with some Account of the Red Book of Derby, the Missal of Robert of Jumièges, and a few other early MS. Service Books of the English Church. Edited, with Introduction and Notes, by F. E. Warren, B.D. 4to. half morocco, 35*s.*

Monumenta Ritualia Ecclesiae Anglicanae. The occasional Offices of the Church of England according to the old use of Salisbury, the Prymer in English, and other prayers and forms, with dissertations and notes. By William Maskell, M.A. Second Edition. 1882. 3 vols 8vo. 2*l.* 10*s.*

Records of the Reformation. The Divorce, 1527–1533. Mostly now for the first time printed from MSS. in the British Museum and other libraries. Collected and arranged by N. Pocock, M.A. 1870. 2 vols. 8vo. 1*l.* 16*s.*

Shirley (W. W.). .Some Account of the Church in the Apostolic Age. Second Edition, 1874. fcap. 8vo. 3s. 6d.

Stubbs (W.). Registrum Sacrum Anglicanum. An attempt to exhibit the course of Episcopal Succession in England. 1858. Small 4to. 8s. 6d.

Warren (F. E.). Liturgy and Ritual of the Celtic Church. 1881. 8vo. 14s.

ENGLISH THEOLOGY.

Butler's Works, with an Index to the Analogy. 2 vols. 1874. 8vo. 11s.   Also separately,

Sermons, 5s. 6d.   *Analogy of Religion*, 5s. 6d.

Greswell's Harmonia Evangelica. Fifth Edition. 8vo. 1855. 9s. 6d.

Heurtley's Harmonia Symbolica: Creeds of the Western Church. 1858. 8vo. 6s. 6d.

Homilies appointed to be read in Churches. Edited by J. Griffiths, M.A. 1859. 8vo. 7s. 6d.

Hooker's Works, with his life by Walton, arranged by John Keble, M.A. Sixth Edition, 1874. 3 vols. 8vo. 1l. 11s. 6d.

—— the text as arranged by John Keble, M.A. 2 vols. 1875. 8vo. 11s.

Jewel's Works. Edited by R. W. Jelf, D.D. 8 vols. 1848. 8vo. 1l. 10s.

Pearson's Exposition of the Creed. Revised and corrected by E. Burton, D.D. Sixth Edition, 1877. 8vo. 10s. 6d.

Waterland's Review of the Doctrine of the Eucharist, with a Preface by the late Bishop of London. Crown 8vo. 6s. 6d.

—— *Works*, with Life, by Bp. Van Mildert. A new Edition, with copious Indexes. 6 vols. 1856. 8vo. 2l. 11s.

Wheatly's Illustration of the Book of Common Prayer. A new Edition, 1846. 8vo. 5s.

Wyclif. A Catalogue of the Original Works of John Wyclif, by W. W. Shirley, D.D. 1865. 8vo. 3s. 6d.

—— *Select English Works.* By T. Arnold, M.A. 3 vols. 1869-1871. 8vo. *Price reduced to 1l. 1s.*

—— *Trialogus.* With the Supplement now first edited. By Gotthard Lechler. 1869. 8vo. *Price reduced to 7s.*

HISTORICAL AND DOCUMENTARY WORKS.

British Barrows, a Record of the Examination of Sepulchral
Mounds in various parts of England By William Greenwell, M A., F S A.
Together with Description of Figures of Skulls, General Remarks on Pre-
historic Crania, and an Appendix by George Rolleston, M.D., F.R S. 1877.
Medium 8vo. 25*s*.

Britton. A Treatise upon the Common Law of England,
composed by order of King Edward I. The French Text carefully revised,
with an English Translation, Introduction, and Notes, by F. M Nichols, M.A.
2 vols. 1865 Royal 8vo. 1*l*. 16*s*.

Clarendon's History of the Rebellion and Civil Wars in
England. 7 vols 1839. 18mo 1*l*. 1*s*.

Clarendon's History of the Rebellion and Civil Wars in
England. Also his Life, written by himself, in which is included a Con-
tinuation of his History of the Grand Rebellion. With copious Indexes.
In one volume, royal 8vo. 1842. 1*l* 2*s*.

Clinton's Epitome of the Fasti Hellenici. 1851. 8vo. 6*s*. 6*d*.

—— *Epitome of the Fasti Romani.* 1854. 8vo. 7*s*.

Corpvs Poeticvm Boreale. The Poetry of the Old Northern
Tongue, from the Earliest Times to the Thirteenth Century. Edited, clas-
sified, and translated with Introduction. Excursus, and Notes, by Gudbrand
Vigfússon, M.A , and F. York Powell, M.A. 2 vols. 1883 8vo. 42*s*.

*Freeman (E. A.). History of the Norman Conquest of Eng-
land;* its Causes and Results. In Six Volumes. 8vo. 5*l* 9*s*. 6*d*.

Freeman (E. A.). The Reign of William Rufus and the
Accession of Henry the First. 2 vols. 8vo. 1*l*. 16*s*.

Gascoigne's Theological Dictionary ("Liber Veritatum"):
Selected Passages, illustrating the condition of Church and State, 1403-1458.
With an Introduction by James E. Thorold Rogers, M.P. Small 4to. 10*s*. 6*d*.

Magna Carta, a careful Reprint. Edited by W. Stubbs, M.A.
1879. 4to. stitched, 1*s*.

Passio et Miracula Beati Olaui. Edited from a Twelfth-
Century MS. in the Library of Corpus Christi College, Oxford, with an Introduction and Notes, by Frederick Metcalfe, M.A. Small 4to. stiff covers, 6*s*.

Protests of the Lords, including those which have been ex-
punged, from 1624 to 1874; with Historical Introductions. Edited by James
E. Thorold Rogers, M.A 1875. 3 vols. 8vo. 2*l*. 2*s*.

Rogers (J. E. T.). History of Agriculture and Prices in
England, A D. 1259-1793.

Vols. I and II (1259-1400). 1866. 8vo. 2*l*. 2*s*.
Vols. III and IV (1401-1582). 1882. 8vo. 2*l* 10*s*.

Saxon Chronicles (Two of the) parallel, with Supplementary Extracts from the Others. Edited, with Introduction, Notes, and a Glossarial Index, by J. Earle, M.A. 1865. 8vo. 16s.

Sturlunga Saga, including the Islendinga Saga of Lawman Sturla Thordsson and other works. Edited by Dr. Gudbrand Vigfússon. In 2 vols. 1878. 8vo. 2l. 2s.

York Plays. The Plays performed by the Crafts or Mysteries of York on the day of Corpus Christi in the 14th, 15th, and 16th centuries. Now first printed from the unique manuscript in the Library of Lord Ashburnham. Edited with Introduction and Glossary by Lucy Toulmin Smith. 8vo. 21s. *Just Published.*

Statutes made for the University of Oxford, and for the Colleges and Halls therein, by the University of Oxford Commissioners. 1882. 8vo. 12s. 6d.

Statuta Universitatis Oxoniensis. 1884. 8vo. 5s.

The Student's Handbook to the University and Colleges of Oxford. Seventh Edition. 1883. Extra fcap 8vo. 2s. 6d.

The Oxford University Calendar for the year 1885. Crown 8vo. 4s. 6d.
The present Edition includes all Class Lists and other University distinctions for the five years ending with 1884.

Also, supplementary to the above, price 5s. (pp. 606),

The Honours Register of the University of Oxford. A complete Record of University Honours, Officers, Distinctions, and Class Lists; of the Heads of Colleges, &c.. &c , from the Thirteenth Century to 1883.

MATHEMATICS, PHYSICAL SCIENCE, &c.

Acland (H. W., M.D., F.R.S.). Synopsis of the Pathological Series in the Oxford Museum. 1867. 8vo. 2s. 6d.

Astronomical Observations made at the University Observatory, Oxford, under the direction of C. Pritchard, M.A. No. 1. 1878. Royal 8vo. paper covers. 3s. 6d.

De Bary (Dr. A.) Comparative Anatomy of the Vegetative Organs of the Phanerogams and Ferns. Translated and Annotated by F. O. Bower, M A., F L.S., and D H. Scott, M.A., Ph.D., F.L.S. With two hundred and forty-one woodcuts and an Index. Royal 8vo., half morocco, 1l. 2s. 6d.

Müller (J.). On certain Variations in the Vocal Organs of the Passeres that have hitherto escaped notice. Translated by F. J Bell, B.A., and edited, with an Appendix, by A. H. Garrod, M.A., F.R.S. With Plates. 1878. 4to. paper covers, 7s. 6d.

Phillips (John, M.A., F.R.S.). Geology of Oxford and the Valley of the Thames. 1871. 8vo. 21s.

—— *Vesuvius.* 1869. Crown 8vo. 10s. 6d.

Price (Bartholomew, M.A., F.R.S.).   Treatise on Infinitesimal Calculus.

> Vol. I. Differential Calculus. Second Edition. 8vo. 14s. 6d.
>
> Vol. II Integral Calculus, Calculus of Variations, and Differential Equations. Second Edition, 1865. 8vo 18s.
>
> Vol. III. Statics, including Attractions; Dynamics of a Material Particle. Second Edition, 1868. 8vo. 16s.
>
> Vol. IV Dynamics of Material Systems; together with a chapter on Theoretical Dynamics, by W. F. Donkin, M A , F R S. 1862. 8vo. 16s

Rigaud's Correspondence of Scientific Men of the 17*th Century,* with Table of Contents by A. de Morgan and Index by the Rev. J. Rigaud, M.A. 2 vols. 1841–1862. 8vo. 18s. 6d.

Rolleston (George, M D., F.R.S.).   Scientific Papers and Addresses. Arranged and Edited by William Turner, M B, F R S.) With a Biographical Sketch by Edward Tylor, F.R.S. With Portrait, Plates, and Woodcuts. 2 vols. 8vo. 1l. 4s.

Sachs' Text-Book of Botany, Morphological and Physiological. A New Edition Translated by S. H. Vines, M.A. 1882. Royal 8vo., half morocco, 1l. 11s. 6d.

Westwood (J. O., M.A., F.R.S.).   Thesaurus Entomologicus Hopeianus or a Description of the rarest Insects in the Collection given to the University by the Rev. William Hope. With 40 Plates. 1874. Small folio, half morocco, 7l. 10s.

The Sacred Books of the East.

TRANSLATED BY VARIOUS ORIENTAL SCHOLARS, AND EDITED BY
F. MAX MÜLLER.

[Demy 8vo. cloth.]

Vol. I. The Upanishads. Translated by F. Max Müller.
Part I. The *Khândogya-upanishad*, The Talavakâra-upanishad, The Aitareya-âranyaka, The Kaushîtaki-brâhmana-upanishad, and The Vâgasaneyi-samhitâ-upanishad. 10s 6d.

Vol. II. The Sacred Laws of the Âryas, as taught in the
Schools of Âpastamba, Gautama, Vâsishtha, and Baudhâyana. Translated by Prof. Georg Buhler. Part I. Âpastamba and Gautama. 10s. 6d.

Vol. III. The Sacred Books of China. The Texts of Con-
fucianism. Translated by James Legge. Part I. The Shû King, The Religious portions of the Shih King, and The Hsiâo King. 12s. 6d.

Vol. IV. The Zend-Avesta. Translated by James Darme-
steter. Part I. The Vendîdâd. 10s. 6d.

Vol. V. The Pahlavi Texts. Translated by E. W. West.
Part I. The Bundahis, Bahman Yast, and Shâyast lâ-shâyast. 12s. 6d.

Vols. VI and IX. The Qur'ân. Parts I and II. Translated
by E. H Palmer. 21s.

Vol. VII. The Institutes of Vishnu. Translated by Julius
Jolly. 10s. 6d

Vol. VIII. The Bhagavadgîtâ, with The Sanatsugâtîya, and
The Anugîtâ. Translated by Kâshinâth Trimbak Telang. 10s 6d

Vol. X. The Dhammapada, translated from Pâli by F. Max
Muller; and The Sutta-Nipâta, translated from Pâli by V. Fausböll; being
Canonical Books of the Buddhists. 10s. 6d.

Vol. XI. Buddhist Suttas. Translated from Pâli by T. W.
Rhys Davids. 1. The Mahâparinibbâna Suttanta; 2. The Dhamma-kakka-
ppavattana Sutta; 3. The Tevigga Suttanta; 4 The Akankheyya Sutta;
5 The Ketokhila Sutta; 6. The Mahâ-sudassana Suttanta, 7. The Sabbâsava
Sutta. 10s. 6d.

Vol. XII. The Satapatha-Brâhmana, according to the Text
of the Mâdhyandina School. Translated by Julius Eggeling. Part I.
Books I and II. 12s. 6d.

Vol. XIII. Vinaya Texts. Translated from the Pâli by
T. W. Rhys Davids and Hermann Oldenberg. Part I. The Pâtimokkha.
The Mahâvagga, I–IV. 10s. 6d.

Vol. XIV. The Sacred Laws of the Âryas, as taught in the
Schools of Âpastamba, Gautama, Vâsishtha and Baudhâyana Translated
by Georg Buhler. Part II. Vasishtha and Baudhâyana. 10s 6d.

Vol. XV. The Upanishads. Translated by F. Max Müller.
Part II. The Katha-upanishad, The Mundaka-upanishad, The Taittirîyaka-
upanishad, The Brihadâranyaka-upanishad, The Svetasvatara-upanishad, The
Prasna-upanishad, and The Maitrâyana-Brâhmana-upanishad. 10s. 6d.

Vol. XVI. The Sacred Books of China. The Texts of Con-
fucianism. Translated by James Legge. Part II. The Yî King. 10s. 6d.

Vol. XVII. Vinaya Texts. Translated from the Pâli by
T. W. Rhys Davids and Hermann Oldenberg. Part II. The Mahâvagga,
V–X. The Kullavagga, I–III. 10s. 6d.

Vol. XVIII. Pahlavi Texts. Translated by E. W. West.
Part II. The Dâdistân-î Dînîk and The Epistles of Mânûskîhar. 12s. 6d.

Vol. XIX. The Fo-sho-hing-tsan-king. A Life of Buddha
by Asvaghosha Bodhisattva, translated from Sanskrit into Chinese by Dhar-
maraksha, A.D. 420, and from Chinese into English by Samuel Beal. 10s. 6d.

Vol. XXI. The Saddharma-pundarîka or the Lotus of the
True Law. Translated by H. Kern. 12s. 6d.

Vol. XXIII. The Zend-Avesta. Part II. The Sîrôzahs, Yasts, and Nyâyis. Translated by James Darmesteter. 10s. 6d.

The following Volumes are in the Press:—

Vol. XX. Vinaya Texts. Translated from the Pâli by T. W. Rhys Davids and Hermann Oldenberg. Part III. The Kullavagga, I-IV.

Vol. XXII. Gaina-Sûtras. Translated from Prâkrit by Hermann Jacobi. Part I. The Âkârânga-Sûtra. The Kalpa-Sûtra.

Vol. XXIV. Pahlavi Texts: Translated by E. W. West. Part III. Dînâ-î Maînôg-î Khirad, Shikand-gu-mânî, and Sad-dar.

Second Series.

Vol. XXV. Manu. Translated by GEORG BUHLER. Part I.

Vol. XXVI. The Satapatha-Brâhmana. Translated by Julius Eggeling. Part II.

𝕬𝖓𝖊𝖈𝖉𝖔𝖙𝖆 𝕺𝖝𝖔𝖓𝖎𝖊𝖓𝖘𝖎𝖆 :
[Small 4to.]

Classical Series. I. i. *The English Manuscripts of the Nicomachean Ethics,* described in relation to Bekker's Manuscripts and other Sources. By J A Stewart, M A. 3s 6d.

—— I. ii. *Nonius Marcellus,* de Compendiosa Doctrina, Harleian MS. 2719. Collated by J. H. Onions, M.A 3s. 6d.

—— I. iii. *Aristotle's Physics.* Book VII. Collation of various MSS.; with an Introduction by R. Shute, M A. 2s.

I. iv. *Bentley's Plautine Emendations.* From his copy of Gronovius. By E. A. Sonnenschein, M.A. 2s. 6d.

Semitic Series. I. i. *Commentary on Ezra and Nehemiah.* By Rabbi Saadiah. Edited by H. J. Mathews, M.A. 3s. 6d.

Aryan Series. I. i. *Buddhist Texts from Japan.* Edited by F. Max Muller, M.A. 3s. 6d.

—— I. ii. *Sukhâvatî-Vyûha.* Description of Sukhâvatî, the Land of Bliss. Edited by F. Max Muller, M.A., and Bunyiu Nanjio. 7s. 6d.

—— I. iii. The Ancient Palm-leaves containing the Pragñâ-Pâramitâ-Hridaya-Sûtra and the Ushnîsha-Vigaya-Dhâranî, edited by F. Max Muller, M.A., and Bunyiu Nanjio, M.A. With an Appendix by G. Buhler. With many Plates. 10s.

Mediaeval and Modern Series. I. i. *Sinonoma Bartholomei;* A Glossary from a Fourteenth-Century MS. in the Library of Pembroke College, Oxford. Edited by J. L. G. Mowat, M A. 3s. 6d.

—— I. iii. *The Saltair Na Rann.* A Collection of Early ' Middle Irish Poems. Edited from a MS. in the Bodleian Library by Whitley Stokes, LL.D. 7s. 6d.

𝕮𝖑𝖆𝖗𝖊𝖓𝖉𝖔𝖓 𝕻𝖗𝖊𝖘𝖘 𝕾𝖊𝖗𝖎𝖊𝖘

I. ENGLISH.

A First Reading Book. By Marie Eichens of Berlin ; and
edited by Anne J. Clough   Extra fcap. 8vo. stiff covers, 4*d.*

Oxford Reading Book, Part I. For Little Children. Extra
fcap. 8vo. stiff covers, 6*d.*

Oxford Reading Book, Part II. For Junior Classes. Extra
fcap. 8vo. stiff covers, 6*d.*

An Elementary English Grammar and Exercise Book. By
O. W. Tancock, M.A. Second Edition   Extra fcap. 8vo. 1*s.* 6*d.*

An English Grammar and Reading Book, for Lower Forms
in Classical Schools. By O. W. Tancock, M A. Fourth Edition. Extra
fcap. 8vo. 3*s.* 6*d.*

Typical Selections from the best English Writers, with Introductory Notices. Second Edition. In Two Volumes. Extra fcap. 8vo.
3*s.* 6*d* each.

   Vol. I. Latimer to Berkeley.   Vol. II. Pope to Macaulay.

Shairp (J. C., LL.D.). *Aspects of Poetry;* being Lectures
delivered at Oxford. Crown 8vo   10*s.* 6*d.*

A Book for the Beginner in Anglo-Saxon. By John Earle,
M.A. Third Edition. Extra fcap. 8vo. 2*s.* 6*d.*

An Anglo-Saxon Reader. In Prose and Verse. With Grammatical Introduction, Notes, and Glossary. By Henry Sweet, M.A. Fourth
Edition, Revised and Enlarged. Extra fcap. 8vo. 8*s.* 6*d.*

An Anglo-Saxon Primer, with Grammar, Notes, and Glossary.
By the same Author. Second Edition. Extra fcap. 8vo. 2*s.* 6*d.*

First Middle English Primer, with Grammar and Glossary.
By the same Author. Extra fcap. 8vo. 2*s.* *Just Published.*

The Philology of the English Tongue. By J. Earle, M.A.
Third Edition. Extra fcap. 8vo. 7*s.* 6*d.*

A Handbook of Phonetics, including a Popular Exposition of
the Principles of Spelling Reform. By Henry Sweet, M.A. Extra fcap. 8vo
4*s.* 6*d.*

The Ormulum; with the Notes and Glossary of Dr. R. M.
White. Edited by R. Holt, M.A. 1878. 2 vols. Extra fcap. 8vo. 21*s.*

English Plant Names from the Tenth to the Fifteenth Century. By J Earle, M.A. Small fcap 8vo. 5s.

Specimens of Early English. A New and Revised Edition. With Introduction. Notes, and Glossarial Index By R. Morris, LL.D., and W. W. Skeat, M.A.

> Part I From Old English Homilies to King Horn (A.D. 1150 to A.D. 1300). Extra fcap. 8vo. 9s

> Part II. From Robert of Gloucester to Gower (A.D. 1298 to A D 1393). Second Edition Extra fcap 8vo. 7s 6d

Specimens of English Literature, from the 'Ploughmans Crede' to the 'Shepheardes Calender' (A D. 1394 to A D 1579). With Introduction, Notes, and Glossarial Index. By W. W. Skeat, M A. Extra fcap. 8vo. 7s. 6d.

The Vision of William concerning Piers the Plowman, by William Langland. Edited. with Notes, by W. W. Skeat, M A. Third Edition. Extra fcap. 8vo 4s 6d.

Chaucer. I. *The Prologue to the Canterbury Tales;* the Knightes Tale; The Nonne Prestes Tale Edited by R. Morris, Editor of Specimens of Early English, &c , &c Fifty-first Thousand Extra fcap. 8vo. 2s. 6d.

—— II. *The Prioresses Tale; Sir Thopas;* The Monkes Tale; The Clerkes Tale; The Squeres Tale, &c. Edited by W. W. Skeat, M.A. Second Edition. Extra fcap. 8vo. 4s. 6d

—— III. *The Tale of the Man of Lawe;* The Pardoneres Tale; The Second Nonnes Tale; The Chanouns Yemannes Tale. By the same Editor. Second Edition. Extra fcap. 8vo. 4s 6d.

Gamelyn, The Tale of. Edited with Notes, Glossary, &c., by W. W. Skeat, M A. Extra fcap 8vo. Stiff covers, 1s. 6d. *Just Published.*

Spenser's Faery Queene. Books I and II. Designed chiefly for the use of Schools. With Introduction, Notes, and Glossary. By G. W. Kitchin, M.A.

> Book I. Tenth Edition. Extra fcap. 8vo. 2s. 6d.

> Book II. Sixth Edition. Extra fcap. 8vo. 2s. 6d.

Hooker. Ecclesiastical Polity, Book I. Edited by R. W. Church, M.A. Second Edition. Extra fcap. 8vo. 2s.

Marlowe and Greene. Marlowe's Tragical History of Dr. Faustus, and *Greene's Honourable History of Friar Bacon and Friar Bungay*. Edited by A. W. Ward, M.A. 1878. Extra fcap. 8vo. 5s. 6d.

Marlowe. Edward II. With Introduction, Notes, &c. By O. W. Tancock, M.A. Extra fcap. 8vo. 3s

Shakespeare. Select Plays. Edited by W. G. Clark, M.A., and W. Aldis Wright, M.A. Extra fcap. 8vo. stiff covers.

> I.   The Merchant of Venice. 1*s*.
> II.   Richard the Second. 1*s. 6d.*
> III.   Macbeth. 1*s. 6d.*
> IV.   Hamlet. 2*s*.

Edited by W. Aldis Wright, M.A.

> V.   The Tempest. 1*s. 6d.*
> VI.   As You Like It. 1*s. 6d.*
> VII.   Julius Cæsar. 2*s*.
> VIII. Richard the Third. 2*s. 6d.*
> IX.   King Lear. 1*s. 6d.*
> X.   A Midsummer Night's Dream. 1*s. 6d.*
> XI.   Coriolanus. 2*s. 6d.*
> XII.   Henry the Fifth. 2*s*.
> XIII. Twelfth Night. *Nearly ready.*

Bacon. I. *Advancement of Learning.* Edited by W. Aldis Wright, M.A. Second Edition. Extra fcap. 8vo. 4*s. 6d.*

—— II. *The Essays.* With Introduction and Notes. *In Preparation.*

Milton. I. *Areopagitica.* With Introduction and Notes. By J. W. Hales, M.A. Third Edition. Extra fcap. 8vo. 3*s*.

—— II. *Poems.* Edited by R. C. Browne, M.A. 2 vols. Fifth Edition. Extra fcap. 8vo. 6*s. 6d.* Sold separately, Vol. I. 4*s*.; Vol. II. 3*s*.

In paper covers :—

Lycidas, 3*d*.   L'Allegro, 3*d*.   Il Penseroso, 4*d*.   Comus, 6*d*.
Samson Agonistes, 6*d*.

—— III. *Samson Agonistes.* Edited with Introduction and Notes by John Churton Collins. Extra fcap. 8vo. stiff covers, 1*s*.

Bunyan. I. *The Pilgrim's Progress, Grace Abounding, Relation of the Imprisonment of Mr John Bunyan.* Edited, with Biographical Introduction and Notes, by E. Venables, M.A. 1879. Extra fcap. 8vo. 5*s*.

—— II. *Holy War, &c.* Edited by E. Venables, M.A. In the Press.

Dryden. *Select Poems.* Stanzas on the Death of Oliver Cromwell; Astræa Redux; Annus Mirabilis; Absalom and Achitophel; Religio Laici; The Hind and the Panther. Edited by W. D. Christie, M.A. Second Edition. Extra fcap. 8vo. 3*s. 6d.*

Locke's Conduct of the Understanding. Edited, with Introduction, Notes, &c., by T. Fowler, M.A. Second Edition. Extra fcap. 8vo. 2*s*.

Addison. Selections from Papers in the Spectator. With Notes. By T. Arnold, M A. Extra fcap. 8vo. 4s. 6d.

Steele. Selections from. By Austin Dobson. *Nearly ready.*

Pope. With Introduction and Notes. By Mark Pattison, B.D.

I. *Essay on Man.* Sixth Edition. Extra fcap. 8vo. 1s. 6d.

—— II. *Satires and Epistles.* Second Edition. Extra fcap. 8vo. 2s.

Parnell. The Hermit. Paper covers, 2d.

Johnson. I. *Rasselas; Lives of Pope and Dryden.* Edited by Alfred Milnes, B.A. (London). Extra fcap 8vo 4s 6d.

—— II. *Vanity of Human Wishes.* With Notes, by E. J. Payne, M.A. Paper covers, 4d.

Gray. Selected Poems. Edited by Edmund Gosse, Clark Lecturer in English Literature at the University of Cambridge Extra fcap. 8vo. Stiff covers, 1s 6d In white Parchment, 3s. *Just Published.*

—— *Elegy and Ode on Eton College.* Paper covers, 2d.

Goldsmith. The Deserted Village. Paper covers, 2d.

Cowper. Edited, with Life, Introductions, and Notes, by H. T. Griffith, B A.

—— I. *The Didactic Poems of* 1782, with Selections from the Minor Pieces, A D. 1779–1783. Extra fcap 8vo. 3s

—— II. *The Task, with Tirocinium,* and Selections from the Minor Poems, A D. 1784–1799. Second Edition. Extra fcap. 8vo. 3s.

Burke. Select Works. Edited, with Introduction and Notes, by E. J Payne, M.A.

—— I. *Thoughts on the Present Discontents ; the two Speeches on America* Second Edition. Extra fcap. 8vo. 4s. 6d.

—— II. *Reflections on the French Revolution.* Second Edition. Extra fcap. 8vo. 5s.

—— III. *Four Letters on the Proposals for Peace with the* Regicide Directory of France. Second Edition. Extra fcap. 8vo. 5s.

Keats. Hyperion, Book I. With Notes by W. T. Arnold, B.A. Paper covers, 4d.

Scott. Lay of the Last Minstrel. Introduction and Canto I, with Preface and Notes by W. Minto, M.A. Paper covers, 6d.

[9]   c

II. LATIN.

Rudimenta Latina. Comprising Accidence, and Exercises of a very Elementary Character, for the use of Beginners. By John Barrow Allen, M A. Extra fcap *2s.*

An Elementary Latin Grammar. By the same Author. Third Edition, Revised and Corrected. Extra fcap. 8vo. *2s. 6d.*

A First Latin Exercise Book. By the same Author. Fourth Edition. Extra fcap. 8vo. *2s 6d.*

A Second Latin Exercise Book. By the same Author. Extra fcap 8vo. *3s. 6d.*

Reddenda Minora, or Easy Passages, Latin and Greek, for Unseen Translation. For the use of Lower Forms Composed and selected by C. S. Jerram, M.A. Extra fcap. *1s. 6d.*

Anglice Reddenda, or Easy Extracts, Latin and Greek, for Unseen Translation. By C. S. Jerram, M.A. Third Edition, Revised and Enlarged Extra fcap. 8vo *2s. 6d.*

Passages for Translation into Latin. For the use of Passmen and others. Selected by J. Y. Sargent, M.A. Fifth Edition. Extra fcap. 8vo. *2s. 6d.*

Exercises in Latin Prose Composition; with Introduction, Notes and Passages of Graduated Difficulty for Translation into Latin. By G. G. Ramsay, M.A., LL.D. Second Edition. Extra fcap. 8vo *4s. 6d.*

First Latin Reader. By T. J. Nunns, M.A. Third Edition. Extra fcap. 8vo. *2s.*

Caesar. The Commentaries (for Schools). With Notes and Maps. By Charles E. Moberly, M.A.

> Part I. *The Gallic War.* Second Edition. Extra fcap. 8vo. *4s. 6d.*
> Part II. *The Civil War.* Extra fcap. 8vo. *3s. 6d.*
> *The Civil War.* Book I. Second Edition. Extra fcap. 8vo. *2s.*

Cicero. Selection of interesting and descriptive passages. With Notes. By Henry Walford, M.A. In three Parts. Extra fcap. 8vo. *4s. 6d* Each Part separately, limp, *1s. 6d.*

> Part I. Anecdotes from Grecian and Roman History. Third Edition.
> Part II. Omens and Dreams: Beauties of Nature. Third Edition.
> Part III. Rome's Rule of her Provinces. Third Edition.

—— *De Senectute* and *De Amicitia.* With Notes. By W. Heslop, M.A. Extra fcap. 8vo. *2s.*

Cicero. Selected Letters (for Schools). With Notes. By the
late C E. Prichard, M.A., and E. R. Bernard, M.A. Second Edition.
Extra fcap 8vo. 3*s*.

—— *Select Orations* (for Schools). In Verrem I. De Imperio
Gn Pompeii Pro Archia Philippica IX. With Introduction and Notes by
' J. R. King, M.A. Second Edition. Extra fcap. 8vo. 2*s*. 6*d*.

Cornelius Nepos. With Notes. By Oscar Browning, M.A.
Second Edition. Extra fcap 8vo. 2*s* 6*d*.

Livy. Selections (for Schools). With Notes and Maps. By
H. Lee-Warner, M A. Extra fcap 8vo In Parts, limp, each 1*s*. 6*d*.

        Part I.   The Caudine Disaster.

        Part II.   Hannibal's Campaign in Italy.

        Part III The Macedonian War.

Livy. Books V–VII. With Introduction and Notes. By
A. R Cluer, B A. Extra fcap 8vo. 3*s*. 6*d*.

Ovid. Selections for the use of Schools. With Introductions
and Notes, and an Appendix on the Roman Calendar By W. Ramsay, M.A.
Edited by G. G Ramsay, M A Second Edition. Extra fcap. 8vo. 5*s*. 6*d*.

Pliny. Selected Letters (for Schools). With Notes. By the
late C E Prichard, M.A., and E. R. Bernard, M.A. Second Edition. Extra
fcap. 8vo. 3*s*.

Tacitus. The Annals. Books I–IV. Edited, with Introduction and Notes for the use of Schools and Junior Students, by H. Furneaux,
M A. Extra fcap. 8vo. 5*s*.

———

Catulli Veronensis Liber. Iterum recognovit, apparatum cri-
ticum prolegomena appendices addidit, Robinson Ellis, A.M. 1878. Demy
8vo 16*s*.

—— *A Commentary on Catullus.* By Robinson Ellis, M.A.
1876. Demy 8vo. 16*s*.

—— *Veronensis Carmina Selecta,* secundum recognitionem
Robinson Ellis, A.M. Extra fcap. 8vo. 3*s* 6*d*.

Cicero de Oratore. With Introduction and Notes. By A. S.
Wilkins, M.A.

        Book I. 1879. 8vo. 6*s*.   Book II. 1881. 8vo. 5*s*.

—— *Philippic Orations.* With Notes. By J. R. King, M.A.
Second Edition. 1879. 8vo. 10*s*. 6*d*.

—— *Select Letters.* With English Introductions, Notes, and
Appendices. By Albert Watson, M.A. Third Edition. 1881. Demy 8vo. 18*s*.

Cicero. Select Letters. Text. By the same Editor. Second
Edition. Extra fcap. 8vo. 4*s.*

Cicero pro Cluentio. With Introduction and Notes. By W.
Ramsay, M A. Edited by G. G. Ramsay, M A. Second Edition. Extra fcap.
8vo. 3*s.* 6*d.*

Horace. With a Commentary. Volume I. The Odes, Carmen
Seculare, and Epodes. By Edward C. Wickham, M A Second Edition.
1877. Demy 8vo. 12*s.*

—— A reprint of the above, in a size suitable for the use
of Schools. Extra fcap. 8vo. 5*s.* 6*d.*

Livy, Book I. With Introduction, Historical Examination,
and Notes. By J. R. Seeley, M.A. Second Edition. 1881. 8vo. 6*s.*

Ovid. P. Ovidii Nasonis Ibis. Ex Novis Codicibus edidit,
Scholia Vetera Commentarium cum Prolegomenis Appendice Indice addidit,
R. Ellis, A M. Demy 8vo. 10*s.* 6*d.*

Persius. The Satires. With a Translation and Commentary.
By John Conington, M.A. Edited by Henry Nettleship, M.A. Second
Edition. 1874. 8vo. 7*s.* 6*d.*

Plautus. The Trinummus. With Notes and Introductions.
Intended for the Higher Forms of Public Schools By C. E. Freeman, M.A.,
and A. Sloman, M.A. Extra fcap. 8vo. 3*s.*

Sallust. With Introduction and Notes. By W. W. Capes,
M.A. Extra fcap. 8vo. 4*s.* 6*d.*

Tacitus. The Annals. Books I–VI. Edited, with Introduction and Notes, by H. Furneaux, M.A. 8vo. 18*s.*

Virgil. With Introduction and Notes. By T. L. Papillon,
M.A. Two vols. crown 8vo. 10*s.* 6*d.*

––––––––

Nettleship (H., M.A.). Lectures and Essays on Subjects connected with Latin Scholarship and Literature. Crown 8vo. 7*s.* 6*d.*

—— *The Roman Satura:* its original form in connection with
its literary development. 8vo. sewed, 1*s.*

—— *Ancient Lives of Vergil.* With an Essay on the Poems
of Vergil, in connection with his Life and Times. By H. Nettleship, M.A.
8vo. sewed, 2*s.*

Papillon (T. L., M.A.). A Manual of Comparative Philology.
Third Edition, Revised and Corrected. 1882. Crown 8vo. 6*s.*

Pinder (North, M.A.). Selections from the less known Latin
Poets. 1869. Demy 8vo. 15*s.*

Sellar (W. Y., M.A.).   Roman Poets of the Augustan Age.
VIRGIL. By William Young Sellar, M.A, Professor of Humanity in the
University of Edinburgh. New Edition 1883. Crown 8vo. 9s.

—— *Roman Poets of the Republic.* New Edition, Revised
and Enlarged. 1881. 8vo. 14s.

Wordsworth (J., M.A.).   Fragments and Specimens of Early
Latin. With Introductions and Notes. 1874. 8vo. 18s.

III. GREEK.

A Greek Primer, for the use of beginners in that Language.
By the Right Rev. Charles Wordsworth, D C.L. Seventh Edition. Extra fcap.
8vo. 1s. 6d.

Graecae Grammaticae Rudimenta in usum Scholarum. Auc-
tore Carolo Wordsworth, D C.L. Nineteenth Edition, 1882. 12mo 4s.

A Greek-English Lexicon, abridged from Liddell and Scott's
4to edition, chiefly for the use of Schools. Twenty-first Edition. 1884.
Square 12mo 7s 6d.

Greek Verbs, Irregular and Defective; their forms, meaning,
and quantity, embracing all the Tenses used by Greek writers, with references
to the passages in which they are found. By W. Veitch. Fourth Edition.
Crown 8vo 10s. 6d.

The Elements of Greek Accentuation (for Schools) : abridged
from his larger work by H. W Chandler, M.A. Extra fcap 8vo. 2s. 6d.

A SERIES OF GRADUATED GREEK READERS :—

First Greek Reader. By W. G. Rushbrooke, M.L. Second
Edition. Extra fcap. 8vo. 2s 6d.

Second Greek Reader. By A. M. Bell, M.A. Extra fcap.
8vo. 3s. 6d.

Fourth Greek Reader; being Specimens of Greek Dialects.
With Introductions and Notes. By W. W. Merry, M.A. Extra fcap. 8vo.
4s. 6d.

Fifth Greek Reader. Part I. Selections from Greek Epic
and Dramatic Poetry, with Introductions and Notes. By Evelyn Abbott,
M.A. Extra fcap. 8vo. 4s. 6d.

The Golden Treasury of Ancient Greek Poetry: being a Collection of the finest passages in the Greek Classic Poets with Introductory
Notices and Notes. By R S. Wright, M.A. Extra fcap.. 8vo. 8s. 6d.

A Golden Treasury of Greek Prose, being a Collection of the finest passages in the principal Greek Prose Writers, with Introductory Notices and Notes. By R. S. Wright, M.A., and J. E. L. Shadwell, M.A. Extra fcap. 8vo. 4*s.* 6*d.*

Aeschylus. Prometheus Bound (for Schools). With Introduction and Notes, by A. O. Prickard, M.A. Second Edition. Extra fcap. 8vo. 2*s.*

—— *Agamemnon.* With Introduction and Notes, by Arthur Sidgwick, M.A. Second Edition. Extra fcap 8vo. 3*s.*

—— *Choephoroi.* With Introduction and Notes by the same Editor. Extra fcap. 8vo. 3*s.*

Aristophanes. In Single Plays. Edited, with English Notes, Introductions, &c., by W. W. Merry, M A. Extra fcap. 8vo.

    I. The Clouds, Second Edition, 2*s.*

    II. The Acharnians, 2*s.*

    III. The Frogs, 2*s.*

          Other Plays will follow.

Cebes. Tabula With Introduction and Notes. By C S. Jerram, M A Extra fcap 8vo. 2*s.* 6*d.*

Euripides. Alcestis (for Schools). By C. S. Jerram, M.A. Extra fcap. 8vo. 2*s.* 6*d*

—— *Helena.* Edited, with Introduction, Notes, and Critical Appendix, for Upper and Middle Forms. By C. S Jerram, M.A. Extra fcap. 8vo. 3*s.*

Herodotus, Selections from. Edited, with Introduction, Notes, and a Map, by W W. Merry, M.A. Extra fcap. 8vo. 2*s* 6*d.*

Homer. Odyssey, Books I–XII (for Schools). By W. W. Merry, M.A. Twenty-seventh Thousand. Extra fcap. 8vo. 4*s* 6*d.*

    Book II, separately, 1*s.* 6*d.*

—— *Odyssey*, Books XIII–XXIV (for Schools). By the same Editor. Second Edition Extra fcap. 8vo. 5*s.*

—— *Iliad*, Book I (for Schools). By D. B. Monro, M.A. Second Edition. Extra fcap. 8vo. 2*s.*

—— *Iliad*, Books I–XII (for Schools). With an Introduction, a brief Homeric Grammar, and Notes. By D. B. Monro, M.A. Extra fcap. 8vo. 6*s.*

—— *Iliad*, Books VI and XXI. With Introduction and Notes. By Herbert Hailstone, M.A. Extra fcap. 8vo. 1*s.* 6*d.* each.

Lucian. *Vera Historia* (for Schools). By C. S. Jerram, M.A. Second Edition. Extra fcap 8vo. 1s. 6d

Plato. *Selections from the Dialogues* [including the whole of the *Apology* and *Crito*] With Introduction and Notes by John Purves, M A, and a Preface by the Rev. B Jowett, M.A. Extra fcap. 8vo 6s 6d.

Sophocles. In Single Plays, with English Notes, &c. By Lewis Campbell, M A, and Evelyn Abbott, M A Extra fcap 8vo limp

    Oedipus Tyrannus, Philoctetes. New and Revised Edition, 2s. each
    Oedipus Coloneus,   Antigone. 1s. 9d. each.
    Ajax,   Electra,   Trachiniae, 2s each.

—— *Oedipus Rex:* Dindorf's Text, with Notes by the present Bishop of St. David's. Ext. fcap. 8vo. limp, 1s 6d.

Theocritus (for Schools). With Notes. By H. Kynaston, D.D (late Snow). Third Edition Extra fcap 8vo. 4s 6d.

Xenophon. *Easy Selections.* (for Junior Classes). With a Vocabulary. Notes, and Map By J S Phillpotts, B C.L., and C. S. Jerram, M.A Third Edition. Extra fcap. 8vo. 3s 6d.

—— *Selections* (for Schools). With Notes and Maps. By J S. Phillpotts, B C L. Fourth Edition. Extra fcap. 8vo. 3s. 6d.

—— *Anabasis*, Book II. With Notes and Map. By C. S. Jerram, M.A. Extra fcap. 8vo. 2s.

—— *Cyropaedia*, Books IV and V. With Introduction and Notes by C. Bigg, D.D. Extra fcap. 8vo. 2s. 6d.

———————————

Aristotle's Politics. By W. L. Newman, M.A. [*In preparation.*]

Aristotelian Studies. I. On the Structure of the Seventh Book of the Nicomachean Ethics. By J. C. Wilson, M A. 1879. Medium 8vo. stiff, 5s.

Demosthenes and Aeschines. The Orations of Demosthenes and Æschines on the Crown. With Introductory Essays and Notes. By G A. Simcox, M A., and W. H. Simcox, M.A. 1872. 8vo. 12s.

Geldart (E. M., B.A.). *The Modern Greek Language* in its relation to Ancient Greek. Extra fcap. 8vo. 4s. 6d.

Hicks (E. L., M.A.). *A Manual of Greek Historical Inscriptions.* Demy 8vo. 10s. 6d.

Homer. *Odyssey,* Books I–XII. Edited with English Notes,
Appendices, etc. By W. W. Merry, M.A., and the late James Riddell, M.A.
1876. Demy 8vo. 16s.

—— *A Grammar of the Homeric Dialect.* By D. B. Monro,
M.A. Demy 8vo. 10s 6d.

Sophocles. The Plays and Fragments. With English Notes
and Introductions, by Lewis Campbell, M.A 2 vols.

> Vol. I. Oedipus Tyrannus. Oedipus Coloneus   Antigone.   Second
> Edition. 1879. 8vo. 16s
>
> Vol. II Ajax. Electra. Trachiniae. Philoctetes   Fragments.   1881.
> 8vo. 16s.

Sophocles. The Text of the Seven Plays. By the same
Editor. Extra fcap. 8vo. 4s. 6d.

IV. FRENCH AND ITALIAN.

Brachet's Etymological Dictionary of the French Language.
with a Preface on the Principles of French Etymology. Translated into
English by G W. Kitchin, D D. Third Edition. Crown 8vo. 7s. 6d.

—— *Historical Grammar of the French Language.* Translated into English by G. W. Kitchin, D.D. Fourth Edition. Extra fcap.
8vo. 3s. 6d.

Works by GEORGE SAINTSBURY, M A.

Primer of French Literature. Extra fcap. 8vo. 2s.

Short History of French Literature. Crown 8vo. 10s. 6d.

Specimens of French Literature, from Villon to Hugo. Crown
8vo. 9s.

————

Corneille's Horace. Edited, with Introduction and Notes, by
George Saintsbury, M.A. Extra fcap. 8vo. 2s. 6d.

Molière's Les Précieuses Ridicules. Edited, with Introduction
and Notes, by Andrew Lang, M.A. Extra fcap. 8vo. 1s. 6d.

Beaumarchais' Le Barbier de Séville. Edited, with Introduction
and Notes, by Austin Dobson. Extra fcap. 8vo. 2s. 6d.

Musset's On ne badine pas avec l'Amour, and *Fantasio.* Edited,
with Prolegomena, Notes, etc., by Walter Herries Pollock. Extra. fcap.
8vo. 2s.   Other Plays to follow.

————

L'Éloquence de la Chaire et de la Tribune Françaises. Edited
by Paul Blouet, B.A. (Univ. Gallic.). Vol. I. French Sacred Oratory.
Extra fcap. 8vo. 2s. 6d.

Quinet's Lettres à sa Mère. Edited by George Saintsbury.
Nearly ready.

Edited by GUSTAVE MASSON, B.A.

Corneille's Cinna, and *Molière's Les Femmes Savantes.* With
Introduction and Notes. Extra fcap 8vo. 2s 6d.

Louis XIV and his Contemporaries; as described in Extracts
from the best Memoirs of the Seventeenth Century. With English Notes,
Genealogical Tables, &c. Extra fcap. 8vo. 2s. 6d.

Maistre, Xavier de. Voyage autour de ma Chambre. Ourika,
by *Madame de Duras;* La Dot de Suzette, by *Fievée.* Les Jumeaux de
l'Hôtel Corneille by *Edmond About;* Mésaventures d'un Écolier, by *Rodolphe
Topffer.* Second Edition. Extra fcap. 8vo. 2s. 6d.

Molière's Les Fourberies de Scapin. With Voltaire's Life of
Molière. Extra fcap. 8vo stiff covers, 1s. 6d.

Molière's Les Fourberies de Scapin, and *Racine's Athalie.*
With Voltaire's Life of Molière. Extra fcap 8vo. 2s. 6d.

Racine's Andromaque, and *Corneille's Le Menteur.* With
Louis Racine's Life of his Father. Extra fcap 8vo. 2s. 6d.

Regnard's Le Joueur, and *Brueys and Palaprat's Le Grondeur.*
Extra fcap 8vo. 2s 6d.

*Sévigné, Madame de, and her chief Contemporaries. Selections
from the Correspondence of.* Intended more especially for Girls' Schools
Extra fcap. 8vo. 3s.

Dante. Selections from the Inferno. With Introduction and
Notes. By H. B. Cotterill, B A. Extra fcap. 8vo. 4s 6d.

Tasso. La Gerusalemme Liberata. Cantos i, ii. With Introduction and Notes. By the same Editor. Extra fcap. 8vo. 2s. 6d.

V. GERMAN.

GERMAN COURSE. By HERMANN LANGE.

The Germans at Home; a Practical Introduction to German
Conversation, with an Appendix containing the Essentials of German Grammar.
Second Edition. 8vo. 2s. 6d.

The German Manual; a German Grammar, Reading Book,
and a Handbook of German Conversation. 8vo. 7s. 6d.

Grammar of the German Language. 8vo. 3s. 6d.

This 'Grammar' is a reprint of the Grammar contained in 'The German Manual,' and, in this separate form, is intended for the use of Students who wish to make themselves acquainted with German Grammar chiefly for the purpose of being able to read German books

German Composition ; A Theoretical and Practical Guide to the Art of Translating English Prose into German. 8vo. 4s. 6d.

Lessing's Laokoon. With Introduction, English Notes, etc. By A Hamann, Phil. Doc., M A. Extra fcap. 8vo. 4s 6d.

Schiller's Wilhelm Tell. Translated into English Verse by E. Massie, M.A Extra fcap. 8vo. 5s.

Also, Edited by C. A. BUCHHEIM, Phil. Doo.

Goethe's Egmont. With a Life of Goethe, &c. Third Edition. Extra fcap. 8vo. 3s.

—— *Iphigenie auf Tauris.* A Drama. With a Critical Introduction and Notes. Second Edition. Extra fcap. 8vo. 3s.

Heine's Prosa, being Selections from his Prose Works. With English Notes, etc. Extra fcap 8vo. 4s. 6d.

Lessing's Minna von Barnhelm. A Comedy. With a Life of Lessing, Critical Analysis, Complete Commentary, &c. Fourth Edition. Extra fcap. 8vo. 3s. 6d.

—— *Nathan der Weise.* With Introduction, Notes, etc. Extra fcap 8vo. 4s. 6d.

Schiller's Historische Skizzen ; Egmont's Leben und Tod, and *Belagerung von Antwerpen.* Second Edition. Extra fcap 8vo. 2s. 6d.

—— *Wilhelm Tell.* With a Life of Schiller; an historical and critical Introduction, Arguments, and a complete Comm' and Map Sixth Edition. Extra fcap 8vo. 3s. 6d

—— *Wilhelm Tell.* School Edition. With Map. Extra fcap. 8vo. 2s

Halm's Griseldis. In Preparation.

Modern German Reader. A Graduated Collection of Prose Extracts from Modern German writers :—

• Part I. With English Notes, a Grammatical Appendix, and a complete Vocabulary. Fourth Edition. Extra fcap. 8vo. 2s. 6d.

Parts II and III in Preparation.

VI. MATHEMATICS, PHYSICAL SCIENCE, &c.

By LEWIS HENSLEY, M A.

Figures made Easy: a first Arithmetic Book. (Introductory to 'The Scholar's Arithmetic.') Crown 8vo. 6*d.*

Answers to the Examples in Figures made Easy, together with two thousand additional Examples formed from the Tables in the same, with Answers. Crown 8vo. 1*s.*

The Scholar's Arithmetic: with Answers to the Examples. Crown 8vo. 4*s* 6*d.*

The Scholar's Algebra. An Introductory work on Algebra. Crown 8vo. 4*s* 6*d.*

Baynes (R. E., M.A.). Lessons on Thermodynamics. 1878. Crown 8vo. 7*s* 6*d*

Chambers (G. F., F.R.A.S.). A Handbook of Descriptive Astronomy. Third Edition. 1877. Demy 8vo. 28*s*

Clarke (Col. A. R., C.B., R.E.). Geodesy. 1880. 8vo. 12*s. 6d.*

Donkin (W. F., M.A., F.R.S.). Acoustics. 1870. Crown 8vo. 7*s. 6d*

Galton (Douglas, C.B., F.R.S.). The Construction of Healthy Dwellings; namely Houses, Hospitals, Barracks, Asylums, &c. Demy 8vo. 10*s. 6d.*

Hamilton (R. G. C.), and J. Ball. Book-keeping. New and enlarged Edition. Extra fcap. 8vo. limp cloth, 2*s*

Harcourt (A. G. Vernon, M.A.), and *H. G. Madan, M.A. Exercises in Practical Chemistry.* Vol I. Elementary Exercises Third Edition. Crown 8vo. 9*s.*

Maclaren (Archibald). A System of Physical Education: Theoretical and Practical. Extra fcap. 8vo. 7*s. 6d.*

Madan (H. G., M.A.). Tables of Qualitative Analysis. Large 4to. paper. 4*s. 6d.*

Maxwell (J. Clerk, M.A., F.R.S.). A Treatise on Electricity and Magnetism. Second Edition. 2 vols. Demy 8vo. 1*l.* 11*s* 6*d.*

—— *An Elementary Treatise on Electricity.* Edited by William Garnett, M.A. Demy 8vo. 7*s. 6d.*

Minchin (G. M., M.A.). A Treatise on Statics. Third Edition, Corrected and Enlarged. Vol. I. *Equilibrium of Coplanar Forces* 8vo. 9s. *Just Published.*

—— *Uniplanar Kinematics of Solids and Fluids.* Crown 8vo. 7s. 6d.

Rolleston (G., M.D., F.R.S.). Forms of Animal Life. Illustrated by Descriptions and Drawings of Dissections. A New Edition in the Press.

Smyth. A Cycle of Celestial Objects. Observed, Reduced, and Discussed by Admiral W. H Smyth, R N. Revised, condensed and greatly enlarged by G F. Chambers, F R.A.S. 1881. 8vo. *Price reduced to* 12s.

Stewart (Balfour, LL.D., F.R.S.). A Treatise on Heat, with numerous Woodcuts and Diagrams Fourth Edition. 1881. Extra fcap 8vo. 7s. 6d.

Story-Maskelyne (M. H. N., M.A.). Crystallography. In the Press.

Vernon-Harcourt (L. F., M.A.). A Treatise on Rivers and Canals, relating to the Control and Improvement of Rivers, and the Design, Construction, and Development of Canals. 2 vols. (Vol. I, Text. Vol. II, Plates.) 8vo. 21s.

—— *Harbours and Docks;* their Physical Features, History, Construction, Equipment, and Maintenance; with Statistics as to their Commercial Development. 2 vols. 8vo. 25s.

Watson (H. W., M.A.). A Treatise on the Kinetic Theory of Gases. 1876. 8vo. 3s 6d.

Watson (H. W., M.A.), and S. H. Burbury, M.A. A Treatise on the Application of Generalised Coordinates to the Kinetics of a Material System. 1879. 8vo. 6s.

Williamson (A. W., Phil. Doc., F.R.S.). Chemistry for Students. A new Edition, with Solutions. 1873. Extra fcap. 8vo. 8s. 6d.

VII. HISTORY.

Finlay (George, LL.D.). A History of Greece from its Conquest by the Romans to the present time, B.C. 146 to A.D. 1864. A new Edition, revised throughout, and in part re-written, with considerable additions, by the Author, and edited by H. F. Tozer, M.A. 1877. 7 vols. 8vo. 3l. 10s.

Freeman (E.A., D.C.L.). A Short History of the Norman Conquest of England. Second Edition. Extra fcap. 8vo. 2s. 6d.

—— *A History of Greece.* In preparation.

George (H. B., M.A.). Genealogical Tables illustrative of Modern History. Second Edition, Revised and Enlarged. Small 4to. 12s.

Hodgkin (T.). Italy and her Invaders, A.D. 376–476. Illustrated with Plates and Maps 2 vols 8vo. 1*l.* 12*s.*

Vol. III. *The Ostrogothic Invasion,* and

Vol. IV. *The Imperial Restoration,* in the Press

Kitchin (G. W., D.D.). A History of France. With numerous
Maps, Plans, and Tables. In Three Volumes. 1873–77. Crown 8vo. each
10*s.* 6*d*

Vol. 1. Second Edition. Down to the Year 1453.

Vol 2. From 1453–1624.

Vol. 3. From 1624–1793.

*Payne (E. J., M.A.). A History of the United States of
America.* In the Press.

Ranke (L. von). A History of England, principally in the
Seventeenth Century Translated by Resident Members of the University of
Oxford, under the superintendence of G. W. Kitchin, M.A., and C. W. Boase,
M.A. 1875. 6 vols. 8vo. 3*l.* 3*s.*

Rawlinson (George, M.A.). A Manual of Ancient History.
Second Edition. Demy 8vo. 14*s.*

*Select Charters and other Illustrations of English Constitutional
History,* from the Earliest Times to the Reign of Edward I Arranged and
edited by W. Stubbs, M.A. Fourth Edition. 1881. Crown 8vo. 8*s.* 6*d.*

Stubbs (W., D.D.). The Constitutional History of England,
in its Origin and Development. Library Edition. 3 vols. demy 8vo. 2*l.* 8*s.*

Also in 3 vols. crown 8vo. price 12*s.* each.

Wellesley. A Selection from the Despatches, Treaties, and
other Papers of the Marquess Wellesley. K G, during his Government
of India. Edited by S. J. Owen, M.A. 1877. 8vo. 1*l.* 4*s*

Wellington. A Selection from the Despatches, Treaties, and
other Papers relating to India of Field-Marshal the Duke of Wellington, K.G.
Edited by S J. Owen, M.A. 1880. 8vo. 24*s.*

A History of British India. By S. J. Owen, M.A., Reader
in Indian History in the University of Oxford. In preparation.

VIII. LAW.

Alberici Gentilis, I.C.D., I.C. Professoris Regii, De Iure Belli
Libri Tres. Edidit Thomas Erskine Holland, I.C.D. 1877. Small 4to.
half morocco, 21*s.*

Anson (Sir William R., Bart., D.C.L.). Principles of the
English Law of Contract, and of Agency in its Relation to Contract. Second
Edition Demy 8vo. 10*s.* 6*d.*

*Bentham (Jeremy). An Introduction to the Principles of
Morals and Legislation.* Crown 8vo. 6*s.* 6*d.*

Digby (Kenelm E., M.A.). An Introduction to the History of the Law of Real Property, with original Authorities Third Edition. Demy 8vo. 10s. 6d.

Gaii Institutionum Juris Civilis Commentarii Quattuor; or, Elements of Roman Law by Gaius With a Translation and Commentary by Edward Poste, M A. Second Edition. 1875. 8vo 18s.

Hall (W. E., M.A.). International Law. Second Edition. Demy 8vo 21s

Holland (T. E., D.C.L.). The Elements of Jurisprudence. Second Edition. Demy 8vo 10s 6d.

Imperatoris Iustiniani Institutionum Libri Quattuor; with Introductions, Commentary, Excursus and Translation. By J. B. Moyle, B.C.L, M A. 2 vols. Demy 8vo. 21s.

Justinian, The Institutes of, edited as a recension of the Institutes of Gaius, by Thomas Erskine Holland, D.C L. Second Edition. 1881. Extra fcap 8vo. 5s.

Justinian, Select Titles from the Digest of. By T. E. Holland, D.C L., and C. L. Shadwell, B.C L. 8vo 14s.

Also sold in Parts, in paper covers, as follows :—

Part I. Introductory Titles. 2s. 6d.   Part II Family Law. 1s.
Part III. Property Law. 2s. 6d.   Part IV. Law of Obligations (No 1). 3s. 6d.
Part IV. Law of Obligations (No. 2). 4s 6d.

Markby (W., M.A.). Elements of Law considered with reference to Principles of General Jurisprudence. Second Edition, with Supplement. 1874. Crown 8vo. 7s. 6d. Supplement separately, 2s.

Twiss (Sir Travers, D.C L.). The Law of Nations considered as Independent Political Communities.

Part I. On the Rights and Duties of Nations in time of Peace. A new Edition, Revised and Enlarged 1884. Demy 8vo. 15s.

Part II. On the Rights and Duties of Nations in Time of War. Second Edition Revised. 1875. Demy 8vo. 21s.

IX. MENTAL AND MORAL PHILOSOPHY, &c.

Bacon's Novum Organum. Edited, with English Notes, by G. W. Kitchin, D.D. 1855. 8vo 9s. 6d.

—— Translated by G. W. Kitchin, D.D. 1855. 8vo. 9s. 6d.

Berkeley. The Works of George Berkeley, D.D., formerly Bishop of Cloyne; including many of his writings hitherto unpublished. With Prefaces, Annotations, and an Account of his Life and Philosophy, by Alexander Campbell Fraser, M.A. 4 vols. 1871. 8vo. 2l. 18s.

The Life, Letters, &c. 1 vol. 16s.

Berkeley, Selections from. With an Introduction and Notes.
For the use of Students in the Universities. By Alexander Campbell Fraser,
LL D Second Edition Crown 8vo. 7s. 6d

Fowler (T., M.A.). The Elements of Deductive Logic, designed
mainly for the use of Junior Students in the Universities. Eighth Edition,
with a Collection of Examples Extra fcap. 8vo 3s 6d

—— *The Elements of Inductive Logic,* designed mainly for
the use of Students in the Universities. Fourth Edition. Extra fcap 8vo. 6s.

Edited by T. FOWLER, M A.

Bacon. Novum Organum. With Introduction, Notes, &c.
1878. 8vo 14s.

Locke's Conduct of the Understanding. Second Edition.
Extra fcap. 8vo. 2s.

Green (T. H., M.A.). Prolegomena to Ethics. Edited by
A. C. Bradley, M A Demy 8vo 12s 6d.

Hegel. The Logic of Hegel; translated from the Encyclo-
paedia of the Philosophical Sciences. With Prolegomena by William
Wallace, M A 1874 8vo. 14s.

Lotze's Logic, in Three Books; of Thought, of Investigation,
and of Knowledge. English Translation; Edited by B. Bosanquet, M A.,
Fellow of University College, Oxford. 8vo. *cloth,* 12s. 6d.

—— *Metaphysic,* in Three Books; Ontology, Cosmology,
and Psychology English Translation; Edited by B. Bosanquet, M.A.,
Fellow of University College, Oxford. 8vo. *cloth,* 12s. 6d.

Martineau (James, D.D.). Types of Ethical Theory. 2 vols.
8vo. 24s. *Just Published.*

Rogers (J E. Thorold, M.A.). A Manual of Political Economy,
for the use of Schools. Third Edition Extra fcap. 8vo. 4s. 6d

Smith's Wealth of Nations. A new Edition, with Notes, by
J. E. Thorold Rogers, M.A. 2 vols. 8vo. 1880. 21s.

X. ART, &c.

Hullah (John). The Cultivation of the Speaking Voice.
Second Edition. Extra fcap. 8vo. 2s. 6d.

Ouseley (Sir F. A. Gore, Bart.). A Treatise on Harmony.
Third Edition. 4to. 10s.

—— *A Treatise on Counterpoint, Canon, and Fugue,* based
upon that of Cherubini. Second Edition. 4to. 16s.

—— *A Treatise on Musical Form and General Composition.*
4to. 10s.

Robinson (*J. C., F.S.A.*). *A Critical Account of the Drawings* by *Michel Angelo and Raffaello in the University Galleries, Oxford.* 1870. Crown 8vo. 4s.

Ruskin (*John, M.A.*). *A Course of Lectures on Art*, delivered before the University of Oxford in Hilary Term, 1870. 8vo 6s.

Troutbeck (*J., M.A.*) *and R. F. Dale, M.A.* *A Music Primer* (for Schools). Second Edition. Crown 8vo 1s. 6d.

Tyrwhitt (*R. St. J., M.A.*). *A Handbook of Pictorial Art.* With coloured Illustrations, Photographs, and a chapter on Perspective by A. Macdonald. Second Edition. 1875. 8vo. half morocco, 18s.

Vaux (*W. S. W, M.A., F.R.S.*). *Catalogue of the Castellani Collection of Antiquities in the University Galleries, Oxford.* Crown 8vo. stiff cover, 1s.

The Oxford Bible for Teachers, containing supplementary HELPS TO THE STUDY OF THE BIBLE, including Summaries of the several Books, with copious Explanatory Notes and Tables illustrative of Scripture History and the characteristics of Bible Lands; with a complete Index of Subjects, a Concordance, a Dictionary of Proper Names, and a series of Maps. Prices in various sizes and bindings from 3s. to 2l. 5s.

Helps to the Study of the Bible, taken from the OXFORD BIBLE FOR TEACHERS, comprising Summaries of the several Books, with copious Explanatory Notes and Tables illustrative of Scripture History and the Characteristics of Bible Lands; with a complete Index of Subjects, a Concordance, a Dictionary of Proper Names, and a series of Maps. Crown 8vo. *cloth*, 3s. 6d.; 16mo. *cloth*, 1s.

LONDON: HENRY FROWDE,

OXFORD UNIVERSITY PRESS WAREHOUSE, AMEN CORNER,

OXFORD: CLARENDON PRESS DEPOSITORY,

116 HIGH STREET.

The DELEGATES OF THE PRESS *invite suggestions and advice from all persons interested in education; and will be thankful for . . . &c. addressed to the* SECRETARY TO THE DELEGATES, *Clarendon Press, Oxford.*